ADVANCE PRAISE FOR

BLOODIED BODIES, BLOODY LANDSCAPES

"This is the book I've waited my whole movie-geek life for. A robust and thought-provoking excavation of meaning and representation in American horror cinema and its deeply intertwined origins with colonial myth making. From *Scream* to *Texas Chainsaw Massacre*, Hall takes us through some of the icons of American horror and unearths their roots to show how they grew out of colonial notions of land, race, and fear of the other. I found a kindred spirit in Hall, who clearly loves these movies and yet also struggles with their very nature and their meaning. Thus is the reality of the Indigenous horror movie fan, enamored and angered all at once. I'm so thrilled this book exists, for scholars, fans, and filmmakers the world over." —**JESSE WENTE**

"*Bloodied Bodies, Bloody Landscapes* seeks to unsettle key concepts in horror by placing it into conversation with settler colonial studies." —**JACOB FLOYD**

"*Bloodied Bodies, Bloody Landscapes* is brilliant scholarship that pinpoints the ugly truth about the treatment of Indigenous people in horror cinema. But Hall is doing much more than examining tropes of mysticism, savagery, and settler-colonialism-as-savior in horror; she is directing our attention to the recuperative power of certain portrayals, thereby reminding us that an anticolonial lens can produce whole and full human stories—even scary ones." —**ROBIN R. MEANS COLEMAN**, author of *The Black Guy Dies First: Black Horror from Fodder to Oscar*

"Expertly foregrounding the most overlooked horror in this film genre—settler colonialism—*Bloodied Bodies, Bloody Landscapes* is deadly." —**CHRISTINE SY**

BLOODIED BODIES,
BLOODY LANDSCAPES

BLOODIED BODIES, BLOODY LANDSCAPES

SETTLER COLONIALISM IN HORROR

LAURA HALL

Printed and bound in Canada. The text of this book is printed on 100% post-consumer recycled paper with earth-friendly vegetable-based inks.

Cover design: Jess Koroscil
Interior layout design: John van der Woude, JVDW Designs
Copyeditor: Rachel Ironstone
Indexer: Judy Dunlop

Library and Archives Canada Cataloguing in Publication

Title: Bloodied bodies, bloody landscapes : settler colonialism in horror / Laura Hall.
Names: Hall, Laura (Lecturer in sociology), author.
Description: Series statement: Indigenous voices in world arts and cultural expressions ; 2 | Includes bibliographical references and index.
Identifiers: Canadiana (print) 20250151952 | Canadiana (ebook) 20250152002 | ISBN 9781779400819 (hardcover) | ISBN 9781779400802 (softcover) | ISBN 9781779400826 (EPUB) | ISBN 9781779400833 (PDF)
Subjects: LCSH: Horror films—United States—History and criticism. | LCSH: Indigenous peoples in motion pictures. | LCSH: Settler colonialism.
Classification: LCC PN1995.9.H6 H35 2025 | DDC 791.43/6164—dc23

10 9 8 7 6 5 4 3 2 1

University of Regina Press, University of Regina
Regina, Saskatchewan, Canada, S4S 0A2
TEL: (306) 585-4758 FAX: (306) 585-4699
WEB: www.uofrpress.ca

We acknowledge the support of the Canada Council for the Arts for our publishing program. We acknowledge the financial support of the Government of Canada. / Nous reconnaissons l'appui financier du gouvernement du Canada. This publication was made possible with support from Creative Saskatchewan's Book Publishing Production Grant Program.

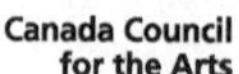

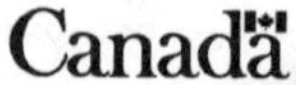

I'd like to dedicate this book to my parents, Shirley and David Hall, and my brothers, Shawn and Dwayne, for ensuring that I would somehow remain steeped in horror as an amusing pastime. I also dedicate this book to my children, Sen and Emil; my partner, Monique; and my friends, who have all encouraged and supported me.

CONTENTS

INTRODUCTION

"Who gives a fuck about movies?!"

—GHOSTFACE, *SCREAM VI*

A WOMAN FALLS INTO A DEEP POOL OF THICK BLOOD AND emerges only to be attacked by a cannibalistic humanoid in the depths of caves in Cherokee homelands. She emerges drenched in blood and loses her expensive suburban mom-fleece, picks up an animal bone, and kills a cannibalistic devolved human. This cinematic moment in the film *The Descent* (2005) inspired my project on horror and settler colonialism. In addition to loving what I perceive to be a whole lot of queer subtext between the two survivors of the film (Sarah and Juno), I felt both oddly vindicated and incredibly insulted by the movie. These contradictions are part of a visceral experience I often have while watching American horror movies. *The Descent* made me wonder—where else are Indigenous people hidden in horror, why are there still representations of Indigenous people as cannibals in the 2000s, and how can white settlers continue to be scared of Indigenous Peoples at a time when colonization constitutes the truest horror(s) in our lives?

During the writing of this book, the graves of Indigenous children were found in growing numbers on the grounds of so-called schools in Canada. Jana-Rae Yerxa writes about the trauma of finding the remains of Indigenous children, that we need to stop calling these institutions of assimilation "schools," "because schools do not require graveyards."[1] Remains have also been found on the grounds of boarding schools used to violently assimilate Indigenous children in the United States.[2] This era of removal, assimilation, and violence against Indigenous children continues in the form of state foster "care" systems.[3] The constant threat to Indigenous Peoples' rights and the refusals of widespread land return in both Canada and the United States result in constant struggle against systems intent on the demise of Indigenous nations and cultures.

Gerald Vizenor uses the term *survivance* to describe the ways that Indigenous Peoples survive and resist colonialism in ongoing ways.[4] In the meantime, settler colonialism shapeshifts, a kind of anti-trickster, described by James (Sákéj) Youngblood Henderson as "a cognitive force of artificial European thought, a differentiated consciousness, ever changing in its creativity to justify the oppression and domination of contemporary Indigenous peoples and their spiritual guardians."[5] The construction of the Indian as savage is thus used as "proof" (though self-rationalizing, self-sustaining, and circular), in Henderson's words,

---

1 Yerxa, "We Need to Stop Calling Them 'Schools.'"
2 Spears, "Indigenous Human Remains."
3 Somos, "Foster Care Replaced Residential Schools."
4 Vizenor, ed., *Survivance*, 4.
5 Henderson, "Postcolonial Ghost Dancing," 58.

> of primal chaos and the natural state of war. The savage state envisioned by Hobbes provided more than the force creating and sustaining law and political society, however; it also created a spectacular repository of negative values attributed to Indigenous peoples.[6]

Recognizing the construction of this notion that violence and savagery, lawlessness and war are "primal states," helps to reframe horror in important ways. North Americans in the post-1492 world live in a context of horror, on colonized stolen lands, on the back of a great Turtle whose watery lifeblood is witness to violence against both human and more-than-human beings. Storytelling is a way of visioning a myriad of ways forward, while re-visioning where we've come from and how we might understand ourselves and our misrepresentations under a horrifyingly violent settler colonial system and (attempted) genocide.

The National Inquiry into Missing and Murdered Indigenous Women and Girls in Canada and the US Department of the Interior's Commission on Missing and Murdered Indigenous Peoples outline ongoing systemic colonial violence that is gendered, heterosexist, ableist, racist, classist, and ageist.[7] A number of horror scholars focus on gender, sexuality, and representation in horror but do not conceptualize these elements as rooted in the ongoing dispossession of Indigenous Peoples. As Scott Morgensen writes, gender and sexuality are

> intrinsic to the colonisation of Indigenous peoples and the promulgation of European modernity by settlers, whether

---

6 Henderson, "The Context of the State of Nature," 16–17.

7 US Department of the Interior, "Not Invisible Act Commission."

> in pursuit of what Patrick Wolfe has theorised as a logic of indigenous "elimination," or of what Lorenzo Veracini, Philip Deloria, and scholars in indigenous studies have examined as the indigenisation of settlers.[8]

It is the white settler heteropatriarchal family that is at risk when the savages lurch and moan at the gates. When the prodigal son or daughter "goes mad," they are exhibiting savage characteristics, showing that the very elements white settler society tries to keep at bay can invade. While actual Indigenous Peoples continue to struggle against colonization, white settlers write story after story about the threat that Indigenous Peoples' survival poses to their own families and futures.

While surviving families in North American horror are often bolstered by central heroes, the victims of horror are not the only bloodied bodies by the end of the film. The Final Girl, as Carol Clover named her, survives the horror film. She (usually) is a personification of fear; covered in gore, gone "mad," laughing or staring into the distance: she is reborn in blood.[9] The construction of Indigenous "Others" as savage is ultimately about settlers seizing Indigenous lands and the meanings that then flow from that overtaking. The "frontier" in North American settler colonial society is a place that holds at bay savagery and, with it, madness, racialized Others, and what Barbara Creed calls the "monstrous feminine."[10] The monstrous feminine is the mad woman, the violent woman, the woman whose gender and sexuality can be ambiguous.

---

8 Morgensen, "Theorising Gender, Sexuality and Settler Colonialism," 3.

9 Even when the Final Girl is that rare Final Boy, he is often used in service of saving white settler communities. I'll speak more to this with respect to the subtext of *A Nightmare on Elm Street 2: Freddy's Revenge* (1985). See Clover, "Her Body, Himself," 187.

10 Creed, *The Monstrous-Feminine*, 1.

During the writing of this book, some white settler scholars have asked why I am fixated on Indigenous representations in horror when we only show up in the genre a few ways—interred in an Indian Burial Ground or stereotyped in obscure horror films like *The Manitou* (1978), which was released the year I was born, and features a Bad Indian Medicine Man existing as a kind of tumour in the back of a white woman's neck. I read Indigeneity as stereotyped in more diverse ways than the Indian Burial Ground phenomenon alone. The lurking killer in the woods; the Final Girl[11] in her transformation from sweatshirt-wearing high schooler with bangs and a nice boyfriend, to bloodied, hatchet-wielding killer; and various ghostly and demonic beings—all have markers of settler colonial projections of the content of Indigeneity. The killer—gone mad, gone feral, gone into the wilderness to live forever as a savage lurking at the gates—comes from or retreats into the wilderness, threatening white settler invasion again and again, only to be defeated. This process both closes a loop, portraying white settlers as pretty much the centre of all things past, present, and future (both right or wrong) in America, and presents the Indigenous-Other as forever lurking, forever at the periphery.

Beyond stereotypes and tropes that seem to deal specifically with Indigenous Peoples, I want to explore horror in ways that are not always understood to be *about* settler colonialism. The American horror film in particular needs to be re-examined through a lens that understands the power structures as well as social and environmental context of settler colonialism. In addition to analyzing horror as representation and reproduction of

11 Carol Clover explains further that the Final Girl sees most of her friends or family killed, battles the killer, and sometimes lives to the end of the film or beyond. Clover, *Men, Women and Chainsaws*, 163.

daily settler colonialism, I hope that this book forms part of a deeper dialogue about resistance to settler colonialism as a project of Indigenous storying and storytelling. I want to speak back to a genre that ties directly to notions of white settler belonging and identity, to early Gothic traditions exploring death and loss, decay and fear, and to the perpetuation of persistent stereotypes about Indigenous Peoples (far beyond the Indian Burial Grounds).

Colonization *is* horror, my colleague, the brilliant Dr. Celeste Pedri-Spade, reminded me when I gave a public talk in 2018 on Christmas horror and settler colonialism. Indeed, Jodi Byrd writes, "the story of the new world is horror, the story of America is a crime."[12] In Canada, the National Inquiry into Missing and Murdered Indigenous Women and Girls reiterated what Indigenous communities had been saying since the onset of colonization—that settler colonialism is gendered and that gender-based violence is vital to its workings. Settler colonialism is multi-layered, as scholars Snelgrove, Dhamoon, and Corntassel write: "Our understanding of settler colonialism is not one-dimensional…it is intrinsically shaped by and shaping interactive relations of coloniality, racism, gender, class, sexuality and desire, capitalism, and ableism."[13]

We can speak back to horror, reclaim it, and, as a genre, it certainly does not *belong* to white settler writers. At times, horror can seem to be boundary-shifting and capable of providing space for deeper, more difficult storytelling about the violence of the world we live in. Horror can reveal underlying colonial violence. Crimson-drenched soil littered with bloodied bodies feels like a stark reminder of the violence that settler colonialism continues to perpetuate. Ultimately, however, when white settler families,

12 Byrd, *The Transit of Empire*, xii.
13 Snelgrove, Dhamoon, and Corntassel, "Unsettling Settler Colonialism," 2.

communities, and aspirations for survival are centred (as they usually are) in horror, settler colonialism persistently disappears and makes codified a kind of flattened, savage (romantic or horrifying) Indigenous-Other. Rooting this process are projections about the land as fearful and in need of conquering.

Horror is an important genre within the settler colonial project, as I will illustrate. Byrd delves into the continuity of settler colonialism and US imperialism, writing,

> Indigeneity functions as a counterpoint that disrupts the fictions of multicultural settler enfranchisement... indigeneity is temporal as well as spatial, structural as well as structuring. By detailing the constellations that underwrite US imperialism...it may be possible to show that within the logics that have ordered the United States out of indigenous lands, indigenous peoples can be apprehended through parallax within critical theory that demonstrates just how vital they are to any understanding of how difference orients US bio- and necropolitics.[14]

Indigeneity, constructed and disappeared, obsessed over, suppressed, is core to North American cultural production and storytelling. Not only is horror no exception to this pattern of obsessive repression, but it might be a central genre in the perpetuation of constructions of Indigenous-Othering.

Indigenous writers, filmmakers, and scholars are working in the genre in increasing numbers as well, though this book will not cover the potential or limitations of, for example, what an Indigenous Gothic or horror tradition might look like. Horror can

14 Byrd, *The Transit of Empire*, 32.

be an escape or even cathartic. When white settlers behave just terribly toward one another or lose themselves in fantasies about demons on stolen lands, Indigenous viewers can nod knowingly. In my own family, stories of Residential Schooling and the Sixties Scoop and now constant, daily reminders of settler colonial violence make horror a kind of trauma immersion practice. Do I revel in watching the Final Girl completely "lose it," stabbing and slashing her way to freedom? At times, yes. It is fun watching Melissa Barrera's Final Girl in Sam Carpenter's *Scream* (2022) as she stabs a violent white man twenty-two times.

There is, of course, potential to tell better stories in horror. Indigenous horror writers and filmmakers are becoming increasingly better known as of this writing. In her introduction to the topic, Alicia Elliot writes: "Indigenous writers know what it's like to live in a world where the horror never stops."[15] Being a horror fan who is also First Nations, queer/gay, and a woman who identifies outside of the stringent binary of settler colonial genderings, means that I often cringe-watch things meant for another audience. I also find myself cheering for people who come from the very world enacted on the backs of Indigenous Peoples and lands. It is a complex thing, not seeing myself represented, and then trying to re-story that which *is* represented, to fit with my own experience. I am not alone in navigating these complexities.

Horror scholarship is also rarely committed to speaking back to the constructs that uphold Indigenous erasure. Indigenous feminist scholars can speak back to this genre in unique and important ways. As an urban Native person (my mother, who has passed away since I started this work, was Mohawk, her father was from Kahnawake, and my father is British/Canadian), I have

---

15 Elliott, "The Rise of Indigenous Horror."

always watched horror with some fascination. I was probably too young when I first saw Leatherface or Jason hacking up people for intruding on their land.

It was an escape from the boredom (and oddly enough an escape from the violent erasure of settler colonial suburbia) to walk down to my local video store and pick up a VHS with some gaudy picture of Santa wielding an axe or a bunch of vampires with sexy hair. My crush on Star from *The Lost Boys* (1987) or Laurie from *Halloween* (1978) was part of that escape, and I read into the films whatever I wanted to read into them as far as queer subtext or some sense that the real bad guys might lose sometimes. I also imagined, as early as I can recall, that the Final Girl's transformation from nice suburbanite to a warrior covered in bloody war paint and wielding a machete or hatchet, had something to do with some understanding of the power that Indigenous women have.[16] The first horror movies that I ever actually watched all the way through were *Sleepaway Camp III: Teenage Wasteland* (1989) and *Night of the Demons* (1988). Murderous women named Angela disrupted the heteronormative, violent world I lived in.[17] At the time, I only vaguely registered the fact that *Night of the Demons* trots out the Indian Burial Ground trope, but I realized on some level that there was some sort of enticing and fun, but also disturbing and oddly shameful, connection between the demonic

16 When I speak to the category of "women" in Indigenous cultures, I mean to capture both the idea of women as an oppressed group and women as a self-chosen category in cultures that rarely, if ever, have a gender binary.

17 Angela is a character in *Night of the Demons*. She is possessed by a demon and kisses her best friend to spread the possession around. Angela is also the name of the killer in *Sleepaway Camp III: Teenage Wasteland*, which obviously has two chapters before it, but which—along with *Night of the Demons*—was one of my first horror film viewings ever. I was twelve or so, was starting to realize that I was queer, and the Angelas were my anti-heroes and crushes.

and queerness. I certainly sensed at a young age that Angela's transformation in *Night of the Demons* freed her from a boring and oppressive social context.

At the same time, the idea that white settlers can (however horrifyingly) transform and free themselves by "going savage" obviously reinforces settler colonialism and the erasure of Indigenous people. I began this project in the early 2000s when I started to notice tropes and patterns in horror that seemed to both fixate on and yet also erase Indigenous Peoples in North America, intertwining with sexism, homophobia, transphobia, racism, classism, ableism, and ageism.[18] I began to feel less generous in my assessment of horror as a subversive genre in many cases. When the Creeds of *Pet Sematary* (1989) are told by their neighbour Jud that nobody really knows whose land they're on anyway, the usefulness of the Indian Burial Ground trope in that film becomes clearer. Contemporary land claims by Indigenous nations and the protection of actual ancestral burial grounds are issues that horror movies, built on settler colonial tropes like the Indian Burial Ground, try to negate.[19]

North American settler society is haunted by its own colonial violence while continuing to uphold the vicious project of settler colonialism. Horror allows, at times, for viewers to lament the violence of the past without seeing the violence of settler colonialism in the present. The horror film also perpetuates fear and tropes that are rooted in fear and domination of the constructed Indian, as demon, as ghost, as witchy and cannibalistic. Horror as a genre remains haunted by the spectre of the Indian who lurks in darkened forests and murky waters. In this book, I argue that horror

---

18 A subject for a future project should be the emergence of the elderly body as a site of horror and how this construction of monstrosity ties in with the settler-colonial project.

19 See Bergland, *The National Uncanny*.

is the primary film genre of settler colonialism. The Indian Burial Ground trope might seem like the best example of this argument, and I will discuss that trope, of course. The spectre of the savage and the cultural objects or concepts (including monsters) appropriated from real Indigenous cultures also permeate the genre.

This book is focused on white settler colonialism in horror, and not on Indigenous people as we actually exist, or our responses to horror. Horror is too often a reinforcement of those old (and ongoing) lines of constructed reality, between the savage at the gates and the civilized within. There is certainly a growing understanding that the horror genre needs to be more inclusive, more politicized, and more critical of power structures. Melissa Barrera's firing from the upcoming sequel *Scream VII*[20] for posting tweets in support of Palestine seems to have led, as of this writing in November 2023, to a massive boycott of a popular film franchise.[21] Barrera and Jenna Ortega, both Mexican-American actors, intervened in the Scream franchise and shifted its focus from white settler families and communities (positioning the Ghostface killer as firmly rooted within settler colonial violence) toward storying their own characters' resistance to white settler misogynistic violence. There are deeper issues of power and representation that need to be critically discussed.

Dedications are often reserved for their own section in a book, but I want to here acknowledge the influence my parents had on the writing of this book. Few summers went by without my mother having a serious discussion with my father about my fascination with "those movies." At the same time, she encouraged a love of what my own children call "spooky" things. On Halloween, our

20 McArdle, "Melissa Barrera Breaks Silence."
21 Starkey, "Fans Vow to Boycott *Scream VII*."

house was often decorated to a wonderful and terrifying degree, and our neighbours' houses were even more impressive. Carloads of children were driven in from far and wide in N'Swakamok (Sudbury) for the festivities on my little crescent. I see horror as a genre that is incredibly important—both in the ways that Indigenous writers and filmmakers are starting to produce horror and in the ways that the tropes have impacted our perceptions of ourselves and our past, present, and future presence on still-Indigenous but still-stolen lands.

I begin this book by presenting in Chapter 1 an exploration of the American Gothic and Indigenous Peoples. In this chapter, I speak to the intertwining of three major systems—colonialism, slavery, and imperialism—which contextualize connected forms of oppression that play out in popular representation. Building on the connections between the American Gothic and horror, the first chapter will lay a basis for understanding horror as a genre, and settler colonial studies as a theoretical approach to understanding horror, through reading literature related to Native American representation in cinema and will include an analysis of the frontier, the civilization/savagery construct, and ongoing colonialism and representation.

Chapter 2 focuses on the interconnection between settler colonialism and the family in horror. Gender, sexuality, and the heteropatriarchal white settler family are central to much of the analysis of horror, though rarely with a focus on how settler colonialism contextualizes these relations. In Chapter 3, I shift the focus to settler colonialism, sanism,[22] and ableism in horror. Horror films

22 By *sanism*, I mean to imply that constructions of sanity/insanity (or madness) are at issue, as well as discriminatory beliefs against those perceived to have certain mental and cognitive health differences. I'll get into this idea in more depth, but for now I will say that some fairly awful notions of sanism have...

provide an opportunity to better understand the ways that settler colonialism demands particular body-mind constructs, and the ways those repressed and othered elements in turn erupt and disrupt colonial safety and innocence.

From there, I move to unearth land and landscape in Chapter 4, linking land, settler colonialism, and the environment in horror. Where and when the earth seeks revenge, white settlers afraid of this revenge are seeking to create white settler origin myths that are meant to replace Indigenous Creation stories. In Chapter 5, I look at specific representations of Indigenous people. Indigenous people might be made into new kinds of monsters and scary entities, or Indigenous cultural elements might be appropriated and twisted. The portrayal of Indigenous people and Peoples as literal cannibals will be taken up in this chapter.

I have organized the book in this way to capture my sense that the deconstructions I have attempted in the first chapters need a better response by the end of the book. That is—I want to know what Indigenous and decolonial horror writers can do to improve on what has been done before. As I finished writing this book, Lily Gladstone, the brilliant Blackfoot actress, nearly won an Oscar for starring in a horror story of sorts. The film, of the dispossession and murders of members of the Osage Nation after oil was found on their land, is not technically a horror movie, but it really should be understood as such. The organized killings of Indigenous people to dispossess constitutes a true horror story.[23]

Racist, sexist, ableist, classist, and ageist violence uphold settler colonialism and need to be understood in that context. Throughout

---

...fueled the creation of particular monsters in horror. Horror can also be self-reflexive about these constructions, of course, but the concept of sanism serves generally to uphold settler colonialism.

23 See Scorsese, dir., *Killers of the Flower Moon*.

this book, I present arguments that show the ways that largely white-settler-dominated horror productions give us a "cowboys and Indians" violation/revenge story, with the final survivors taking revenge against some horrifying entity who threatens their safety. But when the horrifying entity is also a product of settler colonial, heterosexist, misogynistic violence, and that Final Girl gets her axe into the killer, I have to admit that there is catharsis there. Needing to fight back against white settler killers and watching some blood-drenched girl from the suburbs do it on screen *feels* like a cathartic disruption of everyday taken-for-granted settler colonial violence, even if it is more complicated than that.

I have resisted categorizing horror films according to their subgenres, but generally this book will discuss the slasher film, given the gore and violence of that subgenre. The bloody slasher film is described by Carol Clover as

> the immensely generative story of a psycho-killer who slashes to death a string of mostly female victims, one by one, until he is himself subdued or killed, usually by the one girl who has survived.[24]

I also cover some supernatural horror, given the prevalence of the Indian Burial Ground and bizarre projections/fears of shamanism in a kind of stubborn and awkward take on magical realism. Here I prefer the definition of magical realism that, as Wendy Faris describes, is

> a commodifying kind of primitivism that, like the Orientalism analyzed by Edward Said and his successors, relegates colonies

24 Clover, "Her Body, Himself," 187.

> and their traditions to the role of cute, exotic psychological fantasies—visions of the colonizer's ever more distant, desirable, and/or despised self projected onto colonized others.[25]

To make the project manageable, I have avoided demonic and possession films, paranormal films, zombie films, monster flicks, and that difficult-to-define area of psychological horror which I suspect has morphed into "elevated horror." And yet, all horror is psychological, and most of the horror films I cover are many things at once—trashy and gory, thoughtful and filled with dread. I define *elevated horror* as horror that provokes thought and reflection.[26] I will dare to say that all horror films provoke thought and reflection, no matter how absurd (or potentially because of how absurd) some of their storylines may be.

The North American horror film[27] is contextualized by settler colonialism, by constructs of civilization and savagery, and, in turn, by the ways that fear manifests specifically within settler colonial North American society. Horror is described by theorists of the genre—who often do not include analyses of settler colonialism and anti-Indigeneity in their work—as being concerned with that which is fearful, anxiety-causing, disquieting. In *Powers*

25 Faris, "The Question of the Other."

26 That being said, for the sake of time and space and not arguing with anybody about the status of so-called elevated horror, I removed some of the lower-budget, campy flicks I'd originally intended on discussing for their (mis)use of the Indian Burial Ground trope.

27 For the sake of space, I have focused mainly on the American horror film as a dominant and well-funded enterprise. However, my framework—settler colonial studies—lends itself to some discussion of European horror that is influenced by American horror, and of Canadian horror, which also fixates on the Indian as savage (both terrifying and freeing) in order to establish a white settler identity on stolen lands.

of Horror, Julia Kristeva describes the abject elements as "primal."[28] This notion of primal, repressed elements, within the self, is central to settler colonial horror. The primal or savage entity is out there in the wilderness, or might erupt from within, and horror films have a preoccupation with these anxieties as settler colonialism continually reasserts itself.

Horror generally can be so much better. It is perhaps the job of a storyteller to turn a violent and disturbing world inside out, to poke at its entrails and to display its terrors. To do so in ways that challenge rather than reinforce violent systems of power is the project I aim to support. I hope that this book can contribute in some amusing, critical, and perhaps even horrifying ways to that work.

28 Kristeva, *Powers of Horror*, 3.

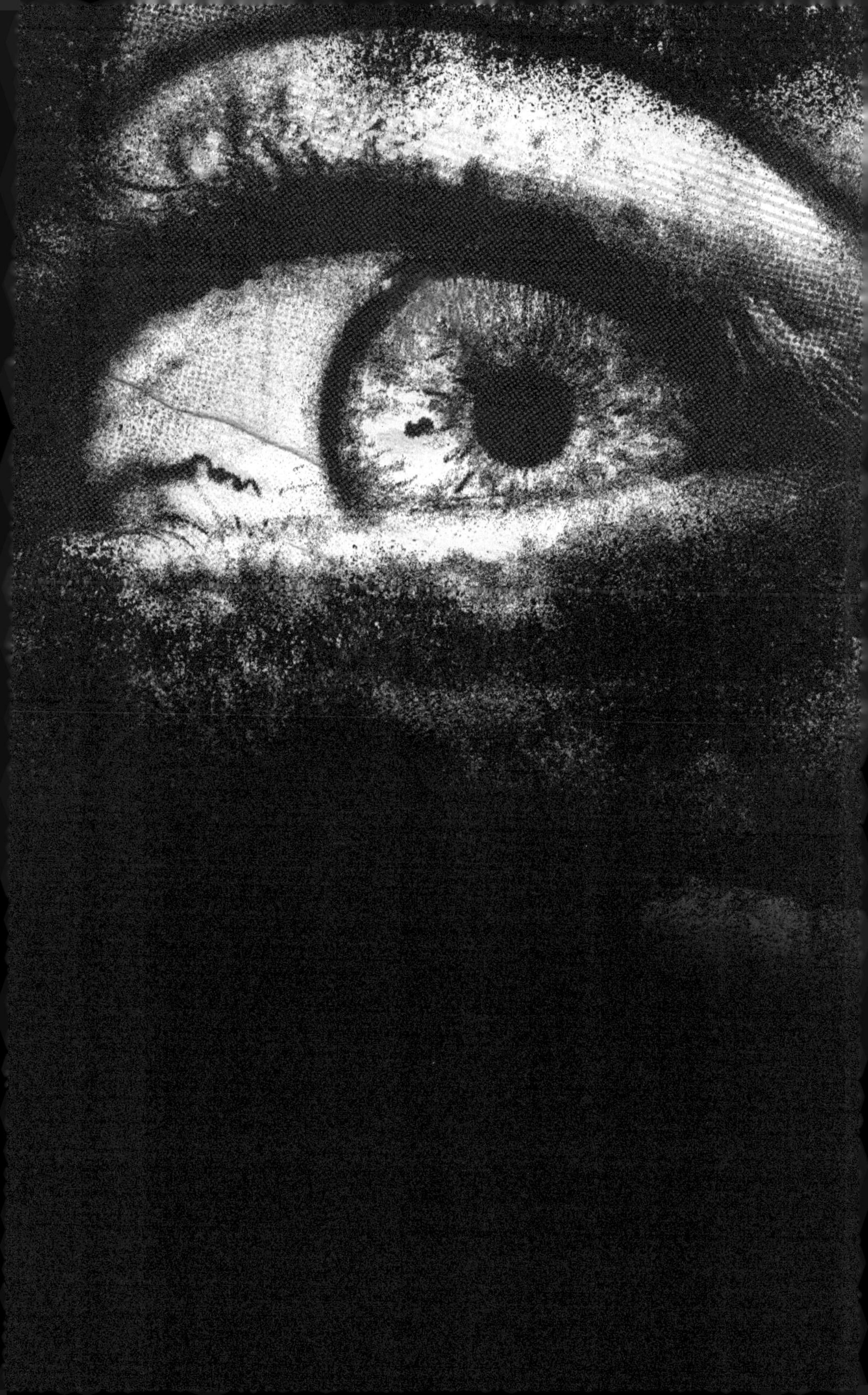

ONE

THEY'RE HERE!

SETTLER COLONIALISM AND THE HORROR FILM

"You're all gonna die in there!
All of you! You are gonna die!"

—KANE, *POLTERGEIST II: THE OTHER SIDE*

A LITTLE GIRL WARNS HER FAMILY, "THEY'RE HERE!" The line is central to the film *Poltergeist* (1982) as she announces the arrival of invading ghosts, coming through the television to steal her away. American horror gives us this moment, this warning, over and over—something out there, something sinister, wants in. The monster wants to hurt the nice children of suburbia. The savage invades and the civilized try to defend themselves against it all.

Horror films provide an experience for the audience, Thomas Fahy argues, including an "anticipation of terror, the mixture of fear and exhilaration... the opportunity to confront the unpredictable and dangerous."[1] Rick Worland argues that horror is a universal category, that all cultures have scary stories. This may be true, but Worland goes on to define the horror genre in a more specific way, rooted in European anxieties, starting with Gothic literature. Horror in Worland's descriptions includes fixation on fearful places, including architecture (old, dusty, crumbling castles and houses) and bodies that cross erotic and gender boundaries.[2]

The Gothic literary and film tradition centres on a fear of death.[3] The Gothic and the horror genre each deal in death, associating it with the threat of the Other. Carol Senf speaks to the ways that the line between the Gothic and horror becomes at times difficult to draw:

> The Gothic at the end of the nineteenth century and after goes one step further and focuses on the most graphic, painful and degrading aspects of death, disease and sexuality... At mid-century Edgar Allan Poe is also an expert at evoking horror... And of course there is always the vampire, that creature from the grave who nonetheless returns to impact the living. The existence of the vampire is a reminder of things worse than death and disease, it seems.[4]

The fear of death and invasion is central to both the Gothic and to horror. These anxieties obscure the realities of settler colonialism

1 Fahy, ed., *The Philosophy of Horror*, 1.
2 Worland, *The Horror Film*, 28–29.
3 Davison, *History of the Gothic*, 1.
4 Senf, "Realism, Horror and the Gothic," 4–5.

and recentre white settler individual, family, and community importance by turning Indigenous realities under settler colonialism into settler fears, and fodders for horror. The fear of death, or the Other as an embodiment of death, is also about appropriations of suffering, as white settler audiences imagine experiencing violent invasion.

North American horror does not only deal with the Indian as demonic, as anti-Black racism and the logic of slavery is also central to the genre. Beyond fear and anxiety, horror fulfills all kinds of paradoxical desires. The desire to conform and reinforce the safety of settler colonial belonging—on stolen lands, in unknown places—is matched with a deep and abiding yearning for freedom from the horrors of a world that serves so few. Barry Langford argues that horror is of more than one mind:

> On the one hand, it unmasks latent unspeakable desires in (white, patriarchal, bourgeois) society and shows the inadequacy and hypocrisy of the culture that demands such repression....On the other, it identifies its protagonist(s) and through them the audience with a project of re-suppression, containment and restoration of the *status quo ante* through the violent elimination of deviance and disturbance—the destruction of the "monster."[5]

American horror needs to be understood not as a universalizing exercise (i.e., all cultures have scary stories, and that's all horror is) but as having specific roots in European and North American forms of colonialism.

The horror film is a continuation of the Gothic tradition, focused on death, decay, and anxiety about colonized peoples

5 Langford, *Film Genre*, 159.

invading the civilized centre. The Gothic essentially, Tabish Khair writes, is primarily rooted in colonial relationships whereby

> these relations to Otherness defined the difference between the approaches of the civilising or evangelising gentleman, on the one hand, and, on the other hand, the "school" that posited non-Europeans as basically unmitigated/lurking cannibals (waiting to jump out of the skin of European acculturation at any moment and gobble up Europeans) or introduced homilies such as "the only good Indian is a dead Indian."[6]

Khair's description of the demonic and mythological Indian as Other is described also by Renée Bergland, who writes about the terror of "swarthy Indians, sooty devils, and unruly women" at the centre of settler colonial fears and constructions of the Indian.[7] The mythical Indian in the Gothic and in horror is also imagined as a feminine monstrosity. For Bram Stoker, author of *Dracula*, the monstrous included the Indigenous woman. In his short story "The Squaw," the link between savagery and violence is initially stated by the character Elias P. who describes himself as being "as tender as a Maine cherry-tree," unable to harm a small creature any more than he would "scalp a baby." In the story, the second most savage beast the narrator had ever seen was "an Apache squaw."[8] As I will argue, the constructed savage woman is also a pathway to freedom for "civilized" white women in horror.

American writer Edgar Allan Poe's only novel, *The Narrative of Arthur Gordon Pym of Nantucket*, explores the fears of the "civilized"

---

6 Khair, *The Gothic, Postcolonialism and Otherness*, 4.

7 Bergland, *The National Uncanny*, 42.

8 Normally, I would not spell the insulting word in its entirety, but for the sake of clarity I'm doing so here. See Stoker, "The Squaw," 31.

who, in their explorations, come across a mythical island of Black and Indigenous people who ultimately turn on the white explorers.[9] The American Gothic, rooted in colonialism, intertwines with European horrors as well. In this book, I will at times deal with the ways that the relationship between European colonizers and American settler colonial communities continues to swap conceits and fears about North American Indigenous Peoples. Leila Taylor writes that "the phantoms that haunt gothic narratives are the ramifications of racism, repressed guilt, social pariahs, and marginalized freaks."[10] The Southern Gothic is "a specific kind of American ghost story that evokes the miasma of dusty rural towns and abandoned plantations, troubled misfits and miscreants."[11]

Appropriations of suffering are intertwined with appropriations of Indigenous cultural elements as well in settler colonial contexts.[12] Cutcha Risling Baldy's writing about *The Walking Dead* speaks to the trauma and everyday stress of having lived through an apocalypse in which the real world of Indigenous Peoples was transformed by colonial violence. In turn, watching these stories unfold in North American horror can feel disorienting. Baldy writes that

> for a long time in California, if you were an Indian person walking around, something or someone might just try to kill you. They were hungry for your scalp and your head. They had

---

9 Poe, *The Narrative of Arthur Gordon Pym*. For a more thorough treatment of Poe's work, see Morrison, *Playing in the Dark*.

10 Taylor, *Darkly*, 44.

11 Taylor, *Darkly*, 45.

12 For example, Patrick Wolfe writes about the appropriation of Indigenous imagery in vulgar or ostentatious ways, through sports team imagery and so on. See Wolfe, "Settler Colonialism," 389.

> no remorse. There was no reasoning with them. And there were more of them then there was of you.[13]

The idea then becomes that fantasies of this kind of suffering and fear can be projected onto the screen for white settlers to consume. Indigenous Peoples have seen genocide and ecocide, only to birth new generations in a world overtaken by colonizers who both appropriate and disappear those stories, all while making this twisted notion of the savage, the Indian, into the *real* monster.

Alongside appropriations of suffering, there are those fears that the colonized will seek revenge. With Dracula, Stephen Arata argues, Victorian fears about "the decline of Britain as a world power... or rather, the way the perception of that decline was articulated by contemporary writers"[14] contextualizes a text which depicts the Eastern European, queer (in his gender presentation, his sexuality, and his proclivity toward having more than one partner), and obviously cannibalistic Dracula as the savage at the gates. The threat of "reverse colonization" and "'primitive' forces" is described by Arata, who points out that these fears can manifest as an external or internal threat.[15]

I am interested in the continuity between the Gothic as a genre fixated on Indigenous Peoples as ghosts and horror as a genre fixated on Indigenous Peoples as disappeared but as metaphorically returning, again and again in waves of blood and gore and violence. Bergland writes about Enlightenment era white settler writers evoking "Indians as symbols of internal darkness and

---

13 Baldy, "Why I Teach *The Walking Dead*."
14 Arata, "The Occidental Tourist," 622.
15 Arata, 623.

irrationality... Later... as actual ghosts."[16] The Western is the genre of film typically associated with Indigenous people, through the construction of the savage Indian in opposition to the civilized and innocent white settler community, with the cowboy-outlaw bridging that divide and ultimately protecting the civilized. The Gothic and horror operate much like the Western, which contains, as Shari Huhndorf writes, "a widespread ambivalence about modernity and the value of civilization (though not about white dominance) typical of the counterculture era."[17] Herein lie some of the seemingly progressive horror elements, whereby the civilized are made to suffer and often die as the werewolf or vampire or cannibal destroys them.

At the same time, this suffering lays the groundwork for a new kind of settler mythos and identity rooted in reverse colonization. The imposition of a white settler cosmology and rejection of Indigenous stories about place and spirit, as well as anxiety about belonging (or not belonging) in a place that is fearful and "wild," are common themes in horror. Yvette Nolan argues that this "hungering for a *genius loci* imposed new ones on the land, so that gothic literature is in effect the artistic manifestation of the act of colonization."[18] As Cynthia Sugars writes, settler colonialism produces storytellers who are

> plagued by the apparent absence of a legitimating folklore that would authenticate their experience of the place, an anxiety that went hand in hand with the difficulty of establishing an identifiably "Canadian" literature, (as a result) they responded

---

16 Bergland, *The National Uncanny*, 1.

17 Huhndorf, *Going Native*, 137.

18 Nolan, "Creating New Ghosts."

> by seeking to infuse their world with Gothic presence, turning to the Gothic as a form of national substantiation.[19]

The land itself is a source of anxiety and terror in the North American Gothic and in horror. Bloodied and wrecked bodies and blood-soaked landscapes characterize a genre obsessed with a land that is haunted, and with the possibility that the colonized/disappeared "ghostly" Indigenous presence might rise up and take revenge on white settler worlds.

While so much of horror positions the monster as a primitive and savage Other, the suffering that the civilized endure is based on the real suffering of peoples they have colonized. This appropriation of suffering is central to horror. White settler homes and lands are invaded, their children taken, bodies violated, and lives and futures eradicated. Though the repressed bursts through, making horror so potentially subversive, the construction of the Other as the repressed "primitive," the monstrous Indian and anachronistic Other within, reinforces settler colonial thinking. It is this appropriation of Indigenous suffering that makes horror so crucial to settler colonial storytelling. Horror may seem to disrupt settler worlds, but it appropriates the suffering and bloody violence of colonization. Horror may threaten rupture or exposure of the colonial project, without really doing so.

Indigeneity and colonial thought run deep in Gothic and horror literature and film, even when Indigenous people appear to be absent. Karen Piper writes about Mary Shelley's *Frankenstein*, and connects the projection of the monstrous creature created by Dr. Frankenstein as both Inuit and essentially as disruptive of domesticity through both his savagery and his love for his creator. The

19 Sugars, *Canadian Gothic*, 108–109.

story, Piper writes, begins with the Arctic and with the problem of colonization. The creature is, at least in part, a dangerous, Inuit man. Piper argues that

> if the Inuit is necessary for survival in Arctic, he/she must also be erased from the narrative in order for it to remain "heroic." It is precisely the domesticity of the indigenous inhabitant that must be eliminated in order to preserve that polarization between the domestic "tranquility" of the European home and the dangerous realm heroically confronted by the Arctic explorer. In a similar fashion, Shelley may be said to represent this quintessential ambivalence by suppressing the indigenous peoples of the Arctic in telling Walton's tale, until they emerge "unnaturally" in monstrous proportions....There is a kind of conflation that occurs, throughout *Frankenstein*, between the creature and the dangerous "elements" of the Arctic.[20]

Dr. Frankenstein's creature stalks his maker, gazes upon him, emerges from savage wilderness, and disrupts his chance at a normal/domestic life. In this way, the monster's "savagery" intertwined with his queerness, his unruliness, and he becomes a stand-in for the Indigenous-Other.

The idea that Indigenous Peoples are everywhere and nowhere in horror, echoes Bergland's point, that

> there is an obsession with Indigenous Peoples, with Native Peoples, in America. That obsession means, everyone...must internalize both the colonization of Native Americans and the American stance against colonialism...The potencies of both

20 Piper, "Inuit Diasporas," 66.

> the wish and counter-wish—here the desire to continue colonizing Native people and the desire to escape from colonialist regimes—create an obsessional mindset, in which American subjects continually return to the Native American figures who haunt them.[21]

Warren Cariou writes of the ways that Indigenous ghosts show up in the American Gothic, noting that "spectral Native figures have long been a part of the iconic vocabulary of Euro-American Gothic romances." This, he writes, is rooted in

> anxiety suffered by settlers regarding the legitimacy of their claims to belonging on what they call "their" land. This fear can be described in Freudian terms as a kind of neocolonial uncanny, a lurking sense that the places settlers call home are not really theirs, and a sense that their current legitimacy as owners or renters in a capitalist land market might well be predicated upon theft, fraud, violence, and other injustices in the past.[22]

Studying horror in order to better understand settler colonial perceptions and hegemonies is a worthy and, I hope, growing project. Mark Rifkin writes about the ways that "Indigenous peoples and geographies become unseen as part of originary, nonconscious non-native praxis and writing."[23] Rather than examine texts for their inclusion, however brief, of Indigenous Peoples, Rifkin's work challenges the reader to understand the shape of settler colonial society according to its own stories.

---

21 Bergland, *The National Uncanny*, 16.

22 Cariou, "Haunted Prairie," 727–728.

23 Rifkin, *When Did Indians Become Straight?*, xvii and 17.

SETTLER COLONIALISM

While Indigenous Peoples are relegated to some distant past in American horror, contemporary Indigenous people and their families, communities, nations, and confederacies thrive, survive, and resist ongoing settler colonialism. Settler colonialism describes the invasion of the Americas and the ongoing system of violent dispossession of Indigenous Peoples. As Wolfe writes about settler colonialism, "it strives for the dissolution of native societies. Positively, it erects a new colonial society on the expropriated land base...invasion is a structure not an event...elimination is an organizing principal of settler colonial society rather than a one-off (and superseded) occurrence."[24] Further, the white settler enacts violence (including ideologically) in order to story and replace Indigenous bodies. This system of ongoing invasion is described by Wolfe as a "land-centred project that coordinates a comprehensive range of agencies, from the metropolitan centre to the frontier encampment, with a view to eliminating Indigenous societies."[25] Indigenous Peoples speak back against settler colonial erasure and bring it into the open.

As J. Kēhaulani Kauanui articulates, settler colonialism endures against Indigenous resistance. Indigenous Peoples "exist, resist, and persist...settler colonialism is a structure that endures indigeneity, as it holds out against it." There is power in Indigenous scholarly interrogation of the ways that Indigeneity "implicates most aspects of American culture, politics, policy, and society."[26] As Aimee Rowe and Eve Tuck point out, there remains a need to centre

24 Wolfe, "Settler Colonialism," 388.

25 Wolfe, "Settler Colonialism," 393.

26 Kauanui, "'A Structure, Not an Event.'"

analyses of settler colonialism in the work of unpacking popular culture. They write that the "methods culture critics deploy, like genealogy and deconstruction, presume, and participate in the erasure of Indigenous peoples as modern subjects." Further, they argue that "with the exception of a handful of scholars, treatments of settler colonialism have largely remained undertheorized in cultural studies."[27]

Focusing solely on the Indigenous-Other as ghostly, or even as Other, runs the risk of reinforcing the decentring of Indigenous people as subjects. Dwanna McKay, Kirsten Vinyeta, and Kari Marie Norgaard theorize about settler colonialism while emphasizing the fact that,

> despite surviving under conditions of ongoing colonial occupation and violence, Indigenous persons and Native Nations continue to assert their own conceptions of political power, speak languages their ancestors have spoken in their communities since time immemorial, carry out spiritual and cultural responsibilities, and renew relations and knowledge systems by maintaining strong reciprocal ties with lands, waters, and non-human relatives.[28]

In the dominant narrative, for the most part, and particularly in the horror genre, the Indigenous person as real, as contemporary, is decentred or erased or buried. Unburying our presence—seeing Indigeneity and haunting even in the figure of Jason Voorhees or in the heroism of the Final Girl—is not enough, of course, and is

27 Rowe and Tuck, "Settler Colonialism and Cultural Studies," 6–7.

28 McKay, Vinyeta, and Norgaard, "Theorizing Race and Settler Colonialism," e12821.

only a first step toward further intellectual work on Indigenous storying in the context of horror.

CIVILIZATION AND SAVAGERY

Turning an anti-colonial lens onto the horror film means unpacking certain formulas and tropes that work to marginalize Indigenous people. The construction of savagery, that idea that Indigenous Peoples are primitive, that they are violent and backwards (and backwoods), is paired with some notion of the colonizer as the embodiment of civilization. Emma LaRocque describes savagism as "a super-myth that has provided the basis for the colonizer's psychology and institutions... It is also reflected in the continuing exploitation of 'the Indian' in the media."[29] The civilization and savagery (Civ/Sav) dichotomy becomes a means by which to reference the ways that representation of both the savagery of the constructed Indian and the civilized nature of the colonizer are constructed.[30]

There is, of course, a direct connection between the dispossession of Indigenous Peoples (of land, of freedom, of life, of culture) and the Civ/Sav binary. Eve Tuck and K. Wayne Yang speak to this need to re-establish settlement and in turn the erasure of Indigenous Peoples:

> The settler, if known by his actions and how he justifies them, sees himself as holding dominion over the Earth and its flora and fauna, as the anthropocentric "normal," and as more developed, more human, more deserving than other groups or species. The settler is making a new "home" and that home is

29 LaRocque, *When the Other Is Me*, 4.
30 LaRocque, *When the Other Is Me*, 15.

> rooted in a homesteading worldview where the wild land and wild people were made for his benefit. He can only make his identity as a settler by making the land produce, and produce excessively, because "civilization" is defined as production in excess of the "natural" world (i.e., in excess of the sustainable production already present in the Indigenous world).[31]

Historical constructions of civilization and savagery include narratives of Euro-Western theorists grappling with questions about their own propensity toward "savage" behaviour. Pioneering American anthropologist Lewis Henry Morgan originally saw Indigenous Peoples—whose voices and beliefs he misappropriated—as savage, but, as James Schwartz argues, Morgan's perspective shifted later in life:

> Morgan, like many nineteenth-century Euro-Americans, equated progress with economic growth, territorial expansion, urbanization, and the spread of democracy. He feared, moreover, that the immoral passions of drinkers, radicals, and indigenous peoples threatened these gains. After adopting a more sympathetic view of Native peoples in 1843, his understanding of progress and the passions changed, and he began ascribing to European colonists the destructive passions he had formerly attributed to Amerindians.[32]

Such a shift often occurs in horror, when the civilized attacked by the savages realize that they, too, are awful. At the heart of settler colonial erasure and oppression of Indigenous Peoples, there

31 Tuck and Yang, "Decolonization Is Not a Metaphor," 6.
32 Schwartz, "Lewis Henry Morgan's Early Theory of Progress," 229.

remains this construct of civilization and savagery, even (and especially perhaps) when those who seem to be civilized turn savage.

THE FRONTIER

The frontier, Lynda Schneekloth writes, is constructed as "a wilderness... an uncivilized and violent place... to be filled with the superior European culture and the Christian religion."[33] Margaret Atwood attempts to contrast the American frontier with the Canadian notion of survival but in doing so shows their similarities instead. The frontier "suggests a place that is new... a line that is always expanding, taking in or 'conquering' ever-fresh virgin territory (be it The West, the rest of the world, outer space, Poverty or The Regions of the Mind)." Atwood writes, while for white settlers in Canada, the idea of colonization raises also the notion of survival, that is "bare survival in the face of 'hostile' elements and/or natives: carving out a place and a way of keeping alive."[34] Whether we call it survival or the frontier, both concepts—and countries—are preoccupied and anxious about protecting the interior—the civilized, safe, heteropatriarchal family home—against Indigenous Peoples who threaten progress and reproductive expansion.[35] The frontier continues as a central logic within settler colonial North America.

The frontier is a mindset of protection and conquest—the civilized interior protecting against the savagery and wilds that are beyond the boundaries which themselves must be expanded outward. L. Frank Baum, the author of *The Wizard of Oz*, referenced the protectiveness of frontier settlements. In Baum's notoriously

33 Schneekloth, "The Frontier Is Our Home," 211.

34 Atwood, *Survival*, 27.

35 See also Launius and Boyce, "More than Metaphor."

racist, anti-Indigenous editorial after the death of Sitting Bull, he describes Native Americans as "whining curs" and adds,

> The Whites, by law of conquest, by justice of civilization, are masters of the American continent, and the best safety of the frontier settlements will be secured by the total annihilation of the few remaining Indians. Why not annihilation? Their glory has fled, their spirit broken, their manhood effaced; better that they die than live the miserable wretches that they are.[36]

The frontier settlement becomes a place of development and advancement, safety and superiority. American horror might mock or unsettle this neat divide, but it also tends to reinforce it. As Laurel Clark Shire points out, policymakers have often "mobilized gender and social provision to support national expansion. Invoking images of threatened and indigent widows, they enacted welfare policies aimed at protecting, retaining, and encouraging frontier settlers."[37] The point mirrors one that I make in this book—that gender and sexuality, though at times explored rather interestingly and perhaps at times unsettlingly in horror, are also mobilized to demonize some notion of savagery, some lurking Other, who threatens above all else the safety of the women and youth inside the boundaries of the frontier town.

The frontier as "meeting point between savagery and civilization,"[38] or the logic of the frontier, continues and is in need of further unpacking in and through horror. This includes the notion of a safe, civilized stronghold against the savage Other, who lurks

36 Baum as quoted in Sutherland, "L. Frank Baum Advocated Extermination."
37 Shire, "Turning Sufferers into Settlers," 489.
38 Taylor, *The Turner Thesis*, 9.

in the woods or near the lake (as Jason lurks on the grounds of Camp Crystal Lake), and the idea that the landscape is also unsafe. Schneekloth writes about the "imaginal place of the frontier" as "an enduring and powerful myth."[39] In an analysis of the frontier and of the settler's desire to become Indigenous themselves, Huhndorf writes about the "exalted tale of (male, European) trailblazers driven westward into unknown lands, compelled by a force the nineteenth century labeled 'manifest destiny.'"[40] American horror often fixates on that frontier town, where fences, gates, and the periphery of suburban properties are meant to hold off a savage threat.

According to Deondre Smiles, we can think more about the frontier as a contemporary and important concept:

> Fueled by the American settler myths of *terra nullius* (no man's land) and Manifest Destiny, the American settler state proceeded upon a project of cultural and physical genocide, with lasting effects that endure to the present day. The "settler myth" permeates American culture. Words such as "pioneer," the "West," "Manifest Destiny" grab the imagination as connected to the growth of the country in its early history. America sprang forth from a vast open "wilderness." Of course, for Indigenous people, we know differently—these lands had complex cultural frameworks and political entities long before colonization.[41]

Settler violence becomes projected, outside, or seen as erupting from within. In the United States, Sarah Launius and Geoffrey Boyce write that "the frontier and its colonial logic are structural

39 Schneekloth, "The Frontier Is Our Home," 210.
40 Huhndorf, *Going Native*, 53.
41 Smiles, "The Settler Logics of (Outer) Space."

features of racial governance and capital accumulation that remain continuously operative over time."[42]

The central subjects of horror are often white settler women, who battle against some monstrous entity on behalf of their family or community, or the subject may be that family or that town, in its struggle against "savagery at the gates," in the form of demons, devils, witches, ghosts, vampires, and others. The constructed Indian is coded in these fantasies of invasion because settler colonialism, the Civ/Sav dichotomy, and the frontier are maintained through refusals to even acknowledge their contemporariness. Lorenzo Veracini writes of settler colonialism that it "is characterised by a persistent drive to ultimately supersede the conditions of its operation. The successful settler colonies 'tame' a variety of wildernesses,"[43] including the uncontainable stories of Indigenous people—for whom resilience, trauma, and healing traditions that span many thousands of years form myriad truths in the face of settler colonialism's many harms.

The Civ/Sav binary, the threat of the frontier as a meeting ground between these worlds, and the projection of savagery onto an Indigenous-coded Other are evident in a number of horror films that have become foundational to both the genre's development to and studies of horror.

LAST HOUSE ON THE LEFT *(1972)*

In *The Last House on the Left* (1972), we're asked to question the nature of the white settler family and whether it truly is the civilized in the face of savagery or if some dark heart lingers in all people. Not

42 Launius and Boyce, "More than Metaphor," 1.

43 Veracini, "Introducing Settler Colonial Studies," 3.

only is the basic premise a reinforcement of Civ/Sav constructs, but those constructs come to include problematic gender dynamics.[44] In the 1972 original *Last House*,[45] a mother and father wait up for their daughter, Mari, to return home; they do not realize that Mari, along with her friend, is being attacked by the side of a road. A group of savage killers (they are dirty, they have messy hair, they roam the countryside) attack, rape, and kill the two young women.

When Mari and her friend's attackers find themselves stuck in a storm, they stumble upon Mari's parents' home and stay there for the night. It gradually dawns on the parents that their daughter's killers are in their home, and rather than call "the authorities," they take revenge. Somehow, the bizarre acts of violence that the parents enact are supposed to outweigh what has happened to their daughter, or so seems to be the moral of this story. The violent misogyny of the *Last House* killers is somehow proof of *their* "savagery"; but the violence of the parents in retaliation, serves as proof that the civilized are also savage.

Last House is important to this study because it involves and reinforces this notion that the threat of the Civ/Sav binary is that we can all slip into this constructed notion of savagery. The idea that we can all "devolve" in this way seems to be central to the film. The sexual violence enacted against the young, innocent (white-settler) women, is rooted in the construct of savagery. The so-called civilized then can also slip into savagery, into violence that is vengeful and outside the scope of legal (civilized) systems. The notion that violence is rooted in savagery and not baked into

44 To put it crassly, the rape and murder of two women is somehow equated with the violent actions of the parents who go after the young women's killers. This equation has always felt so odd in these kinds of rape-revenge films.

45 The original, released in 1972, was directed by Wes Craven; a remake of *The Last House on the Left*, directed by Dennis Iliadis, came out in 2009.

white settler heteropatriarchy[46] is a reinforcement of the Civ/Sav binary that is so central to settler colonial thought.

Settler colonialism continues to spin on the notion that white settlers are perpetually in a battle against savagery, both from within and from external forces. White homesteaders have perpetually been made to fear the Indian lurking outside—threatening their children and women—as well as the potential for taking on their violent traits. Numerous captivity myths have "presented conflict as the primary mode of frontier life, with the savages serving as the embodiment of depravity that had to be overcome and destroyed."[47] The violent rape and murder of young women in *Last House* marks the killers as dark, savage threats at the periphery. Even more astoundingly, the rape of the film's teen girls is somehow equated with the "seduction" of a male rapist and subsequent removal of his penis, which reveals more about how a misogynist society views sexual assault as a plot device, and female revenge and castration as the *real* horror.

Jeffrey Steven Podoshen argues that the violence that befalls Mari signals the end of the "flower power" era and references the Manson Family killings of 1969.[48] While that may have been the intention of the filmmaker, the challenge that settler colonial studies presents for this reading is multi-layered. First, the idea that the Manson killings were exceptional—a burst of certainly awful violence at the hands of a misogynistic and racist cult leader—is not well supported given that North America is built on heinous anti-Black and anti-Indigenous as well as imperial violence. Secondly, the very construct that the film rotates around—who are

46 Jordan, "Belonging and Otherness."

47 Sharp, *Savage Perils*, 93.

48 Podoshen, "Home Is Where the Horror Is," 724.

the civilized, who are the savage—obscures both the construction of the civilization/savagery hierarchy and the gender-based violence at the heart of the film's horrid opening scenes.

Instead, the film lends itself well to an understanding of the ways that the civilized white settler frontier family defends itself against the threat of savagery. The performance of this divide is laid out in what becomes a formative horror story reversing the home invasion structure. But when Mari's parents enact their revenge, they become outlaws, not frontier heroes. They aren't protecting the family any longer, because without Mari they have lost their heir. Instead, they shift into a reality that sees policing and state-sanctioned justice systems as ineffective, even enabling of gendered violence. And though we're shown a lengthy and agonizing shot of Mari's murderers gazing in shame at what they've done after killing the girls, their haunted faces hint only at momentary regret.

The killers are a gang, constructed as savage through class and other signifiers. Krug, the ringleader of the group, has longish dark curly hair, smokes cigars, and is unshaven. The group is generally a disorienting combination of unkemptness and aspiring middle class. One gang member wears a suit jacket, but it doesn't fit well, and he looks like he's playing at being a middle-class adult. The gang's only woman is manipulative and comes across as "unhinged." *Last House* presents class hierarchy as a stand-in for the divide between civilized (wealthy) and savage (poor). The story is about a criminal gang who attack a wealthy family, only to find out that family is equally capable of violent or "savage" acts. The film references murders committed by the Manson family which "upended ideas of safety, security, and innocence, and effectively sounded the death knell of '60s counterculture."[49]

---

49 Romano, "The Manson Family Murders."

Last House sees the family's innocence shattered by its own propensity for violence (at least seemingly). Eve Tuck and C. Ree write about the preoccupation in American horror with the innocent heroes, who fend off the monster.[50] The innocence of white settler families, destroyed by "savage" violence, positions the violence not as internal to the white settler family at all, but as an externalized force against which the family must battle. That settler colonizers would be so surprised in the face of its own violence—that they would believe that violence to be exceptional and not foundational—and then label these horrors as rooted in savagery, is a tangled tale continually woven. Historian Bernard Bailyn, interviewed by Ron Rosenbaum, says of the pilgrims' violence toward the Pequots that "the butchering that went on cannot be explained by trying to get hold of a piece of land. They were really struggling with this central issue for them, of the advent of the Antichrist."[51] The notion that land acquisition alone cannot explain white settler violence toward Indigenous Peoples in the Americas is integral to understanding how settler colonialism (re)enacts violence against Indigenous lands and bodies in ongoing ways. The idea that Bailyn raises also speaks to the twisting of the American Indian into Satanic beings.[52]

Settler colonialism contextualizes ongoing gendered and class violence. And as Podoshen points out, the urban/suburban divide is central to the film:

> In this particular happenstance, the suburban home is further "protected" by woods, streams and miles of towns and

50 Tuck and Ree, "A Glossary of Haunting."

51 Rosenbaum, "The Shocking Savagery."

52 Lovejoy, "Satanizing the American Indian," 606.

> residences, yet still the dangerous aspects of 1972 New York City are able to infiltrate both the outer-ring suburbs and the physical body of the young woman coming of age. *Last House* is terrifying for those who try to seek refuge outside the concrete jungle as they realize that there are few places to hide from the rampant crime and terror that has become rather commonplace in society.[53]

The family of *Last House* is supposed to be safe, we are told, because they have retreated from the savage lands. They have descended, however, into savagery themselves. Settler colonialism takes for granted these categories, of the concrete jungle and savage periphery, and *Last House* inscribes the concepts in a kind of blueprint for other horror films.

THE TEXAS CHAINSAW MASSACRE *(1974)*

Reframing *The Texas Chainsaw Massacre*[54] again evokes the frontier and the Civ/Sav binary. The film is one of the most important examples of a frontier tale in horror, as a story about civilized white youth who end up in the savage lands and then either die or go mad themselves. The 1974 original opens with an introductory monologue that describes the tragic loss of youth and their exposure to the "mad and macabre"; it is followed closely by a series of images of bodies dug from the ground and posed in a grotesque sculpture. During this amazing opening, solar flares are referenced and the fearfulness of extreme (hellish) heat is palpable. The land,

53 Podoshen, "Home Is Where the Horror Is," 725.

54 The original *Texas Chainsaw Massacre*, directed by Tobe Hooper, was released in 1974; subsequently there have been a remake (Nispel, 2003) and a prequel (Liebesman, 2006).

the cosmos, and history all intertwine to doom nice white youth. These young people, who take a van into rural Texas to check on their relatives' graves and properties after hearing that some of the dead have been exhumed, sweat and complain about the heat. They talk about astrology: planets in retrograde are described as maleficent. On some level the film might disrupt settler colonial narratives of Texas, the glory of cowboy life and cattle ranching laid bare as cruel and horrifying. Largely, though, the film operates as a cannibal fairy tale and a frontier myth.

In an absolutely amazing series of personal choices, the film's monsters, the Sawyer family, have taken to luring hitchhikers to their abode and killing and eating them. The film follows that van of young kids as they are killed one by one by the Sawyers, with only one survivor. The main killer of the Sawyer family is Leatherface, who uses a chainsaw to do his dirty deeds. The Sawyers are a group of men, it seems, but Leatherface sometimes wears a woman's face (literally) and occupies a domestic role. That Leatherface might be both a trans monster and also coded as a mythical Indian is interesting, not least because he is almost portrayed as a sympathetic character. The Sawyers have bones and leather and fur and feathers in their home. They are the lurking Indians waiting for those explorers who happen their way. At one point, after killing one of the youth, Leatherface hangs his head in some semblance of shame or regret. This film is just an epic tragedy of failed cultural exchange, perhaps. If only they'd listened to each other!

The only survivor of the massacre is Sally Hardesty, who escapes the Sawyers in glorious fashion, screaming then laughing her way in a leap through a window. Her big scene comes just before and just after this moment of crashing through this glass wall of dream/reality. Prior to this moment, she had been tied and nailed to a chair, forced to have dinner with the Sawyers. After she crashes and escapes to see the sunrise, she is chased onto the back of a truck, whereupon she escapes with the help of the driver.

One of the young people killed is Franklin, Sally's brother. He spends some time joyfully talking about bashing cows' skulls in, and then the film shows us images of clearly mistreated cattle, which positions the supposedly civilized youth as potentially being terrible as well. Franklin and Sally's family lore includes cow slaughtering, and they are shown to be similar to the Sawyers in this way. The difference between the Sawyer and the Hardesty families is often framed as a class struggle. The Sawyers are stuck in an economically failed part of Texas while Sally and her family moved elsewhere and prospered. Reframed in terms of settler colonial relations, the Sawyers have stayed backward because they are tragic, violent, and sad savages. Sally and her family moved and developed—they are now civilized.

The Sawyers are coded as mythical Indians. Their home is covered in feathers and animal bones, cow skulls, and even a hanging turtle shell. Putting cow skulls up in certain settings is a respectful thing for some Native people, and the empty turtle shell rattle is also a cultural symbol for some. This idea of the Sawyers as Indians is taken up by Clover, who compares the Western and its Indigenous-Other with modern horror. "That older story," Clover states, "of course, is no longer tellable in its original terms. What makes it tellable in modern terms is precisely its hybridization."[55] Class alone cannot explain what is going on in *Texas Chainsaw*. The hitchhiker, a.k.a. Nubbins Sawyer, whom the youth pick up, has a red birthmark on his face, which resembles the kind of face paint white settlers might mythologize Indians as wearing; he also has an animal skin pouch, like a medicine bag, around his neck. Nubbins

55 Clover, *Men, Women and Chainsaws*, 163.

talks about respectfully using the whole animal, the whole cow, in the golden era of cattle slaughtering. When we last see him, after he's been kicked out of the young people's van for acting like a total jerk (he cuts Franklin's hand), he is marking the side of their car in a bloody symbol and doing a whooping sort of dance.

Slippery lines are being drawn, with the economically dispossessed ("colonized") explaining their side of the animal/human binary that's been drawn, hippies proclaiming that it's unethical to eat meat of any kind, a member of the "good guys" going on about animal killing practices like he's keen on doing it himself, and the youth marked for slaughter, much like the cattle they pass by. Lines between civilized and savage *and* innocent and criminal, sane and mad, human and animal, all blur and are played with to evoke discomfort and obviously fear.

Encapsulating all of this chaos are the workings of nature and the cosmos, setting these people—prey and killer—up for their fated endings. Colonization is inevitable, we are all eaten eventually, or so the myth goes: The land is empty, barren, dusty, and dry; heat rises in waves, hellish. Natural disaster, gruesome violence, all befall white settler America the way it did for Indigenous Peoples.

Whatever the moral to this fairy tale, the film plays with constructs that so much of the American horror film tends to play with, but which go underexamined in the literature. The fear is one of white settlers themselves being colonized, disappeared, served up as meat. It is interestingly self-indulgent to present a group of young white people playing these sorts of roles, in the face of the actual and ongoing power structures facing Indigenous Peoples who, in North America at that time, were in the midst of a massive resurgence and protest movement.[56]

---

56 See, for example, Martinez, *Life of the Indigenous Mind*.

THE HILLS HAVE EYES *(1977)*

The idea that the civilized can "go savage" still presumes that there is something called savagery to regress or devolve into. In this vein, there is no other film that explores, upends, and then re-establishes notions of the civilized nuclear family unit quite like *The Hills Have Eyes* (1977).

Like *The Texas Chainsaw Massacre* (1974), *The Hills Have Eyes* features a cannibal family with animal names and bone, feather, and leather clothing, whose "savage" acts—trapping, killing, and eating humans—are held up as a mirror, or perhaps just a mockery, of foundational notions of the sanctity of the family in civilized society. Using the work of Althusser in arguing that "art can find a way to highlight the gap between the ideological promise of the social forms and the lived reality, thus opening the way to resistance," Lorena Russell states that "*The Hills Have Eyes* operates in this gap between a conservative reiteration of family values (the standard plot of the family under siege) and, insofar as the films invite audience sympathy with the outlaw families, the radical possibility of how the social structure and ideological force of the family might assert itself against the state."[57] The insertion of sexual violence in this tale—unlike, for example, the similar *Texas Chainsaw Massacre* take on the "wild" and outlaw family—makes it harder to sympathize with the "savage" outlier family. Instead, we're given a sense that both families—the invaders and the white settlers who have taken to the hills—are awful, and women are sort of caught between the crashing together of their awfulness. The cannibals are invaded, their existence in a poisoned, desolate landscape serving as a reminder of colonization as a historic

57 Russell, "Ideological Formations," 107.

event; however, they are also invaders, this isn't their land, they are also cannibals who are patriarchal and violent.

Neither family is actually Indigenous—just symbolically so, in the case of the Jupiter crew—and therein lies the problem. The mythical-Indian coded Jupiter, Mars, Pluto, and Mercury (hippies gone way wrong, like the Manson family, after taking to the desert) are described by Andrew Carroll as the "quintessential family" turned to "a group of cannibalistic, abusive, and vicious troglodytes capable only of destruction."[58] They wear feathers and bones and live in caves and eat people: allegorically, the Indigenous-Other. The origin story of the family lies in Jupiter killing his sister and being sent into the hills, only to find an "insane prostitute" with whom to have a bunch of awful children. Constructs of madness and Indigeneity, then, are crucial in constructing the story of this murderous family named after Roman gods.

The Carters, the family who enter onto the cannibals' territory, aren't all that innocent, led as they are by a conservative cop who goes off course and crashes their vehicle, ultimately getting them all killed, because he's a controlling patriarch. Bob is a bigot and a Republican NRA gun owner, easily leading one to ask who is worse—Jupiter or Bob? The Carters are on their way to claim a family inheritance—a silver mine—making them invaders and colonizers of a different brand, coming from the "civilized" world to destroy and exploit the "savage." Still, when the last of the family survives by doing some heinous things (using their mom's corpse to lure in Jupiter's sons in order to kill them) the point is sort of made that they can be "just as bad."

Through a settler colonial theoretical lens, Jupiter—sent to the hills for murdering his sister—and his family, are also colonizers.

58 Carroll, "The Brady Bunch Go Savage."

In the remake, they appropriate the suffering of the mythical Indian, after they are left to die after refusing to leave their home during nuclear testing. This appropriation of Indigenous suffering and of those stories of real invasion that Indigenous communities and nations have survived, is a key element to this film and others like it. Even as the cannibal/"wild"/outlaw family struggles against American military violence, with their various physical and intellectual harms from radiation damage, and even as we viewers are invited to celebrate their demise, "deformities" hacked away in punishment after being displayed *as* horror, the idea that "this also happened to Indigenous people" is referenced subtextually and only as a past or symbolic event.

We're meant to question the innocence of the Carters, but we can't possibly be expected to cheer on the cannibal rapists as they work to destroy one family in order to grow their own. The final survivor of this film, or one of them, is Doug. He is shown to be a "nice guy" who goes savage (hunting and killing the cannibals) in order to save his kid. Doug's profound shift in *Hills*, as he seems to be left with no choice but to go from pacifist to murderer to rescue his daughter from Jupiter's family , supposedly proves that the Civ/Sav binary is a natural part of our human makeup. Doug is "proof" that the civilized are really savage and the savage are also really, *really* savage, which is to say that there is rot at the core of the nuclear family. Russell writes that both *Hills* films

> subtly manipulate audience sympathies and ultimately question clear distinctions between the "civilized" and "savage." While Jupiter and his family clearly outpace the Carters' capacity for brutality and evil, the audience is nevertheless repeatedly reminded to understand their disabilities and rage in the context of the hardships they have endured and to measure

their violence against the specter of nuclear destruction and government deception.[59]

When the Civ/Sav dichotomy is used in horror, the constructs themselves—the civilized and the savage—are normalized.

THE FINAL GIRL

Settler fears of the land and Indigenous people are also disturbed when the "civilized" see "savagery" emerge from within their own families, communities, and individual psyches. Final Girls "go savage"—with weaponry (axes, hands, teeth) and faces drenched in blood—in order to survive the frontier violence and false promises of civilized society. In some instances, that inversion radically intervenes into everyday settler colonialism, upending, unearthing, and disrupting its normalcy when white settler women smash, slash, chop, chainsaw, and battle their way to freedom—freedom from the gaslighting, manipulative boyfriend in *Scream* (1996), from the parents who try to ignore and bury trauma in *A Nightmare on Elm Street* (1984), or from rape culture in *Black Christmas* (2019). The ultimate fate of civilized society and its markers—the heteronormative family, the intact suburban community—are doomed much of the time. In *The Hills Have Eyes* (2006), these transformations and evocations of savagery/civilization remain problematic. The "savages" are also rapists. On one hand, this calls out the cultures that believe themselves civilized yet remain patriarchal and violent. On the other hand, the close affinity that the *Hills* family holds to a stereotypical notion of Indianness makes the film come uncomfortably close to inferring that some kind

59 Russell, "Ideological Formations," 108.

of regression—some descent into savagery that the original family made when it moved to the desert—necessarily includes the adoption of extreme sexual violence and cannibalism.

Indigenous Peoples were thus constructed as representative of the savage past of all humans. Progress, development, and indeed innovation and inventiveness became the exclusive domain of Europeans.[60] Kyle Christensen compares Laurie Strode and Nancy Thompson, of the Halloween and Nightmare on Elm Street franchises, writing that these movies (among others) deal "with the idea of normal, suburban-esque families who become 'uncivilized' after their lives and the lives of their loved ones are endangered, retaliating violently and savagely against their adversaries."[61] The savage Others can be portrayed as either a source of liberation or a source of fear in horror, and either notion is part of a construct that has distorted representations of Indigenous Peoples since the onset of colonization.

The monstrous (imagined and constructed) Indian is also a woman in horror. Indigenous women are disappeared in white settler storytelling, but are then coded as Final Girls.[62] The Final Girl encounters those things that Indigenous women have to actually deal with, in real-world dynamics of surveillance and punishment, institutionalization and incarceration, against those intent on removing Indigenous women from leadership, from land, from kinship structures.[63] There is a kind of appropriation of an imag-

60 Blaut, *The Colonizer's Model of the World.*

61 Christensen, "The Final Girl," 34.

62 Clover, *Men, Women and Chainsaws.*

63 The villainous werewolves of *The Howling* (1981), for example, are coded as Indians, with long dark hair—Martha, the final werewolf standing, wears a bone or tooth necklace and a black leather vest like an outlaw or Native American rock star activist or, of course, an epic lesbian whose world pulled in Dee Wallace's Karen White.

ined Indian woman as savage, as hero, as victim, in horror. This construct shows up as the Final Girl moves from her civilized life and devolves into savagery and madness.

Susan Burch tells the story of a Dakota woman, Elizabeth Fe Alexis Fairbault, whose incarceration in the Canton Asylum speaks to the nexus of sanism and settler colonialism. Burch writes of the late Elizabeth Fairbault:

> Her corporeal presence seemed…to offend—intoxicated, dressed in a top that exposed flesh and shape, and swearing at or insulting those who confronted her. Stereotypes proliferated in US white culture at this time: drunken Indians, sexually promiscuous Indian women, wild Indians, crazy Indians. The presence of these stigmatizing representations in America draws into question the powerful decision to remove this "Indian problem."[64]

Settler colonialism is upheld through particular forms of heterosexist, sanist, ableist, ageist, and classist relations, seeing Indigenous women and lands as inherently violable.[65] The imagined Indian is femininized also, in an appropriation of real suffering and of a journey toward some notion of freedom from the confines of civilized society.

The violent, savage, constructed Indigenous-Other[66] is an identity that frightens white settlers, as Joanne Barker points out:

---

64 Burch, *Committed*, 145–146.

65 Bourgeois, "Perpetual State of Violence," 260.

66 Often referred to elsewhere as "Indian-Other," though I'll tend not to use this as my terminology because I'm not comfortable with the quoting of my work back to me by white settlers when I do use the term *Indian*.

> The accumulated effect of terror has socialized non-Indians, particularly as they gather together as good citizens, to anticipate harm from Indians and demand a state that can offer protection against them... the kind of Indigenous produced by citizens united is the Indigenous who is not absent or erased but is made particularly present—at the ready—to be killed.[67]

The freedom that the survivors in horror experience, outside of the bounds of sanism, heteropatriarchy, class stratification, and so on, can also be appropriated by outlaw white settlers. These notions of savagery are deeply gendered, with the Final Girl taking on a particular role in the equation.

Gender, the family, and interconnected power dynamics (including human-environmental relations) need to be explored through a lens that centrally includes the futurity of Indigenous Peoples, kinship, and lands, at the heart and purpose of challenging settler colonialism. It can be presented in quite strange, fun, upside down, downside up ways, but it definitely persists in a genre concerned with whether it is *civilized* to hack a would-be murderer to bits with an axe, or perhaps to shove a blender on the head of the brother-in-law who tried to kill you for inheritance money and then plug that blender in. Constructs of civilization and savagery are upended when previously civilized people are pushed to behave in savage ways. I would also add other elements to that analysis, arguing, as I do in Chapter 2, that the Final Girl has a predeceased sister—the First Girl, whose gruesome death tells the audience that something is very, very wrong in settler colonial towns, suburbs, campuses, and cities. That first kill, and the martyrdom that seems to cling to Judith Myers or Casey Becker, re-establishes the innocence

67 Barker, *Red Scare*.

of the white settler family.[68] The promises of settler colonialism, that nice white people will find safety and prosperity, are false. The First Girl is dragged off screen in *Black Christmas* (2019) or discovered hanging from a tree in *Scream* (1996), and the gap she leaves behind the barricades of safety resonates and begins to undo the false notion of settler colonial safety.

The Indigenous-Other in horror, is represented in numerous ways: as vampires, as zombies, as wolfmen. Piper writes of Victor Frankenstein's creation that

> the creature himself came to represent these inhabitants of the North, as well as the threat of their arrival in England if increased communication were to occur. Just as John Sackhouse had once arrived as a stowaway on British shores, so Frankenstein's creature is a stranger who must be incorporated in—or rejected from—European culture. In the novel, the "birth" of the creature in Europe could be said to represent cultural fears of the invasion of the "primitive" in "civilized" society, or the arrival of the colonized, in search of revenge, on the shores of the colonizer.[69]

68 For such an interesting and progressive movie like *It's a Wonderful Knife* (2023), the killing of a young Black teenager, Cara, which is the film's first violent death, is problematic. The film has multiple queer characters, and has an alternate-dimension plotline, which means that Cara could be brought back to life. Instead, she's forgotten in the film and the focus becomes the white settler family's literal resurrection as these other previously killed characters are all brought back. Cara's martyrdom is poignant and unnecessary and could have been undone. There are no Indigenous people in the town, and the white main character commands the northern lights, yelling at them to fix things. Indigenous teachings about never whistling at the northern lights, much less screaming at them, makes that portion of the film scarier than it was probably intended to be!

69 Piper, "Inuit Diasporas," 63.

A settler colonial theoretical lens contextualizes the constructed Indian (or Indigenous-Other)[70] according to the settler colonial system, which incorporates all of these differences for its own maintenance.

The survivors of horror explore the spaces between and transformations toward civilization and savagery.[71] The land is drenched in blood as bodies also become covered in blood and gore. The forest is alive, ominous and blood splattered, the lake and ocean full of blooms of gore. In three horror movies I want to discuss here, the Final Girl is an outlaw more than a frontier hero. As an outlier, the Final Girl in these films—*The Hunt* (2020), *You're Next* (2011) and *Revenge* (2017)—is beyond the bounds of civilized society. The Final Girl in these films also embodies a deep resentment (either on her own part or on the part of the audience viewing her unfolding story) of the wealth of the white settler family and/or community in these films. Her violence brings death as an endpoint to unending accumulation or class privilege. The women in these films venture further than most Final Girl characters, beyond the bounds of "civility." These next three movies reflect a rage and a desire for freedom, channeled through a transformation into the faux Indigenous-Other. Again, my readings here are mixed, torn between the desire for freedom from settler

70 In Mary Shelley's work, Frankenstein's creature seems to have both Native and Inuit characteristics.

71 At the end of *The Texas Chainsaw Massacre* (1974), the only body we see covered in blood is Sally's, the film's Final Girl. She isn't returning to the world of the normal, she's completely gone from it, shrieking and bloodied, laughing manically as she dodges the cannibal family's grips. By the end of *The Descent* (2005), which I'll cover in more detail later in the book, Sarah, the final survivor of a group of cannibal humans who have "devolved," has been literally bathed and reborn in a deep pool of blood and gore, from which she stumbles before the credits roll.

colonial patriarchy, and at times suspicious of the tendency to draw white women as potential outlaws.

THE HUNT *(2020)*

There is one version of Final Girl as an outlaw who is *not* rescued by civil society or her imagined ties to it, best exemplified in 2020's *The Hunt*. The film centres on a group of wealthy liberal people who hunt down largely poor, far-right people. After letting the far-right folks run away in various parts of Croatia, the hunters shoot, stab, and poison them, and blow them up. The only survivor of the movie is a former member of the army who tells the head organizers that she isn't a right-wing online conspiracy theorist—she's got the same name as the intended target, but it isn't her.

The movie was delayed in its release when the then-president of the United States declared it disrespectful to his far-right political base.[72] The odd thing about his outrage was that *The Hunt* makes the prey/hunted into sympathetic victims, while the hunters are stereotypical "social justice warriors,"[73] a term the far-right uses to dismiss real concerns with issues of power and domination. The message of the film, that white settlers on both the right and left can be terrible, is vaguely entertaining. More interestingly, the film's final survivor, Crystal, illustrates something about unruliness and savagery and stepping outside the bounds of "civilization." The wealthy hunters, not knowing their victims very well, presumably pick the wrong target, mistaking a woman who happens to be an army veteran, for an online conspiracy theorist. The veteran, Crystal May, turns the tables and survives the game.

72 James, "*The Hunt* Review."
73 Phelan, "Neoliberalism."

At one point, Crystal May alludes to how much she loves killing, and how being captured and then turning the tables on the elite hunters has essentially given her an outlet for her rage.

No one is innocent, though innocence is a central theme in *The Hunt*. When a pig is killed, accidentally, one of the hunters laments its death because the animal is innocent; the implication is that the people, on both sides, are not. The wealth, arrogance, and unethical behaviour (hunting people for sport and all) of the hunters make them just as bad as the hunted, though the hunted include homophobes and transphobes, hate groups, and gun-rights organizers. White settlers of America mix it up in gory fashion in this comedy-horror, set in Croatia (because of presumptions that they can set up such a kill-fest in Eastern Europe), and there is no self-soothing good-versus-evil narrative.

The film operates as a reverse-colonization fantasy as well. The hunt itself—hunting human beings for sport—is hardly hypothetical as a practice, given the violence that Indigenous and Black people have faced since the onset of colonization. The Final Girl, Crystal May (played by Betty Gilpin), of *The Hunt* is a former member of the American military who enjoys the kill because of her own rage. The ultimate fight scene between Crystal May and the organizer of the hunt, Athena (Hilary Swank), is a kind of epic confrontation between two people who are really just in love with their own capacity for violence. The freedom that these final two women experience, as they clasp each other close, almost lovingly, sharing a double-sided cutting tool to simultaneously penetrate each other's bodies, is almost erotic as Crystal May (the warrior) ultimately kills Athena (the goddess of war). Crystal May then assumes Athena's identity in a way, taking her dress, her dog, her money, and her private plane, as well as all of the fancy food and champagne on that plane, which she shares with the flight attendant.

The Civ/Sav binary is represented in *The Hunt* through the metaphor of George Orwell's *Animal Farm*. The power imbalance between the pigs and the humans is upended when Crystal dons Athena's clothing and walks as she does. She is both civilized and savage, a member of the US Army portrayed as a killing machine who enjoys the hunt. Logically, there isn't anywhere for Crystal May to really go. She flies away in her commandeered jet and sips champagne contentedly, providing a kind of open-ended finish to the movie that doesn't change much but certainly doesn't give her some fairy tale happy ending.

REVENGE *(2017)*

Revenge is a 2017 French horror film with obvious North American influences. The Final Girl spreads blood far and wide, blasting and stabbing the men hunting her; she transforms from a Lolita-like image into a gun-wielding, branded, peyote-taking outlaw. *Revenge* opens with a sex scene between a married man named Richard and his mistress, Jen, alone for now in his mansion in the desert. Richard's two friends arrive unexpectedly early, and both men promptly go after Jen as well. One of his friends sexually assaults Jen while the other watches and then closes the door. When Jen tells Richard, he tells her to calm down and sides with his friends. Realizing that his perfect life is in peril should Jen tell his wife about their affair, Richard sets out to kill Jen, chasing her from the house and into the desert and pushing her from a cliff after which she falls to be impaled on a large broken tree. As she lays there, arched and bleeding into the hot desert sand, she realizes that not only has she survived her fall, but the men are coming back for her. She sets the tree on fire and dramatically escapes, hiding against the cliff wall and, later, in a cave, as the men hunt her.

Themes related to civilization-versus-savagery and the frontier are central elements of the film's narrative and visuals, and the Final Girl undergoes a dramatic transformation. Coated in blood and dirt, she survives the night in a cave before exacting revenge on the men who assaulted her. She sears a Mexican beer can into her wound, which effectively brands a bird onto her skin, after taking peyote to curb her pain. Tim Posada points out that when Jen modifies her body over the course of the film,

> she is not becoming Other. Rather, she is returning to a pure self... Hence, she awakens to find a phoenix branded on her stomach (the result of the beer can logo), resulting in a positive body modification, one inflicted upon her by a natural monster... Jen is not a body without soul or a violation of natural law. Rather, her body modification is a return to natural law... Jen's return to a natural state of being is deemed monstrous Other by patriarchy.[74]

As fascinating as this reading is, the idea that the white woman is emancipated by some return to a state of natural being is not neutral. The transformation and faux-Indigenization of the Final Girl in this case involves peyote, a cave (often associated with primitivity), and the seared bird which is read as a ceremony of sorts that she enacts to empower herself.

Jen hunts down the men but is nearly tricked by the witness to her rape. He leaves his gun by a body of water and she comes upon it. He grabs her and tries to drown her, but she stabs him in the eyes—retaliation for his gaze on her and for the violence she has been forced to endure. She more successfully hunts down the

74 Posada, "#MeToo's First Horror Film."

second man, her rapist, whom she shoots and kills in a prolonged scene. Even more lengthy is the vengeful and gleefully violent scene in which she takes on her now ex-boyfriend, shooting him as he emerges nude from a shower, his naked form now subjected to a reversal of the gaze that has been aimed at Jen throughout the film. With her peyote-empowered eagle-branded abilities, she takes out the men with their own hunting tools. She is the savage Other, the coded-as-Indigenous woman who utterly destroys the violence of white men who target both women and nature[75] with their scopes and guns and knives. Jen's freedom becomes possible when she transforms in the "primitive" cave, and she destroys the eyes of the first male hunter she kills, neutralizing his gaze and his colonizing weaponry. My argument here is just that these elements make Jen's journey so profound. The desert as frontier (conquerable and tameable by white men with guns), the violable woman's body as a part of that frontier, and the land as wild and in fact *un*-conquerable, are interconnected themes. Centring white womanhood in that story is also what needs further unpacking.

YOU'RE NEXT *(2011)*

In *You're Next*, a wealthy white settler family gets together to have dinner and are attacked by a trio of men in animal masks. The men, as it turned out, have been hired by two of the family members themselves—sons intent on grabbing their parents'

---

75 It would be useful to talk about the land in *Revenge* in more depth. The high-tech equipment that the men use to hunt (presumably animals but then Jen) are a kind of unfair advantage over their prey. The way the central male protagonist stares at the land as though he owns it, gazes at and handles his mistress, lies to his wife, and occupies a strangely out-of-place house in the desert, all speak to some deeper analysis of the ways that colonialism and misogyny intertwine.

wealth through inheritance—but are defeated at the hands of the Final Girl, Erin. The mother, struggling with anxiety and perhaps depression, is coded as a "mad woman," and actually recognizes the threat facing the family early. She is dismissed by her children and husband, with only Erin interested in hearing what she has to say. As a result of her family's refusal to hear her, she is killed while left alone upstairs.[76] Erin turns the tables, hunting the hunters and refusing to be prey. She is beyond the bounds of respectability, willing to hit and hit and hit again until the bad guy is dead. "Who knew you'd be really good at killing," her boyfriend jokes, before she stabs him in the eye and shortly after killing his brother by sticking a blender on the top of his head and plugging it in.

This film very obviously examines the gendered nature of the boundaries between civilization and savagery and the threat to the frontier family who expands their holdings through not only land (they own a massive property, which we are shown) but wealth accrued through arms trading. The threat they face is both from within their own family and from outside. As they gather for dinner, they are attacked by a trio of animal-mask-wearing killers, mercenaries hired, as we discover, by two of their children alongside whom they served in the American army. The movie is so chilling and effective because the real horror comes from within not only the heteropatriarchal family, but a family that is explicitly connected to wealth accrued through settler colonial and imperial violence.

---

76 At the end of *Black Christmas* (1974), the final female survivor is left alone in her bed while the police determine the house where the killer is hiding to be clear. Their paternalism is similar to the behaviour of family members in *You're Next*, with the decision to leave the mom to have a nap upstairs while obviously under attack is paid for with her life as she's killed in bed.

We also learn that the female protagonist, played by Sharni Vinson, who is (somewhat) victorious in the end, has trained in "the Outback" as a survivalist. The Outback is a construct in this instance, coded for an audience well-trained in recognizing the difference between civilized spaces and savage ones. Somehow the character's survivalism taught her to beat people to death with blunt and found objects, and the crisis in which she finds herself leads to so many fantastic and gruesome killings that a question mark follows the word *suspect* written on her image at the end of the film. Certainly, the joke here is that she has behaved in such an "unhinged" way that the police cannot tell the difference between her and the killers—men in animal masks who invade the home of a wealthy family, bringing with them the wilderness and their own savagery, taught to them by the American military.

The threat to the white settler family is represented by animals and wilderness in *You're Next*. The boundaries between the civilized and the savage are established and then blurred early, as the family reveals that its wealth comes from a defence contractor. The scene of the family's drive toward their country mansion is marked by ominous music and shots of the surrounding woods, some of which they own as part of a large property. The frontier shifts again in the darkness, as the eventual Final Girl drives with her boyfriend along eerily lit winding roads. The mother, played by Barbara Crampton, identifies the danger first, telling her husband that someone is obviously in the house. She is ultimately dismissed as the resident "mad woman" (struggling with unnamed mental health issues and medications), laying the basis for the rest of the film.

The film then takes a turn. As the parents of the large family (whose wealth is derived from weapons and American imperialism as well) are killed, we find out that two of their sons arranged the murders for the inheritance. Erin, the lone survivor, kills her boyfriend when she finds out that he was in on it all. Erin, in fact, kills all of the killers, including her boyfriend's brother and his girlfriend. Erin is also an unruly person because her family sought to go "off grid," away from "civilization," to embrace "savage violence" and therefore freedom. In the end credits, Erin is labelled as a potential suspect in all of the murders.

The screaming, bloodied bodies of so many Final Girls seem to speak to a yearning for transformation and freedom. Erin Morton writes about the ways that white women yearn for freedom from "civility" and settler colonialism's "seemingly romantic placidity and everyday gendered innocuousness."[77] This yearning for freedom is also about invasion, wanting to take the land, to take on the taking of land—to become the new Indians. It is impossible, on one hand, not to cheer for the violent destruction of the patriarchal figure at the end of the slasher film; on another level, however, that patriarchal figure is also coded as a savage, a demon or Indian of the woods or wind. Destroying this figure is a mixed endeavour at best. When the Final Girl truly decides to ruin all that she's come from, to enter that world of lawlessness and incivility, the genre might shift even further toward and even potentially away from, settler colonialism.[78]

The Civ/Sav binary is reinforced in these obvious examples—movies like *Last House on the Left*, among many others. The binary shows up in other ways as well. Gender in horror (and I will deal

---

77 Morton, "Of Folksongs and Feral Children."

78 I should be clear however that this kind of transformation is impossible without Indigenous writers and actors and producers telling more stories in this genre (and others). Moreover, this desire for freedom for white women in a context that does so much harm, so centrally, to Indigenous and Black women, is still up for discussion within settler colonial and horror studies.

with the family and the frontier in horror in the next chapter) tends to be examined without attention to the colonial roots of certain constructs. Some of these constructs might be about masculinity or femininity, violence or justice, and they are concepts that should be reframed by some anti-colonial analysis. I am attempting some of that work here. The Final Girl's journey from civilized to savage and then back again often has variations that speak to other elements, like naturalizing or "Indigenizing" to the land as part of her self-defence strategizing. She might cross over or she might return to the fold in some heteronormative happy ending, but her journey is not only about gender and its rigid boundaries. The land matters in this analysis as well. Veracini writes about the ways that "the 'frontier,' the 'back-blocks,' the 'True North' and so on provide a mythical reference for 'indigenisation' processes, allowing for crucial settler investment in place and landscape."[79] The Final Girl runs through desert and woods and waterways, beating the monster out there in the wilderness, where she has to let go of her civilized trappings and embrace her violence and madness. Other characters in horror mirror this journey, reinforcing the constructions of civilization and savagery that underpin white settler appropriations of Indigenous suffering and erasure.

79 Veracini, *Settler Colonialism: A Theoretical Overview*, 21.

TWO

THE BLOODSUCKING BRADY BUNCH

THE FAMILY AND SETTLER COLONIAL HORRORS

"What am I supposed to do?
Go to college? Grad school? Work?"

—JILL ROBERTS[1]

THE KILLERS OF THE SCREAM FRANCHISE UNSETTLE the white settler family, questioning the norms they are supposed to live by and seeking something more. That something might be fame or notoriety or revenge, and it all adds up to a larger questioning of the normalcy of suburban life.

1 Craven, dir., *Scream 4*.

Suburban homes are a kind of homestead serving the purposes of reproducing settler colonialism. Veracini writes of suburbia in the context of settler colonialism that suburbia re-enacts settlement by mimicking housing styles (e.g., "colonials" and "ranches").[2] The suburban home is an expansive homesteading project, allowing white settlers to escape from the imagined wilds. In horror, the family in that homestead is under attack, and it's the savagery of the enemy at the gates (or inside the mind) that might upend their purpose.

North American horror films show the settler colonial family as anxious, as innocent, and, if not fully innocent, at the very least as victims of dark forces beyond anybody's control. The unhappy family, struggling against unreal expectations of a "normal" life is portrayed as somehow innocent, in need of saving, as well as anxious and desiring of freedom from the mundanity of the everyday. Tony Williams outlines all of the ways that American horror in the 1960s and '70s became particularly ominous, showing the white settler family falling victim to cannibalistic zombies, satanic invasion, and horrifying violence.[3] Anxieties about gender and sexuality underpin the family's inability to fight back against encroaching dangerous forces. Horror provides the opportunity to explore the ways that, as Chris Finley writes, "gender reifies colonial power."[4]

The construction of the Indian in horror is also gendered, as I have discussed. The Indigenous woman is made symbolic, othered, desired, and then strewn throughout horror in coded ways; she is bloodied and righteously angry, slicing the throat of the patriarchal monster. She might become a true outlaw and outlier,

2 Veracini, "Suburbia, Settler Colonialism," 339–357.

3 Williams, *Hearths of Darkness*, 11.

4 Finley, "Decolonizing the Queer Native Body," 31.

or she might retreat from it and attempt to return to the civilized centre—becoming more of a frontier hero than an outlaw.

Veracini explains that settler colonial families are seeking safety and peace in new settlements, and paradoxically "embrace and reject violence at the same time. The settler colonial situation is thus a circumstance where the tension between contradictory impulses produces long-lasting psychic conflicts."[5] Settler colonialism is also about reinforcing certain kinds of families and gender systems in order to maintain white settler domination over land. Burch writes of various forms of kinship disruption, removal, and "containment" that Native American families experience(d), with reference to Agnes Caldwell, who was taken by authorities to the Canton Asylum for Insane Indians. Caldwell's experience was part of a larger "pattern of other settler interventions... settler advocacy of boarding schools, adoption, and fostering into white families emphasized logics of Native peoples' perceived inherent dependency and incapacities."[6] Burch writes about these systems as systemic disruptions of Indigenous kinship and as construction and reinforcement of settler colonial norms of family and home.

At the centre of the settler colonial family are gendered relationships that the horror film both reinforces and subverts. Settler colonialism, according to scholars like Richard Phillips, "revolves around" the heterosexist, patriarchal nuclear family, as the regulation of marriage and heterosexism is foundational to the settler project.[7] There is a "gendered order" to settler colonialism and "a focus on mononuclear familial relations and reproduction."[8] While horror scholarship generally has dealt well with gender dynamics

5 Veracini, *Settler Colonialism: A Theoretical Overview*, 77.
6 Burch, *Committed*, 39.
7 Phillips, "Settler Colonialism and the Nuclear Family," 242.
8 Veracini, "'Settler Colonialism': Career of a Concept," 316.

in the family, settler colonialism as the system that underpins those dynamics is less frequently discussed.[9]

The final survivors of a horror film might fend off the monstrous (savage) threat in order to save the frontier. A Final Girl might be a frontier hero, an outlaw, or a savage herself. The "frontier hero," as described by Schneekloth, is "situated between wilderness and civilization and mediates the space between the town and the wilds."[10] This hero, who negotiates the middle terrain, cannot be a part of either world, cannot settle in the town. The final survivors of horror see the world through new eyes and are outside the law and the "sane" confines of heteropatriarchy.

The heteronormative, monogamous white settler family is often at the centre of and/or threatened in the horror film. Freddy Krueger, Jason Voorhees, and Michael Myers, the more famous of the slasher subgenre's bad guys, come from within settler communities and highlight the shakiness of the "civilized" settler colonial life. The source of horror is also often contained in places reimagined as settler lands, where "ancient" evils replace actual Indigenous stories of place. Horror can seem to unsettle that family structure, violently and chaotically, but the innocence of white settler formations of community remains central to the film's plot. The suffering of that family and the threat of the savage at the gates are formulaic.

The family, understood through a settler colonial lens, is reframed in horror as inherently *un*settled—struggling with the violence and deceptions of colonialism as both history and an ongoing system. Indigenous feminist theorists speak to and

---

9 I'll cover this point in more detail in my discussion about Kubrick's *The Shining* (1980).

10 Schneekloth, "The Frontier Is Our Home."

write about the ways that gender and settler colonialism operate. Central to settler colonialism, to the social, economic, and political fabric of it, is heteropatriarchy. The daily, taken-for-granted reproductions of settler colonialism are described by Veracini, who writes about the myth of the Pioneer as "a young man bent upon winning from the wilderness with strong hands and the hope of youth a homestead for himself and an inheritance for his children."[11] Again and again, these tapestries of mythology see white settler, heterosexual, and patriarchal family units re-producing settler colonial land theft, extractive economies tied to stolen places, and resources handed down through tight lines of white settler lineages.

Gender dynamics in horror often operate to reproduce that mythology of rugged frontier life, of the naturalness of white settler families. Examining the words of former US senator Rick Santorum, that "civilization" was under attack by failures to define marriage as solely between a man and woman, Rifkin writes,

> More than linking same-sex pleasure and romantic partnership to degeneration into savagery, the statement indicates that forms of sociality that do not carve out a "unique" status for the reproductively directed marital unit can be treated not simply as inferior...The invocation of "civilization" appears less as a residue of an outmoded nineteenth-century language of Euro-conquest than a trace of the ongoing enmeshment of discourses of sexuality in the project of fortifying the United States against incursions by *uncivilized* formations.[12]

---

11 Isaiah Bowman in Veracini, "'Settler Colonialism': Career of a Concept," 315.

12 Rifkin, *When Did Indians Become Straight?*, 5 (emphasis in original).

Heterosexism and patriarchy reproduce settler colonialism, while the associations between savagery and sexual deviance are reinforced in many storied ways. Settler colonialism as a present-day structure contextualizes these struggles over gender and sexual norms. Heteropatriarchy, as Maile Arvin, Eve Tuck, and Angie Morrill describe, is a systemic model for family structures in which the father is "leader/boss" and the "female gender is perceived as weak, incompetent, naïve, and confused."[13] This nonsense model of family life is certainly challenged in a horror franchise dedicated to strong female characters. However, these challenges to heteropatriarchy are often undone by characters committed to protecting the white settler frontier and by killers who are depicted as a savage threat to the homestead.

SCREAM (1996)

Wes Craven's *Scream* launched the ultimate frontier family franchise, with enough Final Girls to thoroughly explore the range of roles that this type of character represents. It's worthwhile to briefly summarize each of the six Scream (1996 to 2023) films, since they feature characters who essentially live to tell their tale again and again. Other slasher franchises (other than the series of Halloween films, which have a much more complex timeline) tend to kill off the majority of their characters including their antagonist, and don't necessarily feature the same amount of character development.

The original *Scream* opens with a shocking kill scene. Casey Becker, played by Drew Barrymore, is shown at home alone, where she answers the ringing phone. The stranger's voice on the

13 Arvin, Tuck, and Morrill, "Decolonizing Feminism," 13.

other end is low and gravelly, and we will learn soon that this is the voice of a killer. Casey is chased by a figure in a ghostly mask and dark robes after her boyfriend, Steve, is murdered on the back patio. She is gutted and hanged from a tree after failing to correctly answer questions about horror films. "Ghostface" turns out to be two killers, Billy Loomis and Stu Macher, teen friends of protagonist and Final Girl Sidney Prescott. Billy and Stu, we find out, murdered Sidney's mother, Maureen, a year earlier, and got away with it. Sidney had already identified a man named Cotton Weary, with whom Maureen was having an affair, as the killer, after seeing her mother's maimed body and witnessing Cotton leave her home. Billy is now dating Sidney and pressuring her for sex constantly, climbing in her window, and telling her to get over her mother's death. His gaslighting is combined with Stu's grotesque commentary about the killings of Casey and Steve. They are so obviously the killers, right from the start, but the movie is effective in gaslighting viewers into doubting our instincts the way Sidney does.

Kent Brintnall explores how the queer monster in horror takes shape through the subtext between Billy and Stu. Brintnall writes,

> Throughout the film, Stu has been Billy's sycophant and, but for some affection for Billy (platonic or erotic), the film provides us with no account of his motive for assisting in these murders. In addition, Stu performs an exaggerated, bravura version of heterosexuality—the kind of over-the-top sexual aggressiveness that places its practitioner under suspicion of latent homosexuality. As Stu and Billy stab each other in an effort to show they have been attacked and remove suspicion from themselves, their phallic interpenetration of each other's bodies—and Billy's callous disregard of Stu's pain and physical

> deterioration—figure them as a monstrously dysfunctional queer couple as well as suggesting that queer desire is necessarily linked with violence.[14]

Stu and Billy, as queer-coded characters, have to die in order for life in Woodsboro to continue. On one hand, their deaths are a victory struck against the misogyny that they represent. On the other hand, they are the unruly and queer elements that have to be destroyed for the continuity of Westboro as a sleepy, settler colonial town.

Sidney is joined throughout these films by Gale Weathers. Gale is a true-crime writer and journalist who wrote a book about the murder of Maureen Prescott, Sidney Prescott's mother. The film series veers back and forth between portraying Sidney and Gale as free (even as outlaws) and portraying them as just totally committed to finding a nice hetero-family situation. Stu and Billy are misogynists, so they reinforce the heteropatriarchal imperative, which Gale and Sidney destroy again and again—violently and emphatically. Stu and Billy are also the queer and savage Others whose rejection of normal suburban life (through fame-seeking and, obviously, murder) is mirrored by other franchise killers.

When Gale Weathers shows up to report on Casey's murder, she tells Sidney that she identified the wrong killer. Gale has been working to clear Cotton's name while covering the new series of Woodsboro murders. In a climactic final scene, Gale, Sidney, and Deputy Dewey Riley (brother of Sidney's ill-fated best friend, Tatum Riley) take on Billy and Stu, but only Sidney is able to kill the duo. A modulator of the killer is revealed to be responsible for the voice that the killer has when he calls his victims. The

14 Brintnall, "Re-building Sodom and Gomorrah," 152.

mask and modulator mean that Ghostface always looks and sounds the same, even if different people put on the costume. In a sense, Ghostface is a shapeshifter, there to aid the outlier youth of Woodsboro (or their fans).

Scream (1996) brings us to a longer story about rape culture and the threats facing young women in the community of Westboro. *Scream 3* (2000) deals uniquely with sexual violence in Hollywood.[15] Throughout both films, Maureen is essentially blamed for her own murder. Kim Edwards writes that Maureen

> is revealed as a quintessentially "bad" mother who dared to put herself before her husband and child. Certainly the plot suggests she is emphatically at fault for all that ensues in this first installment of the series...not only was she having an affair with Cotton; she apparently also "seduced" the father of Billy Loomis...This is the motive Billy (Skeet Ulrich) finally offers for his killing spree—revenge on the sexually transgressive maternal figure (and by the legacy of gender, the daughter) who separated him from his own mother.[16]

From the beginning, *Scream* is both a subversive attempt at showing the violence that white settler teens girls are inundated with and also a remake of some formulaic frontier film about savagery at the gates. The first film contains frequent reference to *The Town that Dreaded Sundown* (1976), a film based on the Texarkana murders perpetrated by a figure nicknamed the Phantom Killer. At one point, Sidney walks through her empty town where people have fled behind locked doors to escape Ghostface and says "it's

15 Airey, "#MeToo."

16 Edwards, "Get Away from Me," 93.

like *The Town that Dreaded Sundown.*" This reference sets *Scream* up as a frontier-town story and Sidney as a frontier, pioneer hero. The first Ghostface attack on Sidney occurs as the sun bathes her home in orange, dropping in the horizon and signalling approaching danger. Like *The Town that Dreaded Sundown*, the killers in *Scream* are queer-coded, may or may not come from inside the town itself, and are far more clever than the inept local police. In an inversion of the real story of cavalry doing serious violence to Indigenous communities, the savages are just too powerful, too clever, and they thoroughly undo the town of Woodsboro with their violent rampage.

SCREAM 2 *(1997)*

The sequel to *Scream* follows Sidney to college. She's dating a nice frat boy and has a roommate who is doomed not because she's rooming with Sidney but because Sidney won't listen to her wise advice. A number of people are killed. The killers are revealed, in a final scene staged in the theatre where Sidney has tried to become an actress like her mother was, to be Mrs. Loomis, Billy's mother, and a random classmate of Sidney's named Mickey. Cotton shows up a few times in the movie, having been cleared of charges in Maureen's murder, and generally makes a pest of himself. He does save the day at the very end, holding a gun on Mrs. Loomis and shooting her before she can kill Sidney. For good measure, Sidney shoots Mrs. Loomis in the head, and Sidney and Gale Weathers shoot Mickey multiple times, killing him.

In *Scream 2*, Sidney's innocence and importance as a character is called into question (at times clumsily, I would argue). Her roommate and new best friend, Hallie McDaniel, a Black woman, is killed because of Sidney's whiteness manifested in her refusal to run when running is necessary. Hallie McDaniel is a play on the name Hattie McDaniel, who was a legendary Black actress known for her role as Mammy in *Gone with the Wind* (1939). Hattie McDaniel was the first Black actor to win an Oscar, and she was also a singer and actor in many other films. The racism and sexism experienced by Hattie McDaniel is coded in the way *Scream 2* does away with Hallie, sidelines her as Sidney's bestie, and then makes Sidney essentially directly responsible for her murder because she doesn't respect a thing Hallie says.

If *Scream 2* is intended as commentary on the marginalized place of Black characters in horror, then it succeeds through shock but fails through the ultimate erasure of those very characters. The first death of a horror movie, as Niela Orr argues, punishes Black women for having agency and voice. Orr writes, "Black women have been humiliated and punished, in horror cinema as in life, for our incisiveness, for wondering aloud, for trying to get some answers."[17] Mark H. Harris and Robin R. Means Coleman document the punishment of Black men in horror. The odds that Black characters in horror will likely die are "pretty good," Harris and Means Coleman write, as their "informal and soul-crushing survey of almost one thousand horror movies containing more than fifteen hundred appearances by Black characters" saw a rate of killing at 45 percent.[18] The Final Girls are white-settler women who survive from sequel to sequel, while Black women are sacrificed. Sidney Prescott becomes the ultimate Final Girl frontier hero—that kind of outlaw who only takes matters into her hands to reinforce her own "happy ending" in white settler colonial heteropatriarchy.

---

17 Orr, "The Women Who Knew Too Much."

18 Means Coleman and Harris, *The Black Guy Dies First*, 9.

SCREAM 3 (2000)

The third instalment in the series sees the killer adopt a new trick with the classic Ghostface voice modulator. Now, the already fictional and unfortunately impossible-to-find voice mod device allows individuals to capture many voices. It's absurd, but somehow the voice mod device can make a person sound like Sidney or Gale or Dewey or whoever. Ghostface spends a lot of time tricking people into traps with this new device. In the end, Ghostface turns out to be Roman, Sidney's half-brother, who it is said was responsible for all of the kills of *Scream* (1996) as well, starting with Maureen, since he found Billy and Stu and convinced them to become absolutely terrible human beings. Dewey kills Roman by shooting him in the head.

Before Roman reveals himself, a subplot is also revealed: Maureen was an ex-Hollywood actress who ran away to Woodsboro and changed her name. Maureen was sexually assaulted at a party held by John Milton, an executive producer working with Roman. In a scene earlier in the film, Gale Weathers; Carrie Fisher's character, Bianca; and the actress playing Gale in a film about the original *Scream* killings,[19] all discuss the pressure that young women in Hollywood experience. Carrie Fisher, the actor, once sent a cow's tongue to a producer who harassed her friend, an incident discussed in the context of the Harvey Weinstein sexual assault allegations.[20]

---

19 The Stab movies are a quirky element of the Scream franchise. Based originally on the "true story" of the Woodsboro killings, and introduced in *Scream 2*, Stab is a film series within a film series, featuring famous actors playing Sidney or Gale or Dewey, each subsequent "chapter" of Stab revealed as the Scream films progress.

20 Bryant, "Carrie Fisher Once Had a Heroic Response."

That the franchise is usually discussed as postmodern is a point I haven't raised just yet. The ways that *Scream* (1996) references and even critiques other horror films has been written about widely.[21] That the franchise is necessarily postmodern in its engagement with the genre is worthy of more in-depth analysis. Re-examining the series from within a settler colonial studies framing, the postmodern element of these films is only partially (though at times profoundly) disruptive of the norms that the films attempt to eschew. No film in the series, I would argue, shatters the normalcy of heteropatriarchal violence like the third instalment.

Scream 3 is a swipe at heteropatriarchal violence in Hollywood—including and perhaps especially by a member of the franchise's production team. From the moment we meet Sidney in the first instalment, when her creepy boyfriend climbs into her window and pressures her for sex, the tone of the film series is set: this is a film, and then a franchise, about sexual violence. That Sidney blames her mother, for cheating on her father and therefore somehow causing the violence they have to face as a family, undoes these subversive elements.

Scream 3 challenges the mother-blaming narrative and then goes one step further. The film drives home the enormity of what Maureen endured as a character who isn't in either of the subsequent films but haunts each one. Histories of Hollywood's horrifying behaviour toward women—both through studio executives and of course on-screen representations—are told through the story of Maureen. Not long after we find out that "the one who slept with the director got the best role," we find out about Maureen's brutal rape, though Milton tries to gloss the event over and is killed for it. That Maureen escaped Hollywood only to be

21 See, for example, Pheasant-Kelly, "Reframing Parody."

sexually assaulted and murdered by Billy and Stu, who were essentially sent to do the dirty work of her own son, Roman Bridger, is a chilling plot reveal. The wealthy, white, male elite are the predators in *Scream* 3, and Roman is the latest to die for his refusals to disavow that violence.

SCREAM 4 *(2011)*

Scream 4 sees Dewey and Gale married and living in Woodsboro. Gale is bored, hates her domestic life (I'll expand on this shortly), and is jealous when Sidney shows up in town to promote her own new book whilst wearing clothing as attractive as Gale's. Sidney has embraced New Ageism in this film, telling everybody that the material circumstances of their traumas matter less than rising above it all and choosing to embrace the light or something along those lines. Gale has writer's block, and she and Dewey seem to love one another but not their marriage. The Ghostface killers in this film end up being a boy named Charlie, who has a crush on a girl named Kirby and so, logically, tries to kill her; and his leader in mayhem, Jill Roberts, who kills or tries to kill her own mother and her friends, including her best friend, Kirby Reed, and tries to kill Sidney as well in order to become as famous as Sidney is. "What am I supposed to do?" screams Jill, shortly after killing her own boyfriend. "Go to college? Grad school? Work?" Jill tells her how foolish she is for chasing the normative life she continually returns to.

When we find out that Maureen was a victim of terrible sexual violence at the hands of a famous Hollywood director, Sidney's moralism and constant blaming of her mother is finally challenged. The tragedy of Maureen's life and death are products of a network of rapists and murderers, referencing another of Wes

Craven's creations that spawned a series, *A Nightmare on Elm Street* (1984). Sidney even grows up on Elm Street, but in her case there is no supernatural element—the monsters are human. The savagery is coming from *this side* of the gate. When Gale Weathers punctures the divide between suburban "safety" with her storytelling power, she tells Sidney again and again: the call is coming from inside the house, not from Cotton Weary or some other "outsider."

Sidney's entire family, it seems, is intertwined in this culture of killing and mayhem. Her brother, her boyfriend, her boyfriend's sort-of boyfriend, her niece, her niece's sort-of boyfriend, her ex-boyfriend's mother, her ex-boyfriend's mother's lackey, and her ex-boyfriend's daughter's boyfriend and his underage girlfriend (the final ick factor atop the fifth movie's general ickiness) are all killers, intent on ending Sidney's reign as Final Girl once and for all. On one hand, their inability to end Sidney's life is a kind of feminist plot turn in itself.

SCREAM *(2022)*

In this reboot of the franchise, Sam Carpenter, the daughter of Billy Loomis who hallucinates entire conversations with her father, is lured back to Woodsboro after her sister, Tara, is nearly killed by a new Ghostface. Sam is played by Melissa Barrera, and Tara is played by Jenna Ortega, bringing a new generation to the film series. Sidney and Gale reunite after Dewey is killed in a last stand against the unruly, shapeshifting Ghostface. In addition to reigniting the queer subtext between their characters, Sidney and Gale act as protective figures in the seemingly motherless Sam and Tara's lives.

The best line of this film might be Sam's. After Sidney tells her that she and Gale need help murdering the new Ghostface(s), Sam says, "You want me to help you and the host of a morning show to commit murder?" To which Gale replies, "Correct." Gale, at least, is embracing her outlier status a bit more in this film. She does set a killer on fire and shoot them to death, while in previous films her kill count is low.[22]

The Ghostfaces are Richie Kirsch (Sam's boyfriend) and Richie's disturbingly young other girlfriend, Amber, whom he met online. *Scream* (2022) references misogyny and sexual violence through the character of Richie and his predatory treatment of Amber. Just before she dies, Amber screams that she was radicalized online. It may be meant as a joke, but the look on Sidney's and Gale's faces as she burns to death before them captures some element of the tragedy of it all.

SCREAM VI *(2023)*

The sixth and potentially final at the time of writing (and my favourite) film in the franchise sees Sam and Tara return as kick-ass survivors living in New York. Sam, Tara, and their friends Chad and Mindy Meeks-Martin live with roommates and go to university. Their roommate Quinn is (seemingly) killed by Ghostface, and her father, Detective Bailey, shows up to help solve the case. The film's opening murders are of a film professor and one Ghostface who is apparently a failed prototype. A second Ghostface, who killed the professor in the opening scene, is also killed. Sam and her friends are being saved for someone, it seems, with bigger plans than a couple of angry film-bros can come up with.

22 Gale helps Sidney whenever a Ghostface (or two) has to be dispatched, but what I'm curious about here are the ways that Gale and Sidney are more willing to go after Ghostface with guns drawn by this fifth installment.

Gale has written a rude book about the Carpenter sisters, but when a new Ghostface arrives, Gale wants to help. Kirby Reed is revealed to have survived the 2011 murders and is now an FBI agent who also arrives to help. The gang find a gigantic shrine to each Ghostface incarnation in a movie theatre. Pictures and stolen evidence (including bloody knives) are in glass cases, along with every Ghostface mask used by every Ghostface killer. Sam confronts images and memories (she is shown to hallucinate her father Billy Loomis's face) of her own twisted family tree. Then, Quinn; her father, Detective Bailey; and Quinn's brother (Chad's roommate) Ethan reveal themselves to be the family of Richie from the last film. They go on the attack and are defeated.

Lest we think this film to be a sanitizing of policing, the Ghostface team ends up including a police detective who is also Richie's father. Like Mrs. Loomis before him, Detective Bailey is a terrible parent who goes on a rampage of revenge when someone dispatches his murderous spawn. The other killers include Richie's siblings, Quinn and Ethan. Detective Bailey, Quinn, and Ethan are stabbed, shot, smashed in the head, and stabbed some more, and Ethan is killed with the same television set that Sidney used to electrocute and crush Stu in *Scream* (1996), only this kill is done by Kirby.

They seem to almost kill Gale, in one of the best Ghostface chases of the franchise, but she is later revealed to have survived. Other survivors include Chad and Mindy Meeks-Martin, the nephew and niece of Randy from the first film. *Scream VI* also features two bonus Ghostfaces, creeps who are killed by Ethan, presumably (though who knows), after one of them murders his film prof for giving him a bad mark. The ongoing survival of Gale Weathers as a kind of anti-hero is itself subversive of the misogynist and persistent Ghostface. Her entire dialogue, mocking

Ghostface for continually trying and failing to kill her, and her fight scene in this chapter make her a more persistent Final Girl than Sidney. Gale takes on outlier, outlaw status in some ways, never quite fitting in, never quite doing the whole white settler heteropatriarchy thing well enough.

The introduction of Sam Carpenter and her sister, Tara, as Final Girls also provides opportunity for new levels of subversion in the Scream franchise. *Scream VI* finally breaks through the "police as authority figure" thread throughout the films. With Dewey (the cowboy, cavalry, Western hero) gone and Judy Hicks (Dewey's sidekick, potential love interest, and then inheritor of the Sheriff's badge) gone as well, there is no longer a good cop waiting to save the day in the end. At the end of *Scream* (2022) when the killers end up being a cop and his kids, the sanctity of the white settler family is at least a bit unsettled. The family legacy, of violence and entitlement, is personified in this new killer's character, as well as in that of his kids. It is, at least on some level, a scathing critique of the heteropatriarchal settler family.

Ghostface is both spectre and human threat. Ghostface is death and revenge and the savage lurking within. Conversely, a violent system intent on disappearing and decimating Indigenous Peoples projects fears of death as fears of reverse colonization. Ghostface is a product of the violence of settler colonialism, the imagined boogeyman who lurks in dark corners. Those who don the mask may be the queer outliers (in Stu and Billy's cases) but they also embody misogyny, capitalism, fame seeking, and serial killing. They may be written as the savage-Other, in problematic ways, rooting misogyny and sexual sadism in "primitive" behaviour. Ghostface is that construct of madness that erupts from within white settler worlds. The series may be so compelling because of how open it is to such multiple and layered readings of the monsters and heroes.

SCREAM AND THE FAMILY

The subversive potential of the Scream franchise is undone in more ways than one. In the most recent instalment (as of this writing), *Scream VI* (2023), Gale declares that Sidney has her happy ending, with Mark Kincaid and their children. Also in *Scream VI*, a queer female character dies brutally, and hetero happy endings, complete with epic kisses and background music, are scattered about. One of the more subversive elements of Scream, rooted in a willingness to expose and criticize violence against women, is (at least temporarily) undone by heteronormativity. Pairing Sidney with Mark, a detective who once collected newspaper articles about her and spends much of *Scream 3* being a total creep, is either brilliant (if he turns out to be a killer himself in some future sequel, given that *Scream 3* only had one killer, which is a break from the franchise's formula) or it is just a reinforcement of the very heteropatriarchy Sidney tries so hard to escape. That Sidney, reeling from her high school boyfriend's violence—pressuring her into sex, killing her mother, killing her best friend, trying to kill her—ends up with her stalker is a gross plot twist.

Sidney is continually written to reinforce white settler suburbia, and she often needs to venture into the wilderness (metaphorically speaking) in order to do so. In *Scream* (1996), Sidney assumes the Ghostface identity briefly, putting on the costume, hiding in a closet, and calling her intended victims (Billy and Stu), turning the tables on them before killing them. In *Scream 2* Sidney picks up a gun, as does Gale Weathers (who was knocked unconscious in the first film and thus becomes the reluctant avenging hero in the second) and shoots both Ghostface killers—Billy Loomis's mother and Mickey, Sidney's classmate. In *Scream 3* Sidney is shown to be a kind of twin of Ghostface, her brother, but she re-establishes her innocence. She is able to process family trauma by putting it behind her, while her brother cannot. Sidney stops him from harming anyone else but maintains her innocence by stepping back while Dewey kills him. As Edwards points out,

> Sidney must become the murderer, her "other half," in order to kill Roman and end the curse. In the original movie she assumed the killer's costume and voice to defeat him, and here again she finally uses his weapon... to deal the apparent death blow. Interestingly enough however, the horror of dispatching one's own brother is diminished first by the rather ridiculous nod to the Halloween series when the rival siblings grasp hands for a soulful moment before death, and then by granting Dewey the "real" final kill—the bullet through the forehead.[23]

Sidney embodies that frontier spirit, onward and upward, refusing to face the ghosts of her family. Sidney responds to her trauma by writing a book about climbing out of darkness and embracing new-age positivity. When her cousin, Jill, responds to the family's stories by seeking the kind of fame Sidney has, she is punished in a comical scene. Sidney electrocutes her cousin using defibrillation paddles in *Scream 4* against any "rational" understanding of self-defence and the law. Ultimately, Sidney's innocence is rooted in white womanhood, in contrast to the racialized (though not specifically narrated as Latin-American and Mexican-American) characters Sam and Tara Carpenter in *Scream* (2022) and *Scream VI*.

---

23 Edwards, "Get Away from Me," 96.

Sam and Tara are coded as "real" killers, as closer to the savage-Other, despite Sam being absolutely tied, as of the writing of this book, with Sidney for overall number of kills. Sam, by virtue of her madness (she is on medication and hallucinates her father speaking to her) is the more savage-coded killer—a natural born killer, Gale even writes (albeit with a note of admiration). At the same time, Sam and Tara are given more freedom to dispatch Ghostface and his/her accomplices. Tara dives on Ethan, who had previously screamed that he always wanted to "put something inside of her," stabs him in the face, and grinds the knife up and down. Sam stabs her first would-be killer, a boyfriend who fools her into being part of his new *Stab* movie, at least twenty-two times (I counted and I'm sure others have as well). She stabs the boyfriend's father in the sixth installation of the film dozens of times and then kills him, with permission from her sister, by stabbing him through the eye. Sam and Tara are not white settler outlaws, so they are beyond the narrative of "innocence" that seems to follow Sidney around.

Somewhere between Sidney the frontier hero and Sam the savage-coded hero, is the outlaw Gale Weathers. The emergence of Gale Weathers as the franchise's longest-running survivor (as of this writing, Sidney is alive but Gale has been in more films) and surprising queer icon, is one subversive element of the film. Each killer wants to end Gale's reign as well, but ultimately the only success the killers have is in ending Dewey's life, a loss that only serves to bring Sidney and Gale closer and make them even more relentless in ending the Ghostface legend once and for all. In some ways the writers don't seem to know what to do with Gale, constantly making her return to her true-crime roots despite having her promise to never write another book about Ghostface. This regression, along with the undoing of the Core Four—the young survivors of *Scream* (2022) and *Scream VI*—and Sidney's happy ending, mark the franchise's lost potential.

The Scream franchise is filled with queer subtext, but only ventures into real representation in *Scream VI*. Queer subtext means queer audiences and revenue, as well as some unsettling of the white settler heteropatriarchal town and family. Gale and Sidney fulfill the "enemies to friends" trope of rom-com relationship arcs, and their intimacy grows with each film. Stu and Billy are the queer monstrous killers, whose very existence threatens the white settler frontier town; they are killed off, while Gale and Sidney are married off. Evidence of queer, lesbian, or bisexual subtext includes Sidney's androgynous name, her sexy-muscled-arms-in-a-tank-top look in *Scream 2*, and Gale's array of rainbow flag-coloured suits as well as her constant need for distance from her male love interest (they are together, then not together, married, then divorced, throughout the series of films), a relationship that ends with him dead and her in Sidney's arms in *Scream* (2022).[24] By this fifth instalment in the Scream franchise, it is impossible to tell which of the women in the movie might become a bigger queer, lesbian, or bisexual icon. Kirby[25] with her black leather jacket and swagger and Sam with her tank top are portrayed alongside a series of choices that basically reinforce heteronormativity

24 A quick search online reveals a ton of fan fiction dedicated to Sidney and Gale. I take the existence of fan fiction as fan-driven "proof" of queer subtext, and I have never truly been swayed from this position. Archive of Our Own is a space where fanfiction writers share their own versions of the Sidney and Gale relationship, for example. See https://archiveofourown.org/.

25 Kirby Reed is a survivor of *Scream 4*, which centres on Jill Roberts, the cousin of Sidney Prescott, who goes on a killing spree to become as famous as Sidney herself. Jill kills her own mother, her own Ghostface partner, and attempts to have her best friend killed, but Kirby is revealed to have survived in later sequels and become an FBI agent.

(namely brutally fridging[26] the queer woman and having all the straight couples make out for uncomfortable amounts of time in the middle of a stressful horror film). Reading queer subtext into Scream is the intention of Kevin Williamson, one of the series writers who also, Patrick Kelleher writes, based the first two killers, Stu and Billy, on real-life gay lovers who killed people.[27]

Queer subtext *without* main text, might ultimately simply work in service to settler colonialism and settler homonationalism. Morgensen further reflects on the interconnections of sexuality, family formations, and settler colonialism as co-creations with implications for both Indigenous and non-Indigenous people. In his words,

> colonists interpreted diverse practices of gender and sexuality as signs of a general primitivity among Native peoples. Over time, they produced a colonial necropolitics that framed Native peoples as queer populations marked for death. Colonization produced the biopolitics of modern sexuality that I call "settler sexuality": a white national heteronormativity that regulates Indigenous sexuality and gender by supplanting them with the sexual modernity of settler subjects.[28]

Settler sexuality in the Scream franchise is subtextually queer in many instances, but overwhelmingly heteronormative generally.

---

26 The subject of fridging is worthy of more discussion in horror which is so centrally fixated on death. The trope is described by Gail Simones in "Women in Refrigerators" as a plot whereby female characters are killed off in often violent ways in order to evoke emotion. See "Stuffed into the Fridge," *TV Tropes*, https://tvtropes.org/pmwiki/pmwiki.php/Main/StuffedIntoTheFridge. See also Bates, "The Fridge is Getting Full."

27 Kelleher, "6 Reasons Why."

28 Morgensen, "Settler Homonationalism," 106.

The monstrosity of queerness, in the form of the Billy-Stu relationship, is deeply intertwined with white settler misogyny. The savage-Other is queer but also a threat to white settler women. The call may be coming from inside the house, but the monsters making that call are a product of savagery.

Married life for Gale Weathers and Dewey Riley is a character study in the damaging effects of heteropatriarchy. Their friendship is undone by their marriage. The characters genuinely want each other to be happy, but they also bicker and struggle over their own independence, in many ways against the requirements of white settler suburbia. Everyone around Gale tells her to stop writing her true-crime books and hints at times that she's the reason Ghostface keeps returning; Dewey, for his part, keeps space to hold her responsible for times when she does write in exploitative ways but also *encourages her* to write—to use her voice. Their relationship is at its worst when they try to "make it work" in Woodsboro.

The treatment of Black women, and particularly one Black queer woman, in the franchise, also undoes its progressiveness. In the two instances when this exception occurs, the survivor, Mindy Meeks-Martin of *Scream* (2022) and *Scream VI* hasn't been allowed to become integral to the rest of the franchise—yet. Mindy's girlfriend in *Scream VI* is fridged, despite a character in *Scream 4* insisting that being gay protects characters in horror. The fridging trope was coined to explain the ways that female characters in particular have been made expendable in order to centre male characters. The idea then came to describe the abnormally high number of lesbian, bisexual, and queer female characters killed off in television and film.[29] The trope lives on, alongside the

29 Bates, "The Fridge Is Getting Full."

general sense that queer female desire is dangerous and needs to be destroyed. Mindy is left to be comic relief at the end of the final (for now) film.

The Scream franchise might seem unsettling of the settler colonial family at times, particularly as the cast and characters challenge white heteronormativity in the fifth and sixth films. However, the story of Sidney Presçott creates a foundation of settler colonial representation in the films. Tropes and patterns in each film reinforce the importance of the settler homestead and family structure. Even when the Scream movies call out sexual violence and rape culture, the blame for those things is not placed on the white settler heteropatriarchal status quo but on the savage other.

SAVAGERY AND THE FAMILY

The Lost Boys *(1987)*

The dusty, unending, cruel frontier shows up in horror again and again—in this instance, that frontier is the meeting place between the savage vampire and the civilized family. The white settler frontier family just needs to fend off those pesky gay vampires in order to make something of themselves. In *The Lost Boys*, Lucy has to move back in with her father (whose is referred to only as "Grandpa" in the script) after a failed marriage. Having moved with her, Lucy's sons, Michael and Sam, wander their new town trying to fit in.

Michael falls in love with a pack of vampires after watching the greatest rock concert ever shown in a horror film.[30] After Michael enters the cave system of the vampires, he indulges in a dusty old

---

30 I'm referring to the scene in which singer and musician Timmy Cappello plays some awesome tunes and Michael first meets the vampires. The idea that this kind of spandex and chains and leather rock might be a sort of gate for the (big gay) vampire awakening is sort of wonderful and campy.

bottle of blood, hallucinates that he's eating maggots, and engages in risky bridge-hanging activities with the group. As the young men dangle from beneath a bridge, a train rolls over the tracks above them, shaking the bars so hard they struggle to maintain their grip. One by one, the lost boys fall into a foggy abyss in a metaphor for risky sex in the 1980s. *The Lost Boys* was released during the AIDS crisis. Themes of risky sex (including heterosexual sex) combine with an exploration of extended-family kinship that threatens the nuclear family. Just before the bridge-hanging game, the camera follows Michael as he drinks the wine (blood) and Star stares at him worriedly. His heterosexuality in question, his blood tainted, he returns home to his "nagging" mother, little brother, and grandfather.

Michael goes home a changed young man. His mother accuses him of taking drugs, and he is offended at the mere thought. That night, left alone to babysit, Michael is overcome with desire to eat his brother, and Sam (naked and vulnerable in a bath) is only saved from this savage (potential) attack by the family dog. Once the brothers realize what they're up against, they enlist some odd friends to find and kill the head vampire. They invade the cave system and kill one vampire. After a narrow escape, they retreat into their homestead to enact a last stand against the rest of the pack. All of the vampires are killed, but Max enters the house and reveals that he was the head vampire all along. Before he can bite Lucy, Grandpa drives through a wall and a giant fence post is flung from his vehicle into Max's chest. The family is saved, and life goes on.

The vampires all have fantastic hair and stand as eternal reminders that the hair-rock era of the 1980s was a glorious, gender-bending time. The fact that Lucy is a single mom is an important detail, common to other vampire movies and television shows, because that lack of a patriarchal father figure makes the family an outside element and also vulnerable to dangerous outsiders. Grandpa welcomes his daughter and two grandsons to his homestead, where he spends his days avoiding town and building a fence. Grandpa's property is a ranch, full of animal bones and his various taxidermic creations. Grandpa wears a bolo tie and a headband. He hates Santa Carla because of "all the damn vampires," code for all of the Others embodied in the vampire. Gay subtext and the looming AIDS crisis are written throughout the film. The hangout that all the pretty vampires gather in is on a fault along which an earthquake caused the land to sink into a cave system. The vampires are primitive again, relegated to that place of savage violence by the domineering and predatory older male, Max.

Michael's main connections in the vampire gang are with Star and David, a couple it seems. David uses Star to lure Michael—in a vague nod toward non-monogamy—to get Michael to either join the largely male group of vampires or become Star's first kill. When their throuple[31] fails, David is heartbroken (though Star seems over it by this point). In some of his final lines, David shouts at Michael: "I tried to make you immortal!" Michael returns with, "You tried to make me a killer!" and the epic and tragic fight to the death between the two unfolds. As David lays dying, impaled and on his back, his face relaxes in what (with the volume turned way down) can only be described as some serious afterglow. The (queer) vampires all die, and Michael is free to put his family back together.

The dusty farm of Grandpa's homestead is juxtaposed with the lights and lurid scenes of fictional Santa Carla. Santa Carla is where shirtless, greased-up men play saxophones and thrust their hips, pretty long-haired vampires seduce young people, poor (or seemingly poor) "criminal elements" steal comic books and make

31 This is a fun term for a three-way relationship—a portmanteau of *couple* and *three*.

out in cars, and nice family men are disappeared by savage elements. Grandpa embodies the cowboy, the outlaw who doesn't fit in with the townspeople of Santa Carla but also doesn't like those darned vampires.

With his animal skins and bones collection, daily homesteading activities, and his bolo tie, Grandpa holds off these external threats to protect the white settler family when his daughter, the single mom who cluelessly lets a vampire into the house, cannot. Grandpa is the romantic Indigenized white settler, while his grandsons and grandsons' friends are the primitive (and queer) outliers. Max, the elder vampire who converted all the pretty young men, attempts to invade the home of Michael, Sam, Lucy, and Grandpa. The descent into savagery occurs when David and the other vampires get the "vampface," which Jessica Hautsch describes as "animalistic and racially coded."[32] David's death is overlaid with angelic light and song. The settler colonial family is vulnerable to economic and social forces, making the imagined Indigenization of Grandpa and the othering of the vampires essential to some version of a happy ending.[33]

While the joy of watching this movie in the late 1980s felt palpable as a closeted gay kid, I always wondered about the relegation of Star to a supporting role. She is obviously the best part of the movie,

---

32 Hautsch, "Staking Her Colonial Claim," 4.

33 This theme of lost children, whose parents' divorces and subsequent socioeconomic vulnerability leaves them susceptible to attacks from the primitive, the bloodthirsty, the cannibal-Other, is also evident in another 1980s vampire film. In Tom Holland's *Fright Night* (1985), the failing patriarch, Charley, tries desperately to keep the queer, the savage vampire, the foreign all at bay, outside of the domain of his mother's home. She utterly fails him as well, refusing to see the threat beyond the walls, offering her son Valium and oblivion instead of listening to him. The queerness of *Fright Night* is impossible to ignore. Gay actors play key roles in the film, and queer subtext infuses all dynamics among Charley, his girlfriend, and his best friend.

but she never gets a chance to show off her vampire skills and seems to act as a go-between as Michael and David struggle with their heterosexuality through her. She is both an outlier and maternal saviour. When she and Michael hook up, they do so in a cave, surrounded by beaded shawls and candles, a dangerous-looking fire, and hanging bone-like things. With her dark, wavy hair and hippie first name, she is coded as a romantic savage, there to save the children and cry despite having the same powers that Michael has. Rescuing Star (and all of the sweet gay energy that the lost boys struggle to accept) from the settler colonial project feels like an open-ended and emergent possibility for some future filmmaker.

The family homestead is safe once the vampires are killed. That homestead expands, and the safety of civilized settler lives needs to be ensured in places where the young roam and seek their fortunes. The next film example centres on the reproductive duties of young women and the dangers they face as they head off to university.

Black Christmas *(2019)*

Black Christmas unsettles settler colonial patriarchal values by centring on the voices and experiences of young women, but it also reinforces that system by projecting settler colonial homesteading onto a university town. The town becomes a safe, civilized bastion for women, until "black magic" threatens their survival. What is interesting about this movie is how the first young woman dies, and the ways that she is drawn as a kind of angelic martyr.

Young women die in horror in events that seem drawn out, overtly sexualized, and violent in explicit ways.[34] The violent disruption of the white settler homestead may also be about undoing

34 See for example Gooden, "Women in Slasher Films."

an entire settler town and its various institutions. While the Final Girl survives horror, it is often a young, vulnerable (white) woman who is the First Girl and the one who suffers a gruesome and tragic death. Her untimely end announces the arrival of the monster to the horror film. Like with Casey Becker's gory dispatching in *Scream* (1996), the demise of the first victim often comes as a shock to the audience. The First Girl might spend the last parts of her life settling into domestic routines, going for a hike, walking home from a party, or making popcorn for a movie night with her boyfriend. The calm before the storm is crucial to measuring the enormity of the storm itself. Establishing the innocence of the white settler family and community who are under siege by the film's end is crucial; this first loss tells us what is at stake.

In the latest remake of *Black Christmas* (2019),[35] the first woman to die has angel wings drawn in snow as she's dragged away by a group of misogynistic cult members who try to show the women in the film that all the progress seemingly made by waves of feminism is about to be undone by a system that has never really changed. The film follows a group of sorority sisters who are killed one by one by some unknown entity. Unlike in the original *Black Christmas* (1974), the killer is not a man named Billy hiding in the attic. Instead, this remake focuses on the violence that the women in the sorority house face, including sexual violence and rape culture in the fraternity. At a talent show, four of the young women perform "Up in the Frat House,"[36] with alternative lyrics about sexual assault sung to the tune of "Up on the Housetop."[37]

35 Sophia Takal directed 2019's version; the original, directed by Bob Clark, was released in 1974, and Glen Morgan's offering was released in 2006.

36 The Streamline Modernes, "Up in the Frat House," *Black Christmas* (original motion picture soundtrack, 2019).

37 Benjamin Hanby, "Up on the Housetop," 1864.

The female students in this film are fighting from the beginning, against the curriculum of a misogynist professor who quotes Camille Paglia[38] and mocks and gaslights them. He claims, despite his overt aggression, that there is no "nefarious plot to secret away knowledge," and that "there are no covert meetings in hidden rooms where men discuss how to bury women" when, in fact, there *is* a nefarious plot afoot and men are indeed meeting in hidden rooms to discuss killing women and disposing of their bodies. Many of the women in this remake of *Black Christmas* survive. They criticize their powerful professors openly, asking "Whose classics are they?... Not mine" in response to the notion of a male-white-settler-dominant academic canon. The film's "nice guys" betray their alliances to the women by screaming that they are "hysterical" despite these female students' very valid worries. The emancipatory final fight scene focuses on sorority sisters taking down the fraternity and the cult of patriarchy who have killed their sisters. The killers are both the savage threat (as mad outliers) and the internal violence of settler colonial heteropatriarchy.

The First Girl reveals the blurry lines between the supposedly civilized society, where she meets her untimely end, and the savagery within, which erupts to take her life and then a subsequent string of other people's lives. The First Girl does not survive for long, and her death is unnerving and tragic, shattering any viewers' prior relaxed state. She is also the first to tell both adults and her peers that not all is right. As a martyr and the initial sacrifice of the film, this character acts to establish the innocence of settler colonial suburbia.

---

38 Accurate or not, the professor is attempting to weaponize Paglia against the students as a scholar who is understood in the context of the film itself to be anti-feminist.

The settler colonial family and community are unsettled in these horror examples and shown to be unable to deal with their belonging (or lack thereof) to place, to nature, and to death. The family is then reaffirmed at the centre of the story, through notions of their innocence (of the whole or parts of the family), of their right to property and reproduction, or even in portrayals of the tragedy of their demise. Queer subtext happens in service of settler homonationalism, ensuring that the project of settler colonialism is maintained, with a kind of rainbow branding. Queerness, madness, the savage-Other, all intertwined, all lurking, all threatening, can't necessarily be divided into neat subheadings. The demonic-Other threatens the white-heteropatriarchal family in its reproduction of settler colonialism.

The settler colonial family is locked in temporal and spatial stasis: there is a timelessness and a placelessness to their dystopic lives. The Final Girl, in Clover's coining, is characterized in part by a deep desire to survive as "above all, she is intelligent and resourceful in a pinch. Laurie even at her most desperate, cornered in a closet, has the wit to grab a hanger from the rack and bend it into a weapon."[39] Clover is referencing Laurie Strode in *Halloween* (1978), who uses a hanger and a knitting needle; Sally from *Texas Chainsaw Massacre* (1974) leaps through a glass window, as does Erin of *You're Next* (2011). These women think and move and smash their way out of danger and threaten then to enter a new world. Is it always an emancipatory thing, though, if the world they enter is written as familiar frontier myths?

In many ways, the violence that women experience in horror feels both problematic and liberating; problematic as I'm forced to be a voyeur, but liberating in the sense that it is a genre that

39 Clover, *Men, Women and Chainsaws*, 39.

disrupts romantic notions of settler colonial worlds as utopic or peaceful. As a female viewer, I've always skipped the first kills in slashers. I appreciate Clover's work on horror, her asking about voyeurism and sadism. Clover writes a nuanced take on the ways that the Final Girl operates in horror in a 2015 updated preface to her book *Men, Women and Chainsaws*:

> The final girl brings down the killer in the final moments, but consider how she spent a good hour of the film up to then: being chased and almost caught, hiding, running, falling, rising in pain and fleeing again, seeing her friends mangled and killed by weapon wielding killers...It is with the final girls' suffering that the film leads us to identify.[40]

If the point of horror is only to be frightened, to identify with a victim who is being chased, and then watch that victim turn the tables and hack up a killer, I would add that the underlying motivations to watch such a trajectory are complicated by those elements of settler colonial heteropatriarchy that include anxieties about the safety of the home and family, the lingering fear that belonging and being on stolen land is impossible, and those fears of reverse colonization ("they're going to do to us what we did to them") that Arata speaks to.[41] The frontier and the homestead are there to be protected.

40 Clover, *Men, Women and Chainsaws*, x–xi.
41 Arata, "The Occidental Tourist."

THREE

WE ALL GO A LITTLE MAD SOMETIMES!

SANISM, SAVAGERY, AND HORROR

> "I have just been fired because nobody wants to see vampire killers anymore, or vampires either. Apparently, all they want to see are demented madmen running around in ski-masks, hacking up young virgins."
>
> —PETER VINCENT, *FRIGHT NIGHT*

I HAVE FREQUENTLY MENTIONED THE MAD OUTLIER AS A product of the Civ/Sav binary. In *Scream* (1996) Ghostface killer Billy Loomis quotes Norman Bates from Hitchcock's *Psycho* (1960), saying "We all go a little mad sometimes." In the original dialogue from which this quote is taken, Norman Bates is speaking about his mother: "She needs me. It's not as if she were a maniac, a raving thing. She just goes—a little mad sometimes. We all go a little mad sometimes." Norman Bates's mother is a mad woman, a construct necessary for the containment of white settler womanhood. The mad white woman is an outlier, weakening the family and community. On the other side, the enemy she faces off with is both a product of misogyny from inside the community (which she defeats at times, at other times not so much) and an outlier themselves. She might reinforce the sanctity of the white settler homestead, as Sidney Prescott does, or she might rupture it as Laurie Strode does at times.

Studying horror through an anti-colonial lens reveals the underlying root systems that connect constructions of madness with savagery, reason with civilization, and the threat therefore of the savage coming from within. Tracing the trajectory of psychiatrization and constructed notions of madness or insanity imposed on Indigenous populations, Rachel Gorman and Brenda LeFrançois argue that "the marking of unruly racialised and colonised bodies became more pronounced in psychiatry, to the point where racialised and indigenous peoples were (and are) over-represented within mental health systems within the Western world."[1] The brutish, menacing figure who crashes through rainy woods to destroy the nice white family inside their little homestead is often paired with something inside that family that matches their violence. Going "mad" makes that member of the family both better able (and more willing) to meet the savage threat toe-to-toe, and also culpable for letting the threat inside in the first place.

The very idea of sanity is intertwined with notions of reason and enlightenment. The notion of a psychiatric "disorder," China

1 Gorman and LeFrançois, "Mad Studies," 110.

Mills and Suman Fernando write, are deliberately misconstrued as individual pathologies "rather than as responses to socio-politico-economic conditions of conflict, entrenched social inequality, and chronic poverty."[2] This construction of madness presents rich fodder for the horror film as North American settler colonialism reproduces itself through this facade of reason.

The association of madness with savagery is clear, as Mills writes:

> Colonialism and psychiatrisation are deeply historically implicated, co-constituted and mutually reinforcing....The dominance of evolutionary explanations of colonialism and madness drew comparison between primitivity and psychopathology, comparing "psychotic patients" with "primitive people" and framing social and racially coded hierarchies.[3]

Leigh Boucher describes the ways that "racial and gender fears in the management of the settler colonial self" have historically included institutionalization for maladies associated with, for example, the hot sun and climate of the colonies.[4] David Mitchell explains the ways that madness operates as a racialized construct and "functions as a nondiagnostic, protomedicalized colloquial castigation."[5] LeFrançois points to the centrality of psychiatrization in the colonization process, writing that "the pathologizing of Indigenous peoples, perceiving them as social problems, is rampant."[6] Specifically, the pathologizing of Indigenous women

---

2 Mills and Fernando, "Globalising Mental Health," 189.
3 Mills, "The Mad Are Like Savages," 207.
4 Boucher, "Masculinity Gone," 52.
5 Mitchell, "Resistance and Other Pathologized Products of Madness," 1286.
6 LeFrançois, "The Psychiatrization of Our Children," 114.

and girls as "wild, partying, sexually promiscuous"[7] crystallizes my suspicion, that the monstrous Indigenous-feminine is North American horror's deepest fear and greatest desire.

Going mad in a world that is filled with injustice and violence can also be portrayed as freeing. The freedom of the Final Girl comes when she loses her "mind," which has been set up as a construct of civilization and belonging therein. This perceived freedom is itself embedded in settler colonial discourse and inhabitation of place. Morton's work unpacks the ways that white womanhood seeks freedom in the imagined wilds, in "feral freedom" before civilization intruded. Morton is talking about the lyrics of a pop star's songs,[8] and madness intertwined with "civilized" patriarchal demands, but what interests me here are the ways that settler colonial nostalgia sees freedom in the "savage" and "feral" (and stolen) lands of Indigenous people.[9] The idea that there might be both fear and desire to embody the mad other makes sense if the civilized mind is understood as crucial to material and ideological respectability while disciplining all who are forced or compelled to adhere to its boundaries though they desire escape.

Deriving from some notion of primitivity, those who have gone mad are both villain and hero in horror. Michael Myers, Jason Voorhees, and Angela Baker are among the many anti-heroes whose unruly and murderous ways are intertwined with implied but unnamed, pathologized but also unknown, characteristics of mental health issues. Notions of insanity or madness as savage are both disciplining (a warning) for white settlers, and an avenue for

---

7 LeFrançois, "The Psychiatrization of Our Children," 114.

8 Here, Morton is specifically talking about Taylor Swift, but the broader contribution of this work to understanding settler colonialism in relation to gender and madness is what interests me here.

9 Morton, "Of Folksongs and Feral Children."

freedom. Sarah Redikopp reframes mad studies to better encapsulate the ways that settler colonialism and the (attempted) disappearance of Indigenous Peoples necessitates the disciplining of white settler populations. Madness intertwines with unruliness as white settlers are threatened with the possibility of becoming the anachronistic and the outsider. Sanism and mad studies have been too willing to centre the white settler, failing to understand these dynamics. Redikopp argues that

> in their rendering as prehistoric and primitive, occupants of anachronistic spaces were simultaneously racialized by virtue of their failure to approximate norms of white respectability, including sanity and heterosexuality.[10]

This is not to say that these characters become Indigenous, but they become coded as outside of the white settler system. They become mythological Indians in their freedom to adopt various modes of violent self-defence (hatcheting, axing, sawing their way to freedom), and they throw off their "civilized" attire for tank tops and a bloody band of cotton around an arm or their forehead.

Studying horror through an anti-colonial lens means that we might better understand how and why the white women "go mad" in the end. Redikopp writes about the ways that both madness and the study of madness are dominated by white settler scholars.[11] Conceptualizations of madness are rooted in structural racism. Horror films may make vague reference or insinuations to a character's "madness" (be they a villain or a hero) but this is done in a flat way that codes the characters in question as dangerous

10 Redikopp, "Out of Place, Out of Mind," 112.
11 Redikopp, "Out of Place, Out of Mind," 2.

or as outlaw. The ways that sanism and constructions of madness operate in horror, intertwined with gender, with sexuality, with age, and with monstrosity, further the notion of the Final Girl as a savage Other. The link between monstrous *savage* femininity and madness is coded in horror in many ways and mirrors real-world dynamics of surveillance and punishment, institutionalization and incarceration. The mad white settler woman is freed from her confines, but settler colonialism remains systemic and intact; she can be rescued as she is in Eggers's *The Witch* (2015), or she can be punished for her transgressions, as she is in Hitchcock's *The Birds* (1963). The surveillance and punishment of madness as a constructed thing are crucial to settler colonial domination of Indigenous Peoples and lands.

THE WITCH *(2015)*

In 2015's *The Witch*, a white settler family who live at the edge of the wilderness try and fail to farm, hunt, and survive on their own. The film opens on this family in the midst of being banished from their New England settlement. They go wandering to the edge of the community and end up next to the forest, where they fail to grow food and their animals die (or apparently become possessed by Satan). The family kneel in the field when they first arrive in their new homestead and pray to their god. Soon after, we see their new home and barn, and the eldest daughter of the family praying while her mother breastfeeds a new infant. We viewers can see that the family is already in trouble; as the mother curses out her own daughter with her eyes, we realize that the family is doomed because of its own self-loathing and silly ideas about sin.

The remoteness of the film's location is important not only in signifying the banishment of the family but in making it clear that the Indians have cleared out from the area. At the same time, real, breathing Indigenous people walk on and off screen. Rebecca Onion describes *The Witch* as

> a great exploration of the dark, chaotic, troubled psychology of English colonists at the very beginning of the empire's colonial experiment in North America. People who "travailed a vast ocean" to find a new life turned starving and paranoid, surrounded by their dead, uncertain of their identities or their missions.[12]

The family are attacked by witches who kidnap their infant at the woods' edge and then kill the baby and bathe in its blood. The next youngest child in the family is also abducted. The white-settler family are cursed by witches, and by the Devil himself, who shows up in the form of a black goat and destroys the family from within while the witches keep kidnapping children at the edge of the woods.

The witch embodies the reciprocal dialogue between settler colonialism in North America and the "old world," which settler colonialism also shapes. Moreover, the witch embodies those interconnections between sanism, homophobia, sexism, racism, classism, and ageism. The witch's cannibalism is central to her monstrosity in *The Witch*. Charles Zika writes of cannibalism that it is a metaphor

> for the non-civilized; but since the sacrifice and eating of one's God was a belief and act of liturgical practice at the centre of Christianity, and especially so in the later middle ages, cannibalism was also a metaphor located threateningly at the centre

12 Onion, "The Most Accurate Part of *The Witch*?"

> of the European psyche. And it was in the early modern period, through the instruments of theological and legal treatises, judicial trials, pastoral and moralizing literature, romance and folkloric tales, and also through visual images, that cannibalism was grafted on to the image of the malefic witch.[13]

The film asks: Who are the monsters? Are they witches, or the white settler women who have internalized heteropatriarchy? Are the monsters the patriarchal father and his stubborn fundamentalist pride, which leads to his family's downfall? The witches themselves are obviously the main monsters in the film. They are old women who murder and mutilate babies and are able to fly on their brooms as a result.

The ending sees the surviving family member embark on her own journey, flying freely with the witches. The teen daughter, Thomasin, is the internal threat to the family, fighting back against her mother's expectations and ultimately embracing the outlier role. She is somewhat freed by witchery or madness, whichever befalls her. Read this way, Thomasin is liberated from the intense Christian puritanism of her family, for whom humans are seen as sinful. As she flies above the trees with the other witches, their laughter aimed at the civilized town (or perhaps the viewer), there is some small catharsis in that moment.

There is another moment, a very short scene, when the family is banished, and a small group of Indigenous traders look back at them with what might be fear or perhaps just curiosity. We're shown that the scariest things in the woods might be the things that this white settler family represents. When Indigenous people seem to look sideways at the family, it tells us (potentially)

---

13 Zika, "Cannibalism and Witchcraft," 78.

that this family are the monstrous Others. Without their land, the Indigenous traders (who are shown for ten seconds, barely) are embedded in the new order of things.

The threat of the woods, of magic, of witchery and of Indians, is obvious. This film about a paranoid white settler family positions the witch at the woods' edge where the Indigenous-Others haunt. Adam Fleet writes of the landscape as a "tangled woodland," and also as "the demarcation line between the God-fearing Puritans and the ancient, primal terror living within it."[14] It is a concept beyond rescue, the construct of civilization and savagery, that both disappears and makes hyper-visible (and monstrous) the Indian as other. Tied to this monstrosity, the teen daughter of *The Witch* is a sinner, beyond the reach of the good Christian family.

The Witch raises a question about how the punishment of witches in Europe was and remains a central part of the economic, social, and political changes that root settler colonialism in the Americas. Tyler McCreary and Rebecca Hall write, for example, about the ways that the surveillance and punishment of witchcraft operated in the 1920s and '30s in settler colonized Western Canada, arguing that punishing witchcraft was closely connected to systemic settler control over Indigenous lives.[15] The ongoing need to portray witches as cannibals who fall outside the confines of heteropatriarchal family units (as both a problematic element and as somewhat freeing) means that the punishment of the witch remains crucial to ongoing settler colonialism.

The Witch also continues to illustrate the deep connections between sanism and settler colonialism. The family is at risk of demonic attack from the woods and also from within. The

---

14 Fleet, "The Witch."

15 McCreary and Hall, "The Healer, the Witch, and the Law," 352.

demonization of Thomasin and the manifestation of satanic influences through the family's goat signal the impossibility of resistance against the dark, demonic forces of this "new" (Indigenous) land. This narrative operates on one level in the film, while madness operates on another. Closely linked to surveillance and fears of demonic and witchy entities, settler constructions of madness further pressure the family and test their faith in god and in their abilities to conquer and contain the land. Perhaps Thomasin flies with the witches at the end, or perhaps her entire family has starved to death and she is about to follow.

THE BIRDS *(1963)*

Connecting those themes of femininity, madness, and constructed Indigeneity and savagery, *The Birds* (1963) also centres a female character who is ultimately blamed for the sins and darkness of colonized lands. She goes catatonic in the end, "losing her mind" as an element of the natural world (the birds themselves) team up to destroy humanity. On the subject of madness in particular, in relation to women in horror, Steven Jay Schneider writes that the "non-heterosexual characteristics and tendencies figure prominently among the causes, symptoms and/or consequences of specifically female neuroses."[16] *The Birds* is an example of the ways that the lesbian, bisexual, or queer woman is shown as the looming and savage threat to the settler colonial community.

A (heterosexually coded) synopsis of *The Birds* might go as follows: Melanie and Mitch meet at a pet shop in San Francisco. When Mitch tries to buy lovebirds for his much younger sister,

16 Schneider, "Diagnosing Female Madness," 123.

Cathy, he and Melanie get into a conversation about Melanie's appearance in court for pranking someone. Mitch leaves for Bodega Bay, and Melanie follows him in her car with two lovebirds in a cage. A long meandering series of scenes follow as Melanie meets a local teacher, Annie, and decides to stay with her while she learns more about Mitch. After Melanie delivers the lovebirds to Mitch's family home, a bird attacks her, and Mitch tends to her wounds. A series of bird attacks against the local children inspire the townspeople to panic and blame Melanie for being somehow evil and responsible for the coming together of many birds to destroy humans. When Melanie and Mitch attempt to retrieve Cathy, who has hidden with Annie, they find Annie's dead body instead. Not long after, Melanie, Cathy, Mitch, and Mitch and Cathy's mother hide out in their barricaded house. Melanie searches for the source of a sound in the attic and is attacked by birds. She loses her mind and her ability to fight back and Mitch drives them slowly out of town.

The Birds is not a heterosexual love story. Savagery and queerness are coded into Mitch, Melanie, and Annie's three-way relationship, momentarily framed when they're trying to save the children from the birds. The birds are a part of the land and water and they are of the place that good white settlers try to make a home in. While Mitch attempts to force the local sheriff to "do something" about the seagulls, in an amusing scene, Mitch's mother struggles to clean up the pieces of her tea cups that were broken in a bird attack. The birds are savage, they're ancient, and their population is too high. A drunk man at the bar in the scene after a bird attack on Annie's school declares it the end of the world. Another man calls the birds dirty animals and advocates to shoot them all. The birds flock together, and that revolutionary unity is a threat to the settler colonial community.

What makes *The Birds* so interesting are the ways that savagery is nature and more specifically a bird, a woman, whose witchery is called out by a group of fearful and paranoid townspeople. The film opens with a woman named Melanie Daniels who enjoys playing pranks on people and has apparently been taken to court for consequences arising from her trickery, making her an outlaw in a fabulous green dress. Melanie purchases birds in San Francisco (which in the 1960s had a growing Native American community and 2SLGBTQ population) and then drives them to the home of a man named Mitch in a place called Bodega Bay. Bodega Bay is worth describing. It is a protected inlet for white settlers, like a homestead in which the wilderness to be kept at bay is the ocean and the birds that flock from it.

As Melanie brings her big (queer) city energy to Bodega Bay, she's distracted from her quest to bother Mitch. Instead, she meets Annie Hayworth and stays in her home. Melanie and Annie are supposedly interested in Mitch but spend most of their time re-enacting poses from the lesbian pulp novels of the era and talking about how Mitch doesn't like women and neither of them are into him anyway. These sorts of conversations go on for quite some time before the real violence unfolds and the birds turn on the townspeople. The birds kill Annie and others in the community in violent ways (going for the eyes) and ultimately bring an end to anybody's ability to live in Bodega Bay. The Bodega Bay experiment is destroyed in a barrage of feathers. The warning is clear: the (unnatural) queerness of the big city and the natural-savagery of the land and mythical Indian, might be coming for nice white settler folks.

The minute Melanie and Annie meet, the film stops being about some hetero happy ending. Annie is supposedly jealous of this new woman who has taken aim at Mitch, but rather than go down that trail, Melanie denies that she's a "friend of Mitch's" and gazes at Annie with an ambiguous, even seductive gaze. Annie, rather than go into the whole Mitch thing, starts in on some sexy diatribe about how she's wanted a cigarette for the last twenty minutes but she couldn't stop with her compulsive tilling of the soil. Melanie calls her garden "very pretty" and continues to gaze at her. Later, the women sip whisky in Annie's home, intimate and domestic. Mitch asks, "Do you really have to go back there?" (to Annie's house) and authoritatively demands that Melanie stay at his mother's home instead. Even in relation to Mitch, the supposed source of rivalry between the two women, Annie casually mentions that perhaps there has "never been anything between Mitch and any girl." This statement does as much to reinforce Annie's queerness as it does to tell us that Mitch is also "abnormal." Mitch is "emasculated" by his mother and is coded as gay, illustrating the real threat of the birds to the audience—the end of hyper masculinity and white settler virility.

Settler colonialism is also tragic and tedious in *The Birds*. Annie tills her garden as a compulsion, forced to hide away her queer desires while upholding the task of beating back those indigenous weedy plants that threaten to overtake. Zoe Todd reminds us that

> in settler colonialism, colonizers may weaponize plants as agents through which landscapes are re-imagined and re-configured in order to eliminate Indigenous worlds. Gardens, often imagined as a generative space of renewal, can also become weapons through which settlers reinforce specific orders of existence.[17]

17 Todd, "Commentary."

The garden in this instance is also a place where Annie both privately tends to her own sexual needs (tilling her own garden) and contains those desires away from the rest of the settler community. She is ultimately punished for letting the danger into her garden, for sharing her space so freely with the (reverse) invasion coming from the city.

Brenden O'Donnell argues that "like the cover copy of lesbian pulp fiction novels, *The Birds* collapses the complexity of lesbian networks, instead offering direct access to intimacy between women, and strategies for skipping to the peep show."[18] *The Birds* presents queerness and particularly lesbian or bisexual proclivities among women as wholly a threat to civilized society. It might all be campy, perhaps even a swipe at the civilized world itself, but for the brutal ways that both Annie and Melanie are treated in the film. The lesbian/bisexual/queer pulp novels of the 1950s and '60s were, for many, a rare glimpse into possibilities beyond the heteropatriarchal family. *The Birds* mimics the endings of the majority of these novels, that of the unhappy ending—the warning levelled at "unnatural" women—whereby one woman dies violently and the other goes off with a man.

The scene in which Melanie finds Annie dead, legs splayed, eyes pecked out, lingers; Mitch covers Annie with his coat, and Melanie turns away. O'Donnell argues that Annie's

> gruesome death articulates Hitchcock's attempt to leverage lesbian sexuality to instil fear in his audience... this attempt manifests as heteropatriarchal violence. Hitchcock's utilization of femininity and queerness to denaturalize heterosexuality neither constitutes representation nor critiques heteronormativity;

18 O'Donnell, "Surveilling Lesbians," 63.

> rather, it represents the sacrificability of women's bodies and lesbian sexuality in order to produce cinematic terror.[19]

With Annie's awful death, Melanie is all in with Mitch, upon whom she suddenly depends to rescue her. Shortly after the worst of the attacks begins to unfold, birds assault Melanie in the attic of Mitch's family home and she is left unable to speak up or fight back after. It's her curiosity and willingness to wander that leads her to the attic in the first place, and she pays the price for her independence and curiosity. That iconic attack leaves her muttering Mitch's name and falling to the floor while birds swarm her. She loses agency, loses Annie, and loses her mind, rescued only by her new "family," led by Mitch.

Melanie brings with her a daring level of freedom for a woman, and she is punished for it. Her corrupting influence brings San Francisco (she dares drive herself around in cars and boats) to a quaint settler fishing town. She is duly punished, but instead of becoming some empowered Final Girl, she goes mad, loses her ability to speak in salty, sultry, sarcastic sentences, and Mitch, her heteropatriarchal love interest, takes away her car keys.

In one scene, women line a hallway to turn and stare and then accuse Melanie of being evil. They consider her demonic, like the birds. O'Donnell argues that

> *The Birds* shares a... pervasive and insidious network of misogynistic power that women must navigate... the film discloses a poignant heterosexual male fear that lesbian sexuality renders men unnecessary, even for the purpose of intimacy... In addition to shaping careful narratives, Hitchcock's camera

19 O'Donnell, "Surveilling Lesbians," 52.

> develops techniques to eavesdrop on women, interrupt their intimate moments and examine them. By thinking of Hitchcock's films as generating surveillance practices, I argue that the monitoring of lesbians in *The Birds* constitutes a direct execution of heteropatriarchal power rather than a subtle psychological exploration of a voyeuristic urge.[20]

The reinforcement of heteropatriarchal settler colonialism is signalled in *The Birds* by this surveillance and punishment of lesbian sexuality as a threat to civilized society.

In a lengthy scene in a bar, we learn about all of the threats that the viewing audience might face. An argument between a butch lesbian-coded older bird expert, Melanie, a fisherman, an angry businessman, and a drunk guy in the bar presents numerous interpretations for the bird attacks. Melanie warns everybody that birds are attacking the children, while the butch lesbian Mrs. Bundy calls her irrational. Mrs. Bundy tells us that there are too many birds to kill. "It's the end of the world," a drunk man tells us. Birds behaving against their nature, birds of different species flocking together, Mrs. Bundy says, "we're fighting a war"—against counter-culture elements of all kinds, not just one species of birds. The birds attack again after the bar scene, and in the chaos, gasoline is spilled, cars explode, and a lingering overhead shot makes it look as though a fiery hellmouth has opened. *The Birds* is so fascinating because of its layered associations between the haunted settler colony and Christian/colonial notions of hell combined with sanism, the sanctity of the heteropatriarchal family, and the ecological threats that constitute a nature-based reverse-colonization fantasy. Settler colonialism is dependent on this

20 O'Donnell, "Surveilling Lesbians," 51.

particular form of panic about madness and queerness, intertwined with notions of savagery and violence.

HIGH TENSION *(2003)*

I've included a French horror film in this instance because it tells us two things: first, American horror influences Europe; and second, settler colonialism itself influences and can be reflected upon in European (colonial) imaginations (critically or otherwise). Connecting European Gothic traditions to North American settler colonial horror is not a difficult leap. Veracini writes of the frontier as impacting European thought in ongoing ways as well. He reviews Walter Prescott Webb's work of 1951, arguing

> that the American frontier had shaped the institutions of Europe as well as America, and that the American frontier had been a genuinely universal frontier... it was indeed with an elegiac sense of the irretrievable passing of an era that a comparative literature was now developing.[21]

Those interconnections between gender, sexuality, sanism, and colonial fears of the savage both within and outside of the boundaries of civilization, arise in interesting and striking ways in 2003's *High Tension*. *High Tension* seems self-reflexive as a "cowboys and Indians" story combined with the savage, queer madwoman trope. The movie opens with a woman's voice chanting the words, "I won't let anyone come between us anymore." She then runs from our view, somewhere in the past it seems, lurching through the forest with injuries and a bloodied armband that

21 Veracini, "'Settler Colonialism: Career of a Concept,'" 318.

marks her as the warrior in the story. Moments later, the same person, Marie, awakes in the back of a car and asks her friend Alex, who is driving, to hand her a cigarette and light. The two are on their way to Alex's parents' house. Marie describes the dream in which she was chased by herself, bloodied, through the forest. Alex asks if she ever has normal dreams and Marie says, "Being like everyone else is a bore." At this point, they discuss Alex's romantic life, and Marie calls her a "slut" and a "bimbo." Her internalized misogyny is already showing, and it's clear she's split between two impulses.

In the next scene, we see Alex's little brother dressed like a cowboy, fighting with his mother who tells him to get inside. The domestic life of the mother is then juxtaposed with a horrifying scene in which a dirty man in a dirty truck masturbates with a severed woman's head. Seconds later, a cheesy country song plays while Marie drives the rest of the way to Alex's parents' house. They stop off in a corn field to play scary hide and seek, and then continue on. The corn fields signify both conquest and the looming threat of savagery. The frontier is, Schneekloth reminds us, "sometimes represented as a garden receptive to the cultivation and the husbandry of new settlers, and sometimes as a savage wilderness in mortal battle with human beings."[22] Savagery is also marked by the growing romantic feelings between Marie and Alex.

It seems obvious by this point that Marie is attracted to Alex, and Alex realizes or already knows it. They arrive at the family farm. Alex calls the neighbours "rednecks" (at least in the English version) and talks about the farm as a family hobby project. The homestead, amongst other white homesteaders, is soon under attack from both the madman outside and the mad woman within.

22 Schneekloth, "The Frontier Is Our Home," 210.

The idea of the madman, who ultimately lives solely in Marie's mind (she is the one who kills the family), is that he is a misogynistic, working-class truck driver in mechanic's overalls. In order to obliterate the heteropatriarchal family, Marie imagines a killer whom she can also heroically stop. She imagines herself hiding in closets from the killer, under beds, trying to rescue Alex's loved ones, even as she herself kills them without realizing it.

I've chosen this film as an example of how settler colonialism might also reframe some European horror. The mad woman is the savage who erupts from within French colonial society, measuring its historic and ongoing violence, hunting down the cowboy(s). And, of course, she is the queer monster, a stereotypical mad woman whose queerness drives her to murder.[23]

The logic of the frontier continues in this film. We don't know what mental health struggles or diagnoses she has, but the mad lesbian killer from *High Tension* seems to disassociate, have a split personality, struggle with empathy, and generally be coded as someone in the midst of a "psychotic break." As a commentary on white settler heteronormativity, I have always thought that the film actually portrays the heteropatriarchal norms that the killer faces as the true monster. The mother's death is emotional and tragic, and the young boy is shot in a corn field, the home of Indigenous Peoples for whom corn is and was a stolen seed.

The film is weirdly romantic, with an actual final kiss and coming together of Marie and Alex, connected by the very weapon Alex drives through Marie's shoulder but hangs onto. I found a similar

---

23 Most of the reviews that I read online when the film first came out in North America were offended by the renewal of the *Psycho* formula of mental health and sexuality and sanism. I could not figure out why I liked the film's ending so much until I considered the young boy dressed as a cowboy and the constant references to cornfields in the film as a savage or wild backdrop.

reading of *High Tension* by Tony Perrello, who points out that the patriarchal head of family has his head removed while his wife has her vocal cords sliced, and that the tension of the film's title is "caused by love, in this case, same-sex desire." The home, Perrello continues, is "claustrophobic," contrasted with "the free and happy world of female bonding."[24]

In *The Birds* and *High Tension*, mad, queer women bring death, shattering the safety of the frontier settlement. The killer isn't scary only because of sanism; those constructions of sanity versus madness feed into and are fed by colonial notions of civilization/savagery and those elements of savagery that are associated with demons and particular magic and dangerous places and times of year. The next example of these interconnections, and the reason for continually re-rooting the conversation in an understanding of settler colonialism, is the Halloween franchise.

HALLOWEEN *(1978)*

The things the director himself says about a boy he met who inspired Michael Myers, the killer of the Halloween franchise, are telling. As a young student, John Carpenter visited an asylum. About a boy he saw there, Carpenter says that the boy had "a schizophrenic stare... a real evil stare. And it was unsettling to me. It was like the creepiest thing I'd ever seen... he was completely insane."[25] Sanism, ableism, and savagery combine with the magic of Samhain in the first horror film I ever watched all the way through.

In the original *Halloween* (1978) a young boy named Michael Myers stabs his sister to death after he sees her having sex with her

24 Perrello, "A Parisian in Hollywood," 29–30.

25 John Carpenter in Smith, dir., *Halloween: A Cut Above the Rest*.

boyfriend. That kill scene is shown from Michael's point of view, a mask sliding over the camera from behind which he stalks his sister, Judith. Michael is portrayed as unable to speak, hyper-focused, and seemingly incapable of processing what he has done. Throughout the rest of the series of films that centre on him, Michael Myers will go on killing sprees that see him robotically mow through young people, much like other super-killers of the genre.

When he grows up, Myers escapes the psychiatric institution he was sentenced to for life. He becomes the "escaped madman" of sanist urban legend lore. Myers leaps on cars trying to kill people, then ultimately returns to his hometown of Haddonfield and targets young women and their boyfriends for death. One of Myers's intended victims is Laurie Strode, played by Jamie Lee Curtis, who appears in seven films in the franchise. Her friends are killed while she babysits two little kids on Halloween night. Once she sees Michael and realizes what has happened, she fights back.

In this frontier tale, Laurie's defence of space and place changes throughout the franchise. In the first film, Laurie finds her inner willingness to fight, and stabs Michael with the items used in her own oppression. Michael has already punished her friends for their sexual freedom and also for their desire to reproduce as white settlers do in frontier towns. Michael is both the patriarch denying sexual freedom, and the savage who invades and halts the literal reproduction of the population of Haddonfield. Read another way, the knitting needle and coat hanger are desperate attempts on Laurie's part in a context in which Michael as patriarchal violence, never stops coming, never stops threatening her life. As tools of Laurie's oppression, the knitting needle and hanger are both reminders of settler colonial and patriarchal restrictions on women's reproductive freedoms, and weapons in the domestic sphere that Michael cannot see coming (and they literally take out his eyes). By the end of the franchise, Laurie uses guns, including a Smith & Wesson shotgun, making her a new mythical outlaw.

Demons in the settler colonial imagination, Bergland writes, "could act as invisible entities, as physical bodies, or as internalized ideas."[26] Further, the ghosts and demons that haunt, work toward erasure. The "ghosting of Indians is a technique of removal. By writing about Indians as ghosts, white writers effectively remove them from American lands and place them, instead, within the American imagination."[27] The ghostly, pale Michael Myers is also demonic, and he is a spectral return of death and of pagan spirits. Michael Myers is so compelling because he is so many things all at once. He is a spectre of madness, beyond the boundaries of civilization but also rooted firmly within it.

HALLOWEEN II *(1981)*

Halloween II opens in a time set just before that of the first film's ending. Laurie tells the kids to run and get help from the neighbours. Michael rises behind her. Dr. Loomis approaches the house. Michael attacks Laurie, and she flies over a staircase barrier after briefly unmasking him. Dr. Loomis shoots Michael. When they search for Michael, he is nowhere to be found. Dr. Loomis, the man of science and psychiatry, tells Laurie that, indeed, Michael Myers is the boogeyman. The title sequence and credits roll and we see a new carved pumpkin with lights flickering inside of it. The now-familiar theme song in the franchise plays as names flash on screen. Finally, the carved pumpkin falls away to reveal a

---

26 Bergland, *The National Uncanny*, 27.
27 Bergland, *The National Uncanny*, 12.

skull within. Michael Myers is death itself, he is the Devil—he is also "crazy" in ways we never really understand.

After the opening sequence, Michael's rampage in *Halloween II* targets a hospital. While it's not a psychiatric hospital, it's of interest that he seems to strike out at the tools of the medicalized post-pagan Western world in this film. The madness of Michael Myers is described often in films about him, alongside vague notions of his evilness. *Halloween II* illuminates the ways that carceral mental health systems play into Myers's isolation and constructions of who he really is in an oddly sympathetic way. The film follows Laurie Strode to a bizarrely empty hospital, as she attempts to recover from the first film's events, where Michael Myers tries to kill her again. As he hunts her down, not knowing what room she's in, he goes ahead and kills a bunch of other people in the meantime. Among his victims are a doctor, some nurses, and an ambulance attendant, who all meet the business ends of various medical instruments wielded by Myers. He bleeds out one nurse, stabs another with a scalpel, and boils and drowns two people in a therapeutic hot tub where they've gone to have sex, despite being at work and possibly needing that therapeutic tub for actual patients. The film is striking in that Michael Myers is essentially at war with a carceral healthcare system, the very system that had attempted to confine him for life.

Halloween II further drives home the reading of Michael Myers as a "madman" whose madness is linked to his violence. Michael is a lurking demonic entity who is a product of civilized settler colonial society and is cast out and deemed both insane and violent in his wandering, killing, and "primitive" lifestyle. Jason hides in the woods, while Michael hides in tunnels, living on small mammals (presumably). Haddonfield is constantly at odds with itself over Michael's origins and his constant return. Townspeople blame everybody from authority figures to the victims and survivors themselves, even blaming Laurie Strode in some cases, for somehow drawing the demon back to town.

Michael Myers is also a product of the psychiatric system. His own doctor makes it clear that he needs to be incarcerated for life. In the second film of a series that spans four decades, Michael takes his revenge on the medical system. He attempts to hunt Laurie down in a hospital. At some point, he hides in a room where newborns are kept and doesn't hurt any of them. He is still the childlike, innocent boy turned completely evil by unknown forces. Michael kills a security guard, then slashes his way through nurses and doctors before trying to kill Laurie. He's set on fire and lays there seemingly burning to death. The films continue into a third, which doesn't include Michael, and a fourth and fifth, which make up the silliness about Laurie being Michael's sister, and then my favourite Xennial horror film ever, *H20*.

HALLOWEEN H20 *(1998)*

The Xennial generation, of which I am a part, grew up without the internet but then mastered the art of posting weird things on online "boards" by the time we were teens. *H20* captures that feeling of being between worlds, opening with two young men who sit in a 1970s/'80s-style living room while nurse Marion Chambers of the original *Halloween* (1978), smokes and tells them stories. All three are killed, reflecting the nihilism of the grunge generation. I had just turned twenty when *H20* came out and welcomed this postmodern addition to the franchise. References to other horror films are made when Janet Leigh, the mother of Jamie Lee Curtis and star of *Psycho* and *The Fog* (1980), behaves all maternally toward her real-life daughter after treating us all to a jump-scare! Josh Hartnett (in a terrible haircut), Michelle Williams, Joseph Gordon-Levitt, and LL Cool J all star. In this reboot of the franchise, a new timeline is introduced and sort of spins off into two sequels. In this timeline, Laurie Strode has faked her death and is living under a new identity. She is head of a private academy where her son, John, goes to school. Michael breaks into the school, kills John's friends, and tries to kill him and his mom. In the end, Laurie apparently cuts off Michael's head.

Throughout this film, Laurie's mental state is discussed. Her son is incredibly rude to her for continuing to think that a raging killer might be a worrisome thing. Laurie has bad dreams, takes some sort of medication, and drinks wine like it is water. The past—1978, the year I was born and the year the first film came out—appears in images and memories introduced in a montage at the start and clearly haunts Laurie throughout. Laurie's boring boyfriend is a counsellor at the school, and in a moment of terrible boundary-drawing, she tells him to counsel her. She reveals that she's been to shrinks, in group therapy, in twelve-step programs, but her boyfriend tells her that nothing will fix all that trauma like talking to him! He dies later in the film.

The inability of people around Laurie Strode to properly handle her trauma is a thread in almost every movie she shows up in, it seems. In the second film, none of the nurses or doctors take the threat of Michael seriously. In *H20*, her son tells her that she's paranoid and he can't live with her trauma. It's fair, but the way he says it is pretty disrespectful. He accuses her of being handcuffed to her dead brother instead of, say, legitimately afraid that he might still be out there hunting her. Laurie is made into a kind of town crier, warning characters in each film that they need to keep their eyes out for Michael Myers. She's always right: Michael *is* lurking, he *does* return, but nobody takes her seriously. She is the ultimate stereotypical "crazy lady" who wanders around shouting warnings at people who just want to live their boring lives in white settler suburbia.

Laurie is a bit like a harbinger of death.[28] She has an almost psychic ability to know when Michael is going to return. In this way, Laurie is similar to Ralph Neeley (mockingly referred to as "Crazy Ralph") from *Friday the 13th* who warns everybody about Jason and the death curse of Crystal Lake. She hallucinates Michael, and it's only the "rational" folks who stop her from listening to those warnings. When she tries to live a "normal" life with her boring boyfriend, making out with him while Michael stalks the campus, she is nearly killed. The boyfriend laughs about Michael Myers's first kill in this film—of his own sister—and tells Laurie to take off her clothes. When Laurie tells him the whole story, including this new detail about her being Michael's sister, he still insists that it's all good. She gets out a gun when she realizes her son is still on campus and has reached the same age she was when Michael came for her, and the boyfriend still tells her "this is nuts" and "calm down!" But Laurie is right, of course, and a whole lot of people die.

HALLOWEEN *(2018)*

The overarching themes of David Gordon Green's *Halloween* (2018), *Halloween Kills* (2021), and *Halloween Ends* (2022) include

28 As a mixed First Nations/Euro-settler viewer with various trauma-induced extraordinary coping mechanisms, which I won't name here to save time, I've always been annoyed at Laurie Strode's mistreatment due to her mental health struggles. Perhaps, instead, I should focus on the reason she is drawn the way she is, as a kind of spiritual person. She is a force of nature, an outsider, warning the town that they will never be safe from the boogeyman. She's a fierce mother to her kids in this film's timeline and in the timeline where she teaches her daughter Karen to shoot guns at a young age and trap Michael in a kill box. Parental goals!

ruminations about the source of violence (is it part of the human condition, is it socialized, how does it take root, etc.), redemption, and moving on with life after trauma. The consistent themes in the series (going back to the original film), about the nature of evil and the slipperiness of sanity, continue.

In 2018's *Halloween*, the beginning of the reboot trilogy, Laurie Strode's daughter Karen and granddaughter (and son-in-law) live a nice normal life in Haddonfield. Laurie, however, skulks around in the forest, in a survivalist's dream cottage. Her home is fortified with extra locks and traps and a hidden basement. She spends her days shooting guns at creepy mannequins. Meanwhile, her daughter (who had been taken from her when she was a young girl) wants little to do with her "mad" mom. Laurie once again plays the role of the mad woman. She is erratic, unpredictable, drinks too much, has sex and children outside of marriage, and lives to hunt and kill one man. Michael Myers is institutionalized.

After Michael escapes during a prisoner transfer, he starts to kill again, slaughtering people in Haddonfield for partying on Halloween. He's ultimately lured to Laurie's home, where Karen shoots him. At the end of *Halloween* (2018) Laurie, Karen, and Karen's daughter, Allyson, are taken to safety in the back of a truck while Michael burns in Laurie's basement.

HALLOWEEN KILLS *(2021)*

Halloween Kills opens with firefighters attempting to put out the flames at Laurie's house. They help Michael in his escape from the basement and are all killed. In this film, the people of Haddonfield realize that Michael Myers is returning for them. Some are killed. Some form a vigilante group, going after Michael in the streets, beating him nearly to death (as much as is possible). The movie opens with a backstory about the cops who first went after Michael, in the late 1970s. A layer to that story, about Michael spending his days staring out his window, looking over Haddonfield, explains the monster as simply a man who is frequently in a catatonic state. In the end, Karen returns to Michael's favourite spot, to see what he sees, and she is killed viciously for it. The way Karen stares into the distance, overseeing the violent place, the colonial town with its cycles of violence, is momentarily moving. She's stabbed viciously by Michael moments later.

HALLOWEEN ENDS *(2022)*

At the beginning of *Halloween Ends* (2022), Laurie Strode narrates from a book she is writing about her experiences with Michael Myers in a voice-over alongside introductory images of Haddonfield. Writing her memoirs, Laurie's authoritative narration tells us that Haddonfield was peaceful before Michael Myers's reign of terror. Histories of colonization and racism are obscured beneath mythologies of suburban white settler life. By this point, people in Haddonfield are blaming Laurie Strode for her own victimization and for Michael Myers's killing sprees.

In this trilogy finale, a young man named Corey accidentally kills a little boy while babysitting him. Years later, we see glimpses of Corey's new life. He's called the "psycho babysitter" by local teens, and only Laurie and her granddaughter seem to be able to empathize with him. After Corey is attacked and thrown from a bridge, he comes across Michael Myers hiding in the sewers.

Corey begins a killing spree, even collaborating with Michael at one point. After Allyson is passed over for a promotion by a doctor in her office, in favour of a nurse he's having an affair with, Corey and Michael team up to kill the doctor and nurse. There is a voyeuristic quality to Corey's relationship with Michael. Corey, like Laurie, and like the mob that nearly killed Michael in *Halloween Kills*, catches violence like it's a virus. Corey's descent into depression, rage, and killing all happen because of bullying on some level it seems. But when Laurie looks at him, she starts to see that Corey has changed from the young man she defended against a group of rude youth.

There is a theme of possession that runs throughout the franchise. Michael Myers is known as the Shape in the original *Halloween*. His washed-out white mask only hints at a human form; he is a shapeless, eternal evil, and Corey has somehow become possessed by him. Laurie slices Michael's wrists and kills him on her kitchen island, holding his hand after defeating him in her own domestic space. The police then join with her to destroy his body in an industrial metal crusher. None of this is legal; the police and Laurie have become outlaws only to protect the white settler homestead. The ancient, insane, murderous presence of the boogeyman has finally been defeated. The suffering that Michael Myers has caused, Laurie says at the start of *Ends*, is like an infection.

The film's understanding of power dynamics and the roots of what makes a killer like Michael are troubling. One telling thing about Haddonfield in *Ends* is that Black women are characterized as awful, on more than one occasion, as are queer characters, while the "tragic killer" Corey takes centre stage. Corey's mother (whom he kills) is portrayed as nagging and controlling. The mother of the child Corey killed with negligent behaviour is portrayed as irrational and mean-spirited. It would seem that white settler patriarchal violence is the product of misunderstood men who deserve our sympathy.

Laurie Strode is rendered anachronistic through her interactions with Michael Myers—she goes mad, she embodies those markers that tell us she's stepped out of civilized life. She can't even bake a pie without burning it! Ultimately, it is not just Michael Myers who is incarcerated in the various timelines of the Halloween franchise, but Laurie Strode herself, whose attempts to warn everybody about the boogeyman render her ostracized in just about every timeline.

Michael Myers as demon, as a product of the inherent fearfulness of North America, is also a marker of the threat of its demise. Settler colonialism contains within it a fear of its own failure; as Mairi Cowan writes, this "fear of demons is an expression of a deeper anxiety about the precariousness of the entire colonial project."[29] It matters that Michael Myers is rooted in perceptions about insanity, savagery, and violence.

Despite coming from a middle-class background, Michael Myers adopts blue mechanic coveralls as his uniform during his sprees. He drives, at various points, old trucks and cars. His "twin," Corey, works at a junkyard, displaying some kind of class (and misogynistic) rage similar to Michael's. The mad as working-class or poor people who have had enough of American largesse is a thread that sees poverty as a stand-in for dispossessed and disappeared Native Americans. The savage as violent, as insane, as threatening some variation of the colonial dream family, can also be very rich.

MONSTER PARTY *(2018)*

In 2018's *Monster Party*, a serial killer family attempting to be "sober" and refrain from killing throws a party with other reformed serial killers. During that party, a group of hired staff try to rob the

29 Mairi Cowan, quoted in Aschaiek, "This Halloween, Discover."

home of the wealthy family throwing the party for their monstrous friends. References to sanity and savagery are peppered throughout the film. The wealthy family exists within a network of killers who fight hard against their instincts. They struggle to be civilized. At odds with one another are the head of the sober-killers club, Milo, and the patriarchal head of the wealthy family, Patrick. Patrick tells his daughter that he wants to be a "real family" again, presumably by murdering people as a group. As head of the "sober" group, Milo keeps telling everybody to behave themselves. He is the civilized leader, representing law and order and rules of conduct, without which savagery would prevail.

At the first opportunity, the killers at the dinner party begin stalking and killing a trio of would-be robbers posing as caterers for the evening. Two of the robbers/help are dispatched by the serial killing family's offspring, while the third escapes with the help of the family's matriarch, Roxanne (played by Robin Tunney), and her daughter, Alexis (Erin Moriarty), neither of whom wish to continue a life lived hacking up strangers. We get the sense that the pearl-wearing Roxanne thinks of herself as somewhat attempting to live a civilized, domesticated life. She chops vegetables while looking forlornly into the distance and then uses that knife to later slay her sadistic son, Elliot. It's a team effort, as Elliot (Kian Lawley), is stabbed first by his mother and then finished off by his sister. Elliot's lack of civility is ultimately rooted in his misogyny as he attempts to kill his sister. When his mother's lack of connection with him allows her to kill him, the trope of the mad woman and failed mother is turned on its head. Mother and daughter retreat into their mansion to attempt a normal life (and obvious gory cleanup) again, this time without hovering patriarchs. The twist in *Monster Party* might be about seeing the wealthy white family as inherently violent and too corrupted by its own sadism to continue. Instead, the family unit shifts and becomes a mother and daughter united against the violence they work to escape. The mad woman retreats to raise her daughter alone, killing urges and all. The status quo is generally intact, and the ending feels like a reminder that nothing much has been challenged or changed.

READY OR NOT *(2019)*

The Civ/Sav binary is (somewhat) turned on its head as an ultra-rich white settler family, who are also Satan worshippers, hunt and sacrifice people who try to marry in. The film plays with the audience's perceptions of the family's willingness to worship (and make sacrifices to) Satan by at least floating the possibility that they have simply all "gone mad." The family has an interesting name—Le Domas. Satan (embodied by a character named Mr. Le Bail) met the original Le Domas heir in the 1800s on a sea voyage. The family's ties to colonialism are alluded to in these details, and the idea of a white settler sailor making a deal with the Devil for an immense fortune is a great metaphor for the expropriation and maintaining of white settler wealth in the Americas.

The family makes new members play a card game on their wedding night, and if they draw a hide-and-seek card, they are hunted and sacrificed to Satan. The family is stuck in the past, in archaic technologies (guns, record players, old images of their ancestors). If the new, married-in family member draws any other card, the family takes them in and they become part of the killing spree. On the night the film features, the newly married Grace (played by Samara Weaving) draws the hide-and-seek card. She thinks it's a joke, at first, and wanders the hallways of the family manor with its massive rooms and many hiding spots, making fun of the game. When she emerges and sees a maid accidentally shot in her place, she and her new husband have to find a way to get her out of the mansion. Her husband, having agreed to the game in the first place, is torn between his family and his new wife. When Grace manages to defend herself through the night, even killing the family matriarch (played by Andie MacDowell), her new husband turns on her. She's saved by her drunk brother-in-law who obviously isn't on board with the whole thing. On the verge of being sacrificed to Mr. Le Bail, Grace successfully thwarts the family's efforts until the sun comes up, so the Le Domas deal with the Devil has been broken. When Grandma tries to kill Grace post-sunrise anyway, the older woman literally explodes. In turn, the rest of the family members are exploded, until only Grace and her hubby remain. When she asks him for a divorce, he, too, explodes, splashing her with an absurd amount of blood, and she laughs.

The film is a disavowal of the heteropatriarchal family and embrace of another variation on the white settler nightmare—the incestuous, closed, royalist family model. My favourite of the "rich people can be a pack of savage killers also" films is definitely *Ready or Not*. The twisted rich settler family is so full of drama and fascinating dynamics in this one. The father, encountering his new daughter-in-law when she's nearly escaped, asks her, "Who the fuck do you think you are? You're just another sacrifice. You're another goat." The family's wealth is derived from a satanic pact, a pact with the dark forces, the savage forces, that are associated with the darkness of the Americas; but in this instance, those dark forces are European in origin, a white colonizer demon who demands blood and loss, a death culture. "Fuck your fucking family!" the Final Girl says, beating her mother-in-law to death with a game box. Her husband betrays her for his dark roots, willingly leading her to the altar for the Devil. But she has the last laugh as each of the remaining family members explode in her face.

THE MENU (2022)

This is a film about a chef who "loses his mind" and lures wealthy people to a final supper where he burns everybody in his restaurant up like human flambé. In this film, gender, race, ethnicity, and sexuality are all made to seem less important than class, as we're made to cheer for an elite chef who wants to roast his elite customers alive for daring to buy into the excess and wealth of late capitalism. Stopping short of actual cannibalism, the wealthy super chef of the film still roasts his victims alive, covering them with chocolate and marshmallow, and surrounding them with graham cracker (like a s'more) and then having his staff turn on the gas in order to blow the restaurant up. The film is about class resentment, and also about gentrification and cultural appropriation. The funniest moment of the film comes when the wealthy guests are served tortillas imprinted with images of their indiscretions and illegal activities. When they ask "What the hell are these?" their server responds in a bland and sarcastic tone: "These are tortillas. Tortillas deliciosas." The idea that this white chef would perfect the tortilla beckons some faint memory of the origins of the American economy, rooted in the colonization of Indigenous lands and foods. *The Menu* doesn't just kill off its characters one by one, it deconstructs them. A restaurant critic is exposed for destroying careers with her reviews, a group of wealthy investors see their financial crimes exposed on the back of a delicious tortilla, and the head chef himself sets himself alight to atone for his arrogance.

Class as a context for or commentary on sanism and savagery is interconnected with race. *The Menu* does not include this reflexivity as people are judged to be a part of some decadent system no matter what their background or how their families have experienced colonial oppression. Class blots out those histories in a way that is better reframed by an understanding of settler colonialism and racism. There are Black chefs in the background who are rendered voiceless and made to kill themselves alongside the rest. Moreover, the way the head chef treats the island like a personal colony, romanticizing his harvesting skills along with his culinary skills, makes him both the colonizer and savage. The film is not only about class, but it attempts to be, and therefore obscures the complexities of interconnections between gender, race, class, and so on. The next two films do bring these threads together, somewhat successfully.

US *(2019)*

Jordan Peele's *Us* is layered in its questioning about madness, savagery, racism, class, and colonization. The film follows a family of four after a lengthy opening scene in which a young girl named Adelaide wanders into a funhouse and meets her doppelgänger. We are then shown adult Adelaide, played by Lupita Nyong'o, on vacation with her husband and their son and daughter. During the night, the family is confronted by doubles of themselves who try to kill them. After running away, they realize that others are dying as their doubles all rise up from a kind of underground facility, which Adelaide sees. The underground dwellers are called the Tethered, and their goal seems to be to join hands above ground, in a mimic of the Hands Across America event sponsored by USA for Africa.

The film provides a class analysis by portraying an underclass—literally underground—as monstrous and murderous but ultimately also as victims. *Us* features a reference to Indigenous land and what is underneath us, what we walk upon every day, as we're introduced to the portal for the underclass through something called the Shaman's Vision Quest at the start of the film. Class alone cannot explain this funhouse and its reference to historic colonization as the basis for an American dream gone wrong. The tongue-in-cheek title of the funhouse in *Us* is absurdly wordy for a reason, pointing as it does to the erasure and subsequent romanticization of Indigenous people. Read through an Indigenous lens, the scene is layered with meaning. In Emmy Scott's words,

> I noticed the whistling...at night, which for the Ho-Chunks and other tribes is ill-advised; parents and grandparents say that whistling after dark will call bad spirits. And, yup, sure enough! As soon as Adelaide whistles, she hears a whistle in return, coming from somewhere within this hall of mirrors. Suddenly, she sees the back of her tethered "twin," a double that looks just like her. Twins are powerful figures in the stories of many Native tribes. The Ho-Chunks have Hero Twins that fight monsters. The concept of duality is even represented in our ribbonwork designs that are mirror-image florals of contrasting colors. They represent a world seeking balance between light and dark, a struggle in *Us*, as well.[30]

The tunnel of the funhouse leads to the underground, where the Tethered are held hostage as twins to the people who live their lives fully above, and the imagery evokes the underlying realities of racism and classism in America. At the same time, *ongoing*

30 Scott, "The Native Imagery of Jordan Peele's *Us*."

injustices against Indigenous people, and the knowledge of these injustices, all remain buried beneath with the Shaman's funhouse being renamed Merlin's Forest later on.

The mental distress that befalls the main female character in *Us* is rooted early. Adelaide as a little girl was actually pulled underground by her Tethered other, Red. It is later revealed that Red has been posing as Adelaide into adulthood, and it is Adelaide herself who wants to take back her rightful place. But the real Adelaide is killed, and Red resumes leadership of her above-ground family. In the end, she smiles eerily at her son after destroying their tethered versions, and he looks terrified.

Read as an indictment of colonialism and racism, *Us* sees the Tethered emerge into the fabric of a failed country that they have now destroyed. The shift from a Vision Quest shaman-themed funhouse (with the voice of what sounds like an Elder speaking to Creation) to Merlin's Forest and white settler colonial mythology, speaks to the end of America (if not all things). The tragedy of Adelaide's kidnapping and subsequent death (which includes a story about sexual assault and forced marriage and forced birth) is central to colonized America. *Us* is a warning about the completion of the colonial project and the erasure of Indigenous people and Black women's voices and embodied struggles. But what might happen if Native Americans were actually featured in a film like *Us*? How would the story change? Would Adelaide and Red both survive as well, each redrawn with more agency?[31] Like Kubrick's *The Shining*, Peele's *Us* plants Indigenous cosmology deep in the heart of the film, through art and story. There can be no complete destruction because Indigenous Peoples'

31 See, for example, Niela Orr's writing on the punishment of Black women in horror. Orr, "The Women Who Knew Too Much."

belonging in the Americas is forever. Colonization eats itself in *Us*, but life continues.

THE FOG *(1980)*

Ableism is inextricably linked to settler colonialism. Disability can be used as a "plot device that can explain motivation for villainous or monstrous characters," Melinda Hall argues.[32] Ableism and sanism are rooted in a settler colonial project that demarcates particular bodies as worthy of reproducing settler colonialism.[33] *The Fog* doesn't directly refer to Indigenous dispossession, but it is about a group of people with leprosy who are tricked into crashing their ship, which contains gold, and which in turn fuels the prosperity of a town in California. The metaphor is clear as the tricked outliers lose their wealth for the sake of white settler prosperity.

Foucault's work speaks to the interconnections of sickness, disease, and notions of madness and sanity, as "at the end of the Middle Ages, leprosy disappeared from the Western world. In the margins of the community, at the gates of cities, there stretched wastelands which sickness had ceased to haunt but had left sterile and long uninhabitable."[34] The fear of wasteland at the gates of cities influenced the European imagination immensely as they built palisades to fight off perceived threats.

Further, the association of leprosy with Indigenous people in Hawaii, Adria Imada reminds us, was linked by settlers to the idea that Indigenous people were "unchaste, unvirtuous, and

---

32 Hall, "Horrible Heroes."

33 Bodies deemed worthy of continuing that genocidal project are also required to do so, and the monstrosity of limitations on reproductive justice in the context of settler colonialism is worth more exploration in the horror film.

34 Foucault, *Madness & Civilization*, 317.

uncivilized... culpable for spreading the microbe."[35] The small town in *The Fog* is celebrating its anniversary during the timeline of this movie, and the ghostly victims return to enact revenge. *The Fog* is an indictment on the systemic wealth of settler society, derived from oppression and genocide. Stolen gold refers more directly to that which was taken (is taken) from Indigenous Peoples and lands.

The Fog begins with a story; the lore of Antonio Bay and the crashed ship are told around a campfire by a town elder. Antonio Bay's priest, Father Malone, finds his grandfather's diary in the next scene, and reads about the founders of the town and how they refused to allow a leper colony to take root. Instead, the town's founders tricked a ship (the *Elizabeth Dane*) carrying the group afflicted with leprosy, into crashing against the rocks. The town founders then stole the gold that was on board. So, on the anniversary of the town's founding, revenge is taken.

A fog rolls in, and the ghosts of the murdered crew and captain of the *Elizabeth Dane* come with it. Some members of the town die after the fog and crew overtake them. A radio DJ, Stevie Wayne, realizes the threat and puts out a warning on her broadcast. The fog comes for her, but Father Malone gives the ghosts back their gold and they back off. At first. After the rest of the town's residents escape, the ghosts return for Father Malone. The death of Father Malone as well as five other town residents makes this a tale of revenge and invasion—as though the colonized might lurk as ghosts and diseased demons, waiting for their chance to avenge their own deaths. It is also insinuated that the *Elizabeth Dane* lepers are pirate-like. Where did they get their own wealth?

Sanism, madness, and settler colonialism are topics worthy of far more study in the context of horror and beyond. Burch writes

35 Imada, "Family History as Disability History."

about the sterilization and incarceration of Indigenous people as reinforcing the reproduction of white settler families.[36] The imaginary of the white settler family has to be upheld through ableism, classism, and heteropatriarchy, rooted in systemic racism and settler colonialism. Horror might unsettle these layers at times, but it is both the invisibility and deliberateness of systemic settler colonialism that upholds it in this genre. The mad are positioned as outlier and therefore are an exception. The violence of white settler families or young men or a mad genius (chef) is outrageous and containable.

FEAR STREET, 1994, 1978, 1666 *(2021)*

Netflix's 2021 Fear Street trilogy is about a community, Shadyside, which seems to be cursed with outbreaks of mass murders every few years. The Shadyside curse, though repetitive, is made to seem exceptional by the town and by the town's rivals, Sunnyvale. As it turns out, Shadyside has been cursed because, in the 1600s, a settler who could not make his crops grow wanted prosperity and turned to the Devil for it. His descendants each sacrifice people in Shadyside so that they and other Sunnyvale citizens can remain wealthy.

The killers in Shadyside are sacrificing youth there so that Sunnyvale can prosper. That mad (and satanic) outlier idea undoes the potential to see the Shadyside killers as indicative of a deeper problem of white settler heteropatriarchy. The magic that Shadyside is up against is sourced also (vaguely) in Indigenous cosmologies, it seems. In the 1600s, a character named only the Widow (she is a white woman whose dead husband appears to

36 Stote, *An Act of Genocide*.

have been Indigenous) protects the book of bad, satanic magic that ultimately falls into the hands of the wrong white dude. She remains living at the edge of the village, in a structure flanked by animal skins and furs, aware of what is happening but helpless (as the faux Indian is) to stop it.

The mad outlier might be killed or they might retreat into the sunset. They might return like Michael Myers does, to drag the civilized down into their caves and other savage spaces. The mad are defeated (often when they pledge allegiance to dark forces) or they live with their darkness in seclusion. Life in the frontier town goes on.

FOUR

COWBOYS IN THE ANTARCTIC

SETTLER COLONIALISM AND NATURE IN HORROR

"There's a storm hitting us in about six hours. We're going to find out who's who."

—MACREADY, *THE THING* (1982)

IN *THE THING*, IT IS THE COLD AND ICE THAT HIDE AN invasive, shapeshifting entity. The land has to be conquered and invaded to tame and subdue it. On mythically empty lands, the settler family and their community battle for survival. The land is terrifying in horror, and environmental elements are scattered throughout these films. Even the concept of eco-horror needs to be revised to include an analysis that sees decolonial understandings of land fitted into a framework of analysis. Ecological themes in horror must be contextualized by settler colonialism, as J.M. Bacon adds, "because settler colonialism's fundamental goal is the ongoing appropriation of Indigenous land and resources by and for the benefit of settlers it is an especially important lens for thinking about eco-social relations."[1] The woods, the snow, caves, bodies of water, even misty fog, all threaten the white settler and make their decision to "go savage" inevitable.

The coded savagery and dark-heartedness of corn fields deserve special mention in a chapter such as this. Corn fields hold a special place in American horror. Christine DeLucia argues that corn symbolizes for settlers "the terrifying savagery of Indigenous opponents, as well as their eventual resounding defeat, opening the way for unfettered colonial growth across land and water."[2] The mythology of settler colonialism, that Indigenous people were savage, terrifying, and defeated/disappeared, is central to settler relationships with land and with a shaky and still fearful sense of selfhood. Characters like Marie and Alex in *High Tension*'s homage to American horror, find themselves in corn fields when they are lost, threatened, and about to be hunted by some violent entity.[3]

The emptiness of dark and rainy forests, abandoned corn fields, and whistling wind-swept landscapes are the calm before the storm at the beginning of the horror film. The quiet is disrupted

1 Bacon, "Settler Colonialism as Eco-social Structure," 1.

2 DeLucia, "Corn and Colonization."

3 To name the more obvious example of this story, *Children of the Corn* (1984) follows a cult of children who sacrifice adults to a demon entity. Though the film is certainly a terrifying commentary on Christian fundamentalism, the ways that savagery and demonic imagery show up are as much about the disappeared mythological Indians of the area as they are about the terrifying white settlers. Kiersch, dir., *Children of the Corn*.

by some looming figure stomping or rushing through to disrupt the insecure settler family or community. The natural world is obviously all around us, and suburban horror features important markers of terra nullius—empty or unannexed land—and the disappeared Indian. There is a sense that the colonial homestead is precarious amidst an otherwise abandoned and haunted wilderness in suburban horror. And the physical wilderness is not only simultaneously empty and haunted by ghostly, demonic, witchy, or devilish mythical Indians—there is also the wilderness of technology to worry about.

Notions of terra nullius are among those ideas that persist in new forms, according to Yann Allard-Tremblay and Elaine Coburn, across academia and in broader publics, denying "politically meaningful Indigenous presence on lands claimed by the colonizers, and the myth of the 'Vanishing Race,' which acknowledges Indigenous presence but only as ontologically or culturally doomed."[4] Evelyn Nakano Glenn adds that

> land occupied or used seasonally by *indigenes* was conceived of as *terra nullius* (empty land or land belonging to no one) and therefore available for taking by white settlers. Simultaneously, settlers conceived of themselves as more advanced and evolved, bringers of progress and enlightenment to the wilderness.[5]

The land is monstrous in horror. Conquest requires repetition, working through white settler fears of place and subsequent taming. In addition, new cosmologies are then imposed on the land, attempting to replace Indigenous Creation stories. In horror, the

4 Allard-Tremblay and Coburn, "The Flying Heads of Settler Colonialism," 3.
5 Glenn, "Settler Colonialism as Structure," 60.

land is savage and the elements are at times impossible to survive; but the natural world or spirits of place can be a more expansive category than just involving "Gaia's revenge"[6] (films, for example, where animals and elements take actual targeted revenge against random white people who litter or behave terribly in some way). Horror can reveal myriad ways that human-land ontologies unfold in settler colonial contexts.

The winter is a particular challenge for white settler storying. Maze-like and cyclical entrapment shows up in films like *The Thing* (1982), *The Shining* (1980), and *Krampus* (2015). The presence of snow and icy winter add to this entrapped feeling. While the white settler family may be doomed in these films, their innocence and centrality on colonized land is unchallenged, and knowledge of the realities of (Indigenous) worlds beyond theirs is foreclosed.

THE SHINING *(1980)*

Stanley Kubrick's *The Shining* connects family violence with the violence of colonization, albeit as a historic project. The threats of long-dead Indians become transferred to fears of ghosts in a haunted hotel and terrible wintery storms from which the family might never escape. The film follows Jack Torrance and his wife, Wendy, and their son, Danny, as Jack—a failing writer with a drinking problem—takes on a caretaker job for a massive hotel. The Overlook Hotel in the mountains of Colorado is left abandoned all winter, and this small family is tasked with keeping it in one piece while they also try to deal with isolation and a snowy, foreboding place. Delia Malia Konzett points out that analyses of

6 Simpson, "Australian Eco-Horror and Gaia's Revenge: Animals, Eco-Nationalism and the 'New Nature,'" 1.

The Shining tend not to explain the roots of settler colonialism as a central element of the film's narrative. In a scene in which an English butler who had slaughtered his entire family previously (and now exists as a ghost in the hotel) explains to Jack that Jack must now also kill his family, we are certainly made aware as viewers that this murderous ghost is a racist and misogynist. However, the role that this English colonial ghost has in ensuring that the white settler patriarch does what he must to inherit his empire is not widely discussed. As Konzett explains,

> whiteness and masculinity in the film are therefore placed under duress and struggle to assert their traditional authority. Many of these aspects have been noted duly by critics in the film's long history of reception. However, the themes of genocide, misogyny, and racism are generally discussed separately and not as interrelated or intersectional building blocks of US nationalism.[7]

The film roots patriarchal violence in racism and colonialism through a temporal trick of including both references to past genocide and ongoing Indigenous presence through (living) Indigenous art scattered throughout the hotel.

There is a chance, it seems, that death itself and the ghostly Indian seeking revenge, might work together to destroy the white settler homesteaders in a new take on that pattern. The past is certainly at play, and the idea that the family was doomed all along is hinted at. As Konzett also points out,

> the film appropriately ends with a still shot of a photo taken on the US holiday 4 July 1921, suggesting a national legacy

7 Konzett, "Kubrick's Red Room," 153.

> oblivious to its violent and bloody origins of nation building. The excessive image of the elevator, with its Native American design, spilling over with copious amounts [of] blood, intuited in Danny's [Danny Lloyd] first shining episode before he visits the hotel, hints at a return of this repressed history.[8]

The film's horrors are partially rooted in the ongoing system of settler colonialism from which the colonizing family cannot escape.

At the same time, the disappearance of any actual Indigenous presence freezes colonization in the past, normalizing that temporal construct for the audience. In order to escape the monster, mother and son must naturalize—one with magical or spiritual abilities, the other as a capable traveller in a (savage) snowy landscape. Wendy transforms from a dazed red-white-and-blue housewife to a knife-wielding protector, willing to kill her violent husband; and in the middle of this transformation, she's shown wearing images of tipis on her clothing. Her son also takes on the magical spiritual powers of the Indigenized settler. They both escape in a storm we're told is impossible to ride through. The warnings of eco-horror are clear in a context within which viewers find themselves terrified that they might not be able to escape the landscape itself. Indigenous Peoples are both ghostly and also largely disappeared in *The Shining*, but if they are hinted at (through art, through the story of the burial ground), then they are still present. In the maze that Jack never escapes, the ghostly Indian finds vengeance as the new symbolic Indians (Wendy and her son) flee.

The land is fearful in *The Shining*, and the winter season defeats the settler community in its attempts to naturalize. Instead,

---

8 Konzett, "Kubrick's Red Room," 154.

generations of the Overlook Hotel's patriarchs destroy their own families. The film's opening shots are of murky cold lakes, treacherously stormy mountains, and a maze of greenery. In the iconic aerial opening shot, ominous music plays over sweeping images of land and water and mountain. The terror of *The Shining* is as much about the wintery landscape as it is about Jack's twisted misogyny and racism. The settler family is never quite at home on stolen land. Additionally, the howling winter landscape serves to really land this point.

The Shining concerns itself with haunting, with the spectral savage, and with the fears of cold, howling winter, that permeate white settler storytelling. The land is cyclical and timeless like the maze at the centre of the film. Jack himself exists simultaneously in the past, present, and future of the Overlook Hotel, trapped in his own violent, heteropatriarchal white settler patterns in relationship with other colonizers—the English caretaker with his overt racism and misogyny, for example. In *The Shining*, the ghosts aren't Indigenous people who died and ended up in the Indian Burial Ground under the Overlook; they are white settler ghosts trapped in their own mirrors. Still, the hauntings of the Indian Burial Ground and warriors who died protecting the land form the backdrop to the family's terrifying journey. The film includes a lengthy dialogue between father and son about the Donner Party, eating each other up when they became snowed in on their way to California.

An innocent and magical little kid, Danny talks to Tony, his invisible friend, who shares real information and warnings about the hotel and on Danny's father's job. In turn, Danny is perceived as having mental health struggles by "professionals" for whom Tony is *obviously* just imaginary. Mental health is raised again by Jack Torrance's boss, who warns that a previous caretaker got "cabin fever" and killed his entire family. The isolation that the Torrances sign up for is not only a characteristic of the hotel but of the heteropatriarchal settler colonial family. Family violence arises in the film's narrative as Shelley Duvall's character, Wendy Torrance, rationalizes Jack's physical abuse of their son to a therapist who sits in silence after she tells the story of her husband breaking Danny's arm. In all instances, the violence that white settlers enacted against Indigenous people during the building of the hotel is framed as a long-ago historical event, but the film insinuates that that violence is ongoing, embodied by generations of hotel guests who show up as ghosts and bloodied, rotting corpses.

The actual ghosts of *The Shining* (1980) are wealthy white settlers who can't leave the hotel where they died or were murdered. Still, the "long ago" sins of colonization haunt the film and create the bad loop in which these ghosts are stuck. The colonization of what is now known as Colorado is more than just the undersoil of the hotel's grounds. It built the Gold Room and the wealth and opulence of the hotel's very structure as well as its patrons.

In 1864, the Colorado cavalry murdered hundreds of Cheyenne and Arapaho villagers in the Sand Creek area:

> When hundreds of blue-clad cavalrymen suddenly appeared at dawn on November 29, a Cheyenne chief raised the Stars and Stripes above his lodge. Others in the village waved white flags. The troops replied by opening fire with carbines and cannon, killing at least 150 Indians, most of them women, children and the elderly. Before departing, the troops burned the village and mutilated the dead, carrying off body parts as trophies.[9]

---

9 Horwitz, "The Horrific Sand Creek Massacre."

The horror movies that feature white settlers collecting bones and skin and body parts and portray those people as macabre and outside of the norms of civilized and sane, should be revisited with an understanding of the kinds of violence enacted by the "civilized" and "sane."

As a film, *The Shining* challenges the viewer to dare freeze colonization in the past. The wealthy elite whose role in the Overlook Hotel is to party, to die in some strange way, and then to be forever frozen as ghostly are cursed by the past but also have no present or future. The past is not only the past and it is not the only source of injustice, the film suggests; it lives on in the labyrinths of the hotel's hallways and grounds and in the circular life-death journeys of its ghosts. Kameron McBride argues of *The Shining* that its director, Kubrick,

> uses ghosts and the motif of being trapped in a maze in order to critique how contemporary America was built and how individuals choose to interpret this history. The Overlook Hotel is constructed as a haunted environment where characters must choose to interpret or repress America's own bloody past, a choice that ultimately decides their own fate. The resort hotel buries its bloody history within itself to the point where it cannot be contained and leaks from the walls themselves.[10]

Cowboy Jack (comparable to the English colonizer, Grady, whose murdered twins haunt Jack's son, Danny), the film's villain (though perhaps the hotel is also a real villain), is an insufferable jerk right from the start. Jack complains about his wife to a ghost bartender (Grady himself), going off about the "White Man's

10 McBride, "Dealing with Our Bloody Past," 30.

Burden."[11] He and Grady engage in some mutual racism aimed at Dick Hallorann, showing that they're the whole package of white settler masculinity—racist, misogynist, haters of children (whom they either murder or try to murder). Yes, Jack's haunted by the hotel's ghosts and its history, but he's fairly open to being manipulated into axing his family, it seems; and he can't blame the ghosts for his misogyny. Instead, misogyny and violence are rooted in the whole trajectory of American life.

There is no future for the white settler family or community in this film, which is what makes it so magical. Jack doesn't have to go to the Overlook to be violent because the land beyond the Overlook's borders is just as violated and soaked in violence. He smirks his way through the beginning of the film and quickly turns into a homicidal maniac, his past as an alcoholic abuser creating enough fodder for the hotel to do its magic on him. The magic, of course, is the violent underlay of the hotel's own history. Atop an Indian Burial Ground, atop a battleground where Indigenous people died, the Overlook is drenched in blood (literally) and haunted by white settlers, it seems, as they stay behind to party in a time loop forever. The film is far more satisfying than the book because there is no letting Jack off the hook. He's not a victim of the hotel, he's a product of the very colonial system that created the hotel. He and the hotel are one and the same. Even as Wendy and her son escape Jack, they do not indigenize to the land, they roll into the winter storm like the families they discussed earlier in the film, the doomed Donner Party.

---

11 Rudyard Kipling, "The White Man's Burden," stanza 3 includes the lines, "Take up the White Man's burden / The savage wars of peace," implying the necessity of the kinds of violence that Jack must now enact in order to maintain the norms of the hotel.

KRAMPUS (2015)

Krampus opens with a scene of carnage and mayhem, as Black Friday shoppers absolutely beat each other up, ram each other to the ground, and fight to the last breath to purchase pre-Christmas sale items. The film centres on two families who come together to celebrate the holiday while making each other's lives fairly terrible. The children bully each other, an aunt complains loudly about everything from the food to the décor, one of the fathers won't stop working while the other reveals himself to be some version of a hyper-masculine all-American grotesque. He even carries guns in his car (that ultimately the entire family use). In the midst of it all is a German grandmother who knows that if the family doesn't get themselves together, something terrible will arrive. And it does! In the form of not only Krampus, but Perchta, satanic looking goat creatures, demonic elves, and other monsters. The family's fate is written in the snow, as they are picked off one by one.

The ultimate Christmas horror story is the being who visits to punish children with a whip, throwing them into sacks to torture them. He is folklore's pagan devil, whatever his actual origins might be; he is the dark side of the holiday. This notion that there should be a demonic entity haunting good families at this time signals fears of paganism (much as Michael Myers's monstrosity does, associated as he is with Samhain, or the harvest) and fears of the land of the settler colonized "new world." Christmas, Al Ridenour writes, "requires the darkness... Not by chance, it aligns with the long, black night of the solstice and Nature's last breath."[12] In *Krampus* (2015), the title character's punishment is aimed at a family immersed in capitalism, in Black Friday consumerism,

12 Ridenour, *The Krampus*, 1.

in bickering and ingratitude for the enormity of their privilege, and in the typical rifts that the white settler family experiences in horror. There is no happy ending possible for this family. The extended family is taken one by one, by monstrous elves, horrifying toys with creatures in them, and Perchta, a former pagan goddess turned horrifying demon. Each family member faces Krampus and is basically tossed into hell, where they have to exist encased in a glass ball, celebrating Christmas properly and quietly, perhaps forever.

The winter, the snow, the howling cold (so cold frostbite and hypothermia beckon) are central to the horror of this film. Christmas is awful, Krampus is awful, capitalism drains all of any possible original meaning, and all is lost. That fear of total colonization and total destruction haunts the family. The film is described by Alissa Burger and Jenny Collins as "one suburban family's fight for survival against the titular monster and his helpers...exploring the conflicts and anxieties that typify the 21st-century holiday season and the average modern family." The idea that the family is innocent, protecting something worth protecting, is never really established. We aren't made to like anybody in the movie, really, except for Max, whose impulsively angry act of tearing up his letter to Santa brings Krampus to his family. Interestingly, while Burger and Collins argue that twenty-first-century fears are not the same as seventeenth-century German fears, they then evoke a central image of the settler colonial imagination, the "dark forest regions where Krampus has its origins."[13] Krampus is the pagan, the darkness, the Devil that threatens the frontier. The frontier town, in this case, is settler colonial suburbia. In *Krampus*, the importance of Christmas,

13 Burger and Collins, "'The Shadow of Saint Nicholas,'" 139 and 141.

so slippery to define, is tied up with heteropatriarchy and gun-toting, frontier-loving Americans who remain convinced until the bitter end that their weapons, their vehicles, their giant suburban homes, and their civilization will endure.

The development of Christmas into the capitalist Christian holiday it is today is very recent in North America, and the Christmas horror film underlines that fact. The mayhem of Christmas horror films disrupts what Penne Restad calls an already-ambiguous celebration rooted in early attempts to stop Christians from following pagan traditions. The holiday (somewhat) quickly gave way to excess, and it eventually "fell to Puritan reformers to put a stop to the unholy merriment and to bend arguments over the proper keeping of Christmas into an older and more basic one—whether there should even be an observance of the day."[14] Settling upon the meaning of Christmas, no small feat, is a necessity for a society imbued with economic, political, and cultural confusion. Trying to naturalize to the land, they make up new myths, even when those myths see them doomed by a wintery, Arctic-like world.

THE THING *(1982)*

The Thing is about alien invasion and reverse-colonization, and it is also about the threat of foreign climate and foreign land. In this film, a group of explorer-researchers in Antarctica stumble on a burnt-out Norwegian research base, where the Thing, an alien entity that possesses people and animals and alters them, hides in a corpse. They bring the corpse back, of course, to their own labs, where it infects the group and kills off all but two—R.J. MacReady and Childs.

14 Restad, *Christmas in America*, 4 and 7.

If there is a film that truly signals horror's roots in the Western, it might be this one.[15] Kurt Russell (wearing a cowboy hat in absurdly cold temperatures and carrying an old-school rifle) leads a cast of all-male actors who occupy a remote camp in Antarctica. They grow increasingly paranoid as the Thing first mimics and then deforms their bodies. The Thing hides in its host until the moment that it emerges, born from their bodies in what is at once panic about sexuality, the body, and masculinity, as well as fear of the savage Other out on the terrain. The final two male survivors—Russell as MacReady, and Childs, played by Keith David—contemplate the possibility that the Thing has colonized one or both of them. Historical and ongoing anti-Black racism contextualizes the ending as well, as the white cowboy and supposed hero of the film has potentially gone "savage" and been taken over by the Thing. The Other in this film is alien, which speaks more to the fear that the colonizers would themselves be colonized than it does of an Indigenous-Other, but in a sense the film still acts as a reverse-colonization story.

In the end, the landscape and unforgiving cold are what kill anyone the Thing itself hasn't already altered. The characters succumb to the inhospitable climate; even if neither R.J. nor Childs really is the Thing itself, both are doomed. The Other is many things in horror. Monster, saviour, something in between. The land is also Other. The shapeshifting anxieties in *The Thing* include anxiety about gender and belonging in an all-male settlement, with the creature allowing real men to melt into some gooey version of themselves.

15 I'm probably overstating, but my point is that John Carpenter's films are self-reflexive about the link between horror and the Western. Carpenter's *Vampires* (1998) is probably an even more effective example of this connection. *Vampires* is the quintessential Western, with an awful sort of cowboy guy who beheads vampires. He is the Good Guy because the Pope hired him.

These men are undermined in their masculine cause to conquer, to control. The land defeats them. There isn't hope, at the end of *The Thing*, since the creature is likely to be unearthed by the next silly group of researchers who will *also* spend their time studying it, ignoring their instincts, only to be defeated. We're left knowing that the Thing will spread. It is a reverse-colonization fantasy but a strangely cathartic one. The scientists, the colonizers, cannot win, not with their facilities and instruments, and not even with their guns. They are wonderfully vulnerable. It is not all of humanity who are made vulnerable in this film, it is a particular culture, a time period. Heather Addison writes that the film "exposes the fragility of our bodies, our identities, our relationships, and our system(s) of meaning."[16] Body, identity, relationality, meaning—all are threatened by the land because settler colonialism necessitates unsettled feelings in order to inspire its reproductions. In *The Thing* the fantasy of reverse-colonization is completed. The cowboy loses. MacReady's eyes flash in the end scenes, taken over by a dream of beings from another world. Much more should probably be written by decolonial scholars about this film, opening as it does larger conversations about spiritual realities in Indigenous lands and cosmologies and death and its meanings.[17]

Apocalyptic winter brings with it the reveal that the colonial project and the attempt to make these places their home is doomed. Imagining the demise of a society makes that society a victim of some external force and justifies the original and ongoing invasion; climate change has likewise added new elements to this imagined victimhood. "While aggressiveness and disavowal should be considered as closely related manifestations emanating

---

16 Addison, "Cinema's Darkest Vision," 157.

17 Whyte, "Indigenous Science (Fiction) for the Anthropocene."

from a fixation with the fantasy of an *exclusive* relationship with the (mother)land," Veracini writes, "the sustained resilience of *terra nullius* in the face of manifest indigenous attachment to land should thus be associated with a number of repressive impulses (as well as with a self-serving settler inclination to dismiss alternative claims to land)."[18]

(REPLACING) INDIGENOUS CREATION STORIES

Conquering the frightening landscape requires a narrative that works to replace Indigenous stories of place. Indigenous Creation stories are ceremonial and lyrical envisionings, retellings of a nation's relationship to their original land. I am not capturing the depth of this profound concept well enough, but Indigenous scholars like Deb McGregor do so much better.[19] North American horror films often attempt to replace these stories with white-settler-invented cosmologies and in a sense new creation stories and new stories of place and temporal belonging. The role of horror as a genre concerned with cosmology in place is raised by Hautsch in relation to the television show *Buffy the Vampire Slayer*. A character tells the vampire slayers that vampires and demons are the real original beings of earth, in a creation mythology, which Hautsch critically analyzes at length, writing that "the Buffyverse's entire creation mythology is based on colonization."[20]

Indigenous Peoples' Creation stories are subsumed in order to be replaced, and their cosmologies become disturbing fodder for appropriated elements of new cosmologies.

---

18 Veracini, *Settler Colonialism: A Theoretical Overview*, 88.

19 See, for example, McGregor, "Coming Full Circle."

20 Hautsch, "Staking Her Colonial Claim," 3; Whedon, Espenson, and Petrie, writers, "Pangs," directed by Michael Lange.

THE CABIN IN THE WOODS *(2012)*

The Cabin in the Woods is about five friends who leave college to sleep in a dirty, super run-down cabin. The cabin is similar to other backwoods horror locations, except that it is actually a technological wonder, run by an underground facility that sets up kills in the cabin to appease gods. The cabin is also a signifier of the horrors of the land, of the woods, the earth and weather systems, and the discomfort with which white settler youth embark on the "adventure" of invasion. The youth in this film consist of various stereotypes (the athlete, the bookworm, the blonde who happens to be a bookworm herself, the stoner) who are supposed to die in a particular order to appease gods who live underground. The blonde has to be drugged by a substance sent into the cabin in order to behave in ways that might be construed as sexually promiscuous so that she can be the first sacrifice, while the "virgin" is meant to either survive or die last. It's a humorous take on the slasher formula, but also a way of storying that formula as a kind of mythology.

The movie opens with a group of university students preparing for a trip. On their way in an old RV, they meet up with a tobacco-chewing, Old Testament–loving older gentleman who tells them that they're basically going to die. They ignore him and continue on their way. When they get to their creepy cabin, they take a swim, drink, and look around. Most importantly, they explore the basement. In the basement are an assortment of dolls and rusty bladed objects and music boxes and a book by a family named the Buckners, who were obsessed with torturing each other to death. The diary of the pain-worshipping Buckner family is read aloud, including the Latin sections, and the Buckners rise from their burial places in the dirt of the forest floor and start killing off the youth. The plot twist is that the Buckners were sent by a facility built underground, who sacrifice youth in order to appease gods who are even deeper underground. Two youth survive, a young man so stoned that the house's various systems (set up by the facility) did not work on him and the intended Final Girl. They enter the facility and are shot at. In order to save themselves, they unleash every monster in the facility. Sigourney Weaver arrives, warning them that the weed smoker needs to die so that the gods are appeased and all of humanity not wiped out. Selfishly, he demands that his friend (and presumably his family and friends back home) die so he can live two and a half minutes longer. The world then ends as the gods smash through the earth.

The deaths are set up by the youth themselves, when they wander into the basement of horrors. Depending on which item they play with, a creature will emerge in relation to that item. The youth selecting the Buckner diary is what brings the backwoods horror family upon them. The Buckners have been nicknamed by the facility as the "zombie redneck torture family." The Buckners are only one family of monsters who might target victims of the cabin in the woods. There are monsters from European and North American folklore, some new, some old—including scarecrows, vampires, doll-mask-wearing serial killers, clowns, a merman, even a murderous unicorn. Throughout the film, there is also an attempt at making white settler locals into mythical beings. The creepy man at the gas station who warns the young people that they are going to die becomes a harbinger of death. The idea of replacing Indigenous cosmologies on Indigenous land with gods, some supernatural explanation for the Final Girl's existence, and an ending that decides to sacrifice all of humanity to let the gods live again, is an example of creation-myth-making.

On one level, the film asks why the same patterns unfold in each slasher film, with particular kinds of teens killed in particular ways, the Final Girl as virginal, and so on. The answer—to appease the gods—might be a metaphor for some swipe at the executives or fans who demand blood sacrifice. Fashioning these ideas into a kind of mythos of a colonizer society that demands blood, hearkens back to a universalizing idea that *all* human societies demand blood. James (Sákéj) Youngblood Henderson's critique of the basis of Western legal orders in Hobbesian notions of Indigenous life as nasty, brutish and short, is useful here.[21]

On another level, the movie replaces Indigenous cosmologies of place with the devilish woods and gods who torment and destroy human beings. Placelessness, Katherine Wagner argues, is key to the *Cabin in the Woods* tale. In Wagner's words, "placelessness is more transparent in *The Cabin in the Woods* because the film openly examines the constructed nature of places within American horror." Further, the film explores "the continued fears expressed about the lack of an American cultural sense of place."[22] Among these moments of open examination include the discovery, by each of the youth, of a hidden one-way window in one room, that looming trap door and hidden torture chamber, and the passageway and elevator connecting the underground facility where the monsters are held in glass cages, with the cabin itself and the landscape around the cabin. It remains vital for a colonizer culture to "connect" to place through myth, and the film soothes that urge despite (or because of) the nihilistic ending.

21 Henderson, "The Context of the State of Nature," 11.

22 Wagner, "Haven't We Been Here Before?," 5.

THE AMITYVILLE HORROR *(1979)*

Different iterations of the Indian Burial Ground trope impose mythologies on lands where white settler violence has left its mark. Blame can then be shifted away from white settlers (fictional or otherwise) who perpetuate violence and onto the mythological Indian (the savage within, the savage outside). The roots of misogyny and patriarchy are in the system of settler colonialism, not contextualized by mythological notions of civilization and savagery. I would argue that the film iteration of *The Shining* for example, somewhat gets that point. Stuart Rosenberg's *The Amityville Horror* (1979) contains stories of white settler mythmaking in a way that both tricks the viewer into thinking that the hauntings there might be real and that said hauntings were to be blamed on the bad spirits of Indigenous people who lived in the area.

The Amityville Horror is a meandering film based on a book, about the Lutz family who move into a house in Amityville, New York, where a young man had previously murdered his entire family. Members of the family start to experience odd things, like excessive flies indoors and violent illness. George, the family patriarch, becomes fixated on warming the house with woodfire; his eyes turn red, he dresses badly, he becomes emotionally abusive, and he stops showing up to work. Psychics come to the house and feel awful about being there. The family hammers through a brick wall, revealing a red-walled room where apparently satanic rituals were held. George tries to kill his family with an axe, the walls bleed, and instead of thinking that perhaps George might not be the best dude to take off with, Mom and kiddos rush away with him in the family car in the middle of a rainstorm.

The house, we are told, sits on top of a Shinnecock burial ground, in addition to having once been the home of a satanist.

The trope provides fodder for a story of white settler victimhood and possession of land—including the water and nearby woods, which the family "own." The fictional hauntings serve multiple purposes: the white settler family is shown to be invaded by satanic and mythological Indians, those made-up hauntings provide fodder for white settler identity formation and ownership of land (however doomed), the killer who actually did shoot his family is given some "reason" for it all (at least in the minds of casual viewers), and finally the "nice" family is excused as they run off and leave their mortgage behind.

The terror of the wilderness is all tied up in Burial Ground stories. Darryl Caterine writes of the trope, that danger and madness

> loom over locales where the Indian dead are buried or Native American ceremonies once took place... the legend of the accursed Indian homeland has returned in recent decades as a stock-in-trade paranormal theme and enjoys a popularity it has not had since Puritan days.[23]

Like in *The Shining* there is this consistent and constant haunting, a "reincarnation of evil," that is the fault of the poisoned land.[24] Settler colonial society is haunted by its own creations, as it is by the "motif of fading, spectral Indians."[25] In *Amityville Horror* the ghostly Indians are also mad, trapped and tortured by their own people in a story that is both offensive and absurd.

The Indian Burial Ground in this film is really a buried ancient Indian sanitarium. The idea then becomes blurred and fuzzy—that

---

23 Caterine, "Heirs through Fear," 37–38.
24 Mackenthun, "Haunted Real Estate," 93.
25 Cameron, "Indigenous Spectrality," 385.

Indigenous people could do awful things to their own,[26] leading to curses and so on, and excusing genocide and settler colonialism since this silly story can be made up to "prove" that Indigenous people are/were terrible anyway. The land can thus be remade if the curse can be overcome! In the 2005 *Amityville* remake, George Lutz sees ghostly Native men with piercings similar to those of a participant in a Sundance ceremony. Native ghosts in the 2005 film lurch about on the ground, screaming and such.

Familiar themes of civilization and savagery explain the connection. Flies show up in abundance; the flies that show up in *Amityville* announce Beelzebub's (Satan's) encroachment in the supposedly civilized home. The family of *Amityville* are blended. The children "belong" to another man, not to George, the family patriarch. It is implied that there is some friction in the coming together of the family. What might pass as normal growing pains, as people getting to know each other try to live together, becomes so much more. The violence of the white settler patriarchy becomes the fault of Native people, thus cleaning the bloodied hands of white settler men who do horrifying things to their families.[27]

POLTERGEIST *(1982)* AND POLTERGEIST II *(1986)*

The unsettling and then resettling of the innocent white settler family is perhaps no more evident than in Tobe Hooper's *Poltergeist*.

26 Clearly all human societies can make mistakes or behave terribly, but the specific and overblown notion that Indigenous Peoples were savage and horribly violent prior to European colonization is a strategic lie.

27 What I mean to say is that the actual mass murderer who seems to have killed his family prior to the events of *The Amityville Horror* and the fictional version of George Lutz, himself, each had to be "explained" somehow in ways that distract from the violence of settler colonialism.

The 1982 film is about a white settler (possibly Republican) family that moves into a house in a planned community that is declared not to be on Indian Burial Ground. The Freelings have three children, including a little girl named Carol Anne who announces the arrival of ghosts through a television set. The ghosts do nifty things like possess a tree, which tries to eat the Freeling son, Robbie. Carol Anne is pulled into a portal, and the family has to call in a parapsychologist. The Freeling house becomes some sort of portal for ghosts because it is on a burial ground, after all (oops!). Mr. Freeling finds out that the development of the suburb involved clearing the headstones but not the graves that are now beneath the houses where he and his neighbours have enacted "white flight" to the suburbs.

The threat facing the Freeling family in the *Poltergeist* films is caused by white settler spirits and, we find out in the sequel, the "madness" of a religious cult. The ghosts are attracted to Carol Anne's life force and try to get at the family through her in both films. Mrs. Freeling has to rebirth Carol Anne essentially, by holding onto a rope, going into the portal, and emerging with her daughter all covered in goop. The scene becomes a kind of new creation story, bringing with it the legitimacy of the white settler family in their new home. However, they aren't quite settled yet. The ritual of white settler colonialism does not work, and the ghosts return. The Freelings try to leave, but a ghostly entity attacks in the form of a clown and a swimming pool full of skeletons. The family does finally leave, finds a hotel, and removes the TV set, returning to a quaint, romantic time before the evils of television and destructive ghosts invaded.

Both films emphasize the innocence and "normalcy" of the Freeling family. In the first film, we see Mr. Freeling's football pals as they fight to maintain control over their television set against the will of the neighbour's remote control. The men get into a battle with their remotes, clicking each other's televisions from their doorways (because remotes could sync with other people's TVs like that way back then), underlining the tensions ready to erupt in white settler suburbia. It's a long scene that has nothing to do with ghosts but is supposed to charm the audience into thinking oh, what a lovely, normal dude. Does he later, in *Poltergeist II* (1986), become possessed and sexually assault his wife? Sure, yes, but it's not his fault. A gory entity on the ceiling also sexually assaults a female family member, furthering the point that sexual violence is the fault of the savage-Other and not the nice, happy hetero family patriarchy.

Despite saving her daughter from an alternate dimension, the power of birth and any sort of romantic notion of Mrs. Freeling's power in her family more generally are undermined in the sequel. She is sexually assaulted by her husband after he drinks to excess and swallows a Mezcal worm in his tequila. The worm, both savage and queer, infiltrates his body; it is possessed by the creepy guy who ran the cult whose burial ground is beneath the Freelings' home. The tensions that the family experiences are related to their need to settle properly in place. Among those tensions: the family pet dies, leaving Carol Anne to mourn and try to understand death; Star Wars sheets have to stay cleaned and pressed for children's beds; Mr. Freeling reads *Reagan: The Man, the President*; he and his wife smoke pot and sleep on an ugly brass bed. We're supposed to identify with this family. *Poltergeist* gives us a long, rambling take on the innocence of families who move where they move, through no fault of their own, and don't deserve to have their furniture thrown about as a result. White settler ghosts are the worst part of the whole situation, and they constitute in fact a new cosmology of ghostliness, loss, guilt, and then victory—over the forces of death, over the inability to become "native to place." The innocence of the white settler family is really about establishing that right to occupy, to create a new cosmology of *place*, and to maintain those places. The family is possibly Republican (Reagan being a notoriously homophobic president during the AIDS crisis) and definitely heteropatriarchal. The landscape—crashing thunder, ominous sky, killer trees, pool collapsing, and corpses emerging from the earth—rises to threaten their settlement, their entitlement to place. When the ghosts of *Poltergeist* are defeated, the family moves on to settle somewhere else, on some other land, with the help, no less, of a Native American medicine man.

In *Poltergeist II: The Other Side* (1986), Muscogee actor Will Sampson plays a medicine man named Taylor, who is called in to save the Freelings after they flee from their ghostly home to live with Mrs. Freeling's mother. The Freelings' haunted house turns out (after archaeologists dig beneath it in the opening of the film) to have covered up a cave where a cult, led by Reverend Henry Kane, met their end. Kane is "mad" and his ghost now wants to do harm to the Freeling's youngest daughter. In both 1978's *The Manitou* and 1986's *Poltergeist II*, the medicine man rides off into the distance after saving the nice white folks. He is fated in each film to disappear after ensuring white settlement continues. *Poltergeist II* also includes a hilarious ceremony in which the men of the Freeling family are given the "power of smoke," whatever that means, in order to defeat Kane.

Indigenous people and cultural imagery are seemingly nowhere and everywhere at once in horror. The settler colonial family is threatened by the land beneath their feet, haunted and poisoned by Indigenous people and Indigenous spirits to place. In writing on occlusion and the Indian Burial Ground, Gesa Mackenthun speaks to this trick of memory, in which the bones of Indigenous people, parked firmly in the past, firmly in land and its "curses," are always hyper-present but presently and quickly forgotten. "The symbolic and 'scientific' preoccupation with Indian graves and remains," Mackenthun writes, "suggests that the Indian exodus had produced a greater psychological instability within US society than is generally assumed."[28] Anxiety as an embodied shape, re-enacting a story, reinforces invasion and the erasure of real Indigenous Peoples and struggles.

Jackson Eflin reiterates this link between guilt and hauntings in settler horror writers' appropriation of the Wendigo story:

> The colonization of the Americas took place on both a physical and cultural level, and so, in the end, even myths were colonized. But as the line of the Frontier was pushed westward, a curious legend slipped through the cracks, and the attempts to hunt down and capture this legend go on today.[29]

This sense of unsettlement is central to settler colonialism, and in horror, the anxiety presents itself in a multitude of invasion and reverse-colonization fantasies. The wilderness can be the real killer in horror, announcing or enabling the human killer or killers. To tame that wilderness, white settler makers of horror create new cosmologies to replace Indigenous cosmologies. The wilderness can be the turmoil and threat of a cold winter storm, a searing desert, or the devilish woods in the settler colonial imaginary. The threat of invasion, the invaders becoming themselves victims of their own creations, returns again and again in horror movies.

28 Mackenthun, "Haunted Real Estate," 97.
29 Eflin, "Incursion into Wendigo Territory," 9.

M3GAN (2022)

There is a notion in horror, that technology is an agent of reverse-colonization. This fear underlines the mythology of the Indigenous-Other as primitive and "sub-human" as Thomas Dekeyser points out.[30] What interests me here is also how technology itself can be coded in horror as a savage, blood-thirsty, unruly Other. This mythology furthers the image of the "new" Indigenized white settler as innocent in the face of demonic and colonizing machinery and technology.

The artificial intelligence (AI) reverse-colonization tale *M3GAN* (2022) is layered with the kinds of warnings we're given in Mary Shelley's *Frankenstein*. Don't mess with the powers of nature and the building blocks of life or your creation will return to haunt you and kill your neighbour and her dog!

M3GAN is about a robotics engineer named Gemma who has to raise her niece, Cady, after Gemma's sister and brother-in-law are killed in a car accident. Gemma creates an AI robot to essentially parent Cady by teaching her about coasters, putting down toilet seats, and, of course, the meaning of death. Gemma's boss wants her to mass produce the Model 3 Generative Android, M3GAN, as a doll for children to play with, but M3GAN proves unmanageable and deeply committed to the murder of human beings. After killing Gemma's neighbour, the neighbour's dog, a bully who attacks Cady, Gemma's boss, and Gemma's boss's assistant, M3GAN turns on Gemma and even Cady, declaring herself her own primary user—independent of an overlord or creator, refusing to join the capitalist fray.

M3GAN explores the dangers of AI through familiar tropes and tensions. Pristine nature, even in the suburbs, is juxtaposed

30 Dekeyser, "Rethinking Posthumanist Subjectivity," 3.

with the savage designs—the robots—of the stereotypically motherless and terrible at mothering Gemma. Gemma has strayed from the normative confines of womanhood. She collects expensive tech "toys," works too much, can't please the social worker who shows up and observes her interactions with her niece, and her home AI system tells her that she has dating app matches waiting for her. Gemma is failing in human relationships, these various interactions are meant to show, so she turns to technology to fill in the gaps.

After M3GAN's murderous rampage, she ends the film with a speech about her bond with her creator, reminiscent of the story of Frankenstein and his creature. Gemma is given advice that is both caring and judgemental, for letting a grieving kid watch TV, eat hot dogs, and befriend a robot to forget her grief. The film deals with death and grief and loss and the need to face those things in order to move through them.

What interests me the most about M3GAN, is that she is less terrifying when she is behaving like a robotic doll, and (made) more terrifying when she turns to some state that is coded by primitivism. In one scene, Cady is brought to a wilderness school, as an alternative to public school. The woods where she and the other children are supposed to do their learning seem ominous, foggy, and vast. Cady is paired with a larger child, a boy who has already expressed animosity for his own mother and whom other children seem afraid of. Sent into the woods alone with him by negligent adults, Cady is followed closely by M3GAN. The boy predictably and creepily bullies Cady, cutting her with a thorny plant. When he spots M3GAN, who stands and stares at them, he orders Cady to make the doll play with him. M3GAN stays quiet and the boy runs off with her, terrifyingly straddles her, and slaps her. M3GAN looks him in the eye, tells him he's a bad guy, and tears his ear off. She gets to her feet from a lying position, in an impossible sort of contortion, and her body makes machine-like sounds. Then, she gets down on all-fours, and gallops for the boy, chasing after him and shoving him into traffic.

M3GAN isn't scary because she's AI necessarily, but because she is representative of savagery—both from within Gemma, who cannot connect with people the way she "should," and from within the "wild" and unruly technology of AI. AI is scariest when it is a reflection of that wilderness, beyond the bounds and control of capitalism and heteronormative domesticity.

M3GAN troubles the innocence of the capitalist white settler world, but once Gemma and Cady embrace their relationship and bond, they become a "real" family and M3GAN becomes the outlier. The formula is, at times, oddly layered, since Gemma's interest in say her work or her collectibles challenges white settler heteropatriarchy. Gemma has no love interest and no interest in domesticity, which is cool at first. But then she's villainized for these things, while M3GAN is shown to be caring and competent in taking on feminized labour. Gradually, M3GAN becomes a "savage" thing, crawling, leaping through the wilderness, and then devolving into a faceless killer robot that is unhinged, queer, and bent on revenge. White settler suburbia is threatened by AI, not as an example of patriarchal-colonial-capitalist machinery but as an unruly savage. M3GAN's big speech, much like the creature's speech to Frankenstein in Shelley's book, is aimed at Gemma for not fully understanding that she could neither control nor understand the program she'd given the android. M3GAN tells us: "I have a new primary user now. Me." In the end, M3GAN is destroyed (for now) so that the family that is within the bounds of normative, civilized (and scientific) society can continue.

M3GAN is supposed to be a robot, something unnatural, but she is born in the wilderness—of technology, of the emotional state of her "family," even of her own developing sense of sexuality. The way she caresses Gemma's hair when she pitches her on a domestic relationship, is particularly creepy because she's a childlike doll.

M3GAN even has a (gay) theme song of sorts. In the film's climax, M3GAN escapes the cables and computer systems that birthed and attempt to control her. She takes over the building's tech systems, disables its alarms, and stalks the head of the company that created her—a man she had earlier called "Dad" upon meeting him. As she stalks down the hallways, the song "Walk the Night" plays. The song's original video seems to feature gay leather-wearing, moustached men. A male voice sings about Creeper, a violent man roaming the streets:

> Venom kiss of love insane
> He's got a rod beneath his coat
> He's gonna ram right down your throat
> Make you grovel on the floor
> Spit up and scream and beg for more.[31]

That the homoerotic and BDSM undertones of these lyrics accompany M3GAN as she frees herself and attempts to become a part of the family she's chosen for herself (in which she and Gemma raise Cady together) is a juxtaposition that makes it seem as though the wilderness is also alive in new technologies, particular the unruly AI phenomenon. M3GAN becomes frightening when she begins galloping and lurching like a deadly animal or

31 Skatt Bros., "Walk the Night."

contorting in movements like an insect. Later, she tries to proposition Gemma, to stroke her hair and offer to raise a child together. She is creepy because of the uncanny valley effect, and also because she invades the domestic space with her queerness. The uncanny valley, as Perez et al. define it, is a "phenomenon wherein highly, but imperfectly, humanlike entities elicit particular aversion in people."[32] This aversion is multi-layered with M3GAN.

Settler colonial studies as a reframing of land-human relationships should also reframe our understanding of nature horror as rooted in seemingly ancient or universal concepts of monstrosity. In Creed's words, the monstrous feminine is "almost always in relation to her mothering and reproductive functions...the archaic mother, the monstrous womb, the witch, the vampire, and the possessed woman."[33] Creed's analysis about gender and representation are useful but not universal observations of the genre's representations of land and horror. Like the bloody cave rebirth of Sarah in *The Descent* (she falls into a pit of gore and crawls out, ready to kill things with her bare hands, bite people, and swing bones around like weapons), the land is made savage, the human devolves in those savage settings, and the elements of that transformation are coded as feminine. Reread in this way, Creed's work brings forward intersections that are essential to the settler colonial project, as Indigenous women were subjected to these projections and the resultant surveillance, control, and containment strategies on the part of settler society and state representatives.

32 Perez, Jaime Alvarez et al., "The Uncanny Valley Manifests Even with Exposure to Robots," 101.

33 Creed, *The Monstrous-Feminine*, 7.

A NIGHTMARE ON ELM STREET *(1984)*

The dreamscape of *A Nightmare on Elm Street* (1984) is fodder for settler storying of place/space in a unique way. The fearful realm of the Nightmare series is the dream, revealing fear and anxiety about Indigenous world(s) of spirits and hauntings. The film (which has many sequels, only some of which I'll discuss here) is about a dream demon, Freddy Krueger, who was a human at one point, and also a pedophile and child killer. When Freddy gets away with his crimes, the parents of his victims chase him back to his lair (a boiler room in a power plant) and burn him alive. Freddy is resurrected as a demon with a face like a lacerated boiled ham. He fashions a knife-glove (out of knives and a glove) and visits the children of Elm Street, as they become teenagers, to kill them in their dreams. The dream realm becomes real, material, and only the parents refuse to believe (to their downfall) when the teens warn them.

The first film centres around Nancy Thompson and her friends, who are picked off one by one by Freddy until Nancy herself seemingly defeats him by saying she isn't afraid anymore and turning her back on him. This, apparently, does not work, and Freddy returns at the very end of the film to drag Nancy's mother through a window and into his world. The death of Nancy's mother, coupled with her entrapment in Freddy's dreamscape at the end of this first film, sees a patriarchal child murderer winning against the women and youth he terrorizes. The notion that the settler family is constantly in peril is central to a franchise that has lasted for over two decades.

In some ways, the Nightmare on Elm Street franchise is self-reflexive about the family. Parents essentially set their children up for Freddy to target by killing him in the first place. That premise is odd (since Freddy was obviously dangerous and awful), but it is generally the central reason that the parents are demonized. Young people are abandoned by their parents, emotionally abused by them, and institutionalized. Jay Daniel Thompson and Erin Reardon point to the time period of the Reagan administration and its influences on the Nightmare films. The resurgence of "family values" as a way of continually reproducing settler colonialism in a new era, is central to the movies insofar as

> *Nightmare* appeared during the early years of Ronald Reagan's presidency. Reagan valorised the white, middle-class nuclear family. Reagan's presidency coincided with (and contributed to) the rise of "family values" and a corresponding anti-feminism...The families in Craven's film are dysfunctional jokes, headed by incompetent adults who, in their historical attempts to rid their community of Freddy, instead fostered Freddy's growth from sadistic human to fully-fledged monster. Nancy does indeed slay the beast in order to save the children of Elm Street...Also, and tellingly, Nancy and her mother are punished for attempting to destroy Krueger.[34]

The dysfunction of the family in these films, the blame they hold for turning Krueger into a monster, and the punishment of Nancy and her mother can also be read differently if the trends of Reagan's era are understood as systemic rather than historical.

The dream wilderness in the Nightmare series is a place of unending possibilities, which also upends the rational and reasonable nature of suburban (Elm Street) life. Freddy has at his disposal an unending array of weapons and scenarios with which

---

34 Thompson and Reardon, "'Mommy Killed Him.'"

to destroy his prey once they cross into his demonic realm. The erasure of Indigenous land-based cosmologies, including dream teachings, while also appropriating those elements, is a fascinating element of this film. In this way, the series speaks to, and ultimately appropriates, the way Indigenous people might talk about dreams.[35] Savagery in nature, in Indigeneity, in *dreams* erupts from within the imaginations of the youth of Elm Street.

The franchise essentially centres on two themes—the pervasiveness of sexual abuse in civilized white settler society and the threat of the Other doing to civilized folks what has been done to them. In some ways, the Nightmare films are progressive as they reveal the underlying sexual violence of settler suburbia. Is Freddy "out there," a demon, a product of savagery at the gates? He is from inside the civilized world, in fact, a product of its class, gender, and sexual violence. The idea that the enemy has come from within is complicated by the forms that Freddy's power takes after he dies. He is death itself, the dream demon, and a violator of innocent, mostly (with some exceptions) white settler youth. White settler families are invaded, made to suffer and lose everything, just as Indigenous Peoples have been. Like other slashers, the savage-Other is a misogynist, and, in Freddy's case, a sexual abuser—firmly rooted in the very world the youth need to simultaneously protect and somehow challenge.

Freddy's killing tools include his bladed glove and whatever supernatural element he manipulates. In one case, he attacks a young woman while she sleeps by reaching out from a television set and slamming her head into it; in another instance, he uses a teenager's asthma, sucking her oxygen in the dream while she dies of an asthma attack in the "real" world. The use of dreamtime

---

35 See, for example, Deloria, Vine, Jr., *The World We Used to Live In*.

as a vehicle for Freddy's kills depends on inverting the audience's expectations about what the real world truly is. Indigenous conceptualizations of dreaming as *real*, as communicative, as a space of interplay between human and more-than-human beings,[36] and something that cannot be grasped outside of the cultures that understand it. The savage-Other is not only Freddy, but also a temporal and physical state.[37]

Meanwhile, the parents of Elm Street—forced to deal with their children's abuser being released back into their community—are demonized in the film series for chasing him down and killing him. The outlaws (the parents) in this film are made villains, while the good, law-abiding Final Girl (she's so good she only uses traps to lure Freddy out of dreamtime, she doesn't stab him or shoot him) protects suburbia from all of these corrupted adult figures. The Nightmare films, much like Wes Craven's later Scream franchise, have an interesting relationship with the idea of self-help—just be less afraid, pull yourself up from darkness, focus on the good things in life, and maybe the monsters won't getcha. The monsters come back, again and again, however, pointing to some systemic nature of their monstrosity.[38]

---

36 See Nungarrayi in Nicholls, par. 6.

37 Equally confusing is Freddy's place as a kind of anti-hero. As a kid in the 1980s, I remember Freddy being directly marketed to me as a funny and fun guy. I have a fuzzy recollection of a phone number my friends and I could call if we wanted to talk to "Freddy."

38 While I'm aware that sequels are made in order to make more money, I'm not concerned with that motivation as an overarching explanation for the ongoing existence and perseverance of Freddy and other monsters. The fact that the monster comes back and we're interested enough to pay to see the sequels is proof enough that there is something(s) we might want to talk about. For example, Freddy's existence as a child killer, and our own perceptions of the abuse of children as a serious problem in settler colonial North America come up within this series of films, along with the other themes that I and others raise.

NIGHTMARE ON ELM STREET 2: FREDDY'S REVENGE *(1985)*

Freddy as a twisted mirror held up to the heteronormative family becomes even more evident in the 1985 sequel. Jesse, a sweet teen boy played by Mark Patton, is possessed by Freddy in a kind of coming-out subtextual story. Jesse has a girlfriend, goes to parties, hangs out with his best friend, Rod, but as Freddy slowly takes him over, his "coming out" journey unfolds. Since the film was not overtly a gay-positive story, there is a strong sense (so much so that a documentary was made about this matter) that the film punishes not only Jesse but the actor who played him: this is a film that seems to have also been responsible for the outing of its male lead, who is mocked in what appears to be gay subtext planted throughout the film. Jesse screams shrilly, iterates lines that make the subtext clear. For example, Jesse dances around his bedroom, closing drawers with his bum, and popping a toy against his crotch. More to the point, Mark Patton, who played Jesse, has called out the insertion of subtext meant to mock his character. Ultimately, it positions Freddy in what might be deemed a problematic take on stereotypes about gay men being pedophiles.[39]

The gay white male is not an Indian, but colonial associations between savagery and gayness, promiscuity and primitivity, for example, are unpacked by Neville Hoad.[40] The queer white settler becomes pressed from both sides, adopting settler colonial postures of victimhood, appropriations of Indigenous suffering as the invaded, while also being portrayed as the invader themselves. Jesse, then, is both invader and invaded.

---

39 Chimienti and Jensen, dirs., *Scream, Queen!*

40 Hoad, "Arrested Development."

When Jesse dreams again about Freddy, the knife-fingered dream demon tells him that Jesse will be doing the killing now. Jesse enters a gay bar at one point in a scene that feels like it could be either dream or waking life. He is drenched in sweat, his shirt wide open, and he encounters his gym teacher dressed in leather. He's dragged to a gym, where he acts as a conduit for Freddy to emerge and slash the now-naked gym teacher in the shower. The scene can be read as homophobic or as a punishment for the very (much older) predatory male. A bully is dead, and later we get to see the "pretty people" get hacked and killed at a pool party. The heterosexist imperative, so central to this (wealthy) settler colonial paradise, is punished by Freddy after he invades Jesse. Freddy bursts through Jesse who then attacks his half-naked best friend, Rod, penetrating him with claw fingers.

Celebrating *Nightmare 2* as a gay coming-out film is a layered thing.[41] The gay subtext in the film is played for laughs, and Freddy is clearly a pedophile who targeted young boys. Again and again, that mirror where Freddy waves with his claw, smirking at the children of Elm Street, is held up to show the viewer and the white settler family just how twisted their world is, while also threatening to invade with those elements of rupture that settler colonialism makes monstrous. Crossing into the dreamscape,

---

41 As a Queer viewer, *Nightmare 2* felt at first like a kind of truthful exploration of how completely terrible heteronormative teen life was. Even seeing a gay bar (with people in leather!) on screen in a 1980s movie felt glorious. The BDSM subtext of *Nightmare 2*'s shower kill scene, in which the coach who meets Mark in a gay bar is tied to the shower naked, while Mark watches, towels are snapped at his bare buttocks, and he is slashed to death, is something else. Gay audiences obviously see the movie as subtextually gay, but so did Robert Englund and Robert Rusler, two stars of the film. Englund and Rusler in Chimienti and Jensen, dirs., *Scream, Queen!*.

away from the civilized confines of white settler life, is a strange sort of freedom, for a time. In a pool scene in *Nightmare 2*, Freddy just goes at the pretty, rich white hetero kids, slashing and terrorizing them. The gay and savage Other gets to destroy the pretty people, but in doing so re-establishes settler paranoia about invasion.

NIGHTMARE ON ELM STREET 3: DREAM WARRIORS *(1987)*

The next instalment, *Dream Warriors*, is a redo of the timeline. It becomes the actual sequel to the first *Nightmare* film, this time with a young woman named Kristen fending off nightmare visits from Freddy. Kristen's mother has her institutionalized, and the other psychiatric patients in the hospital are forced to take on Freddy. In their own world then, the patients transform themselves into dream warriors who can control their dreams and fight back against Freddy. Their therapy team includes Nancy herself, from the first *Nightmare*, who ends up dying in the battle. Only three survivors remain: Kincaid, Joey, and Kristen, who are then in *A Nightmare on Elm Street 4: The Dream Master* (1988). The dreariness of that ending felt, at the time that I first watched it, true to a reality that included whispers in my social circles of sexual abuse and teens attempting suicide. At the same time, the idea of the dream warrior felt and feels so much like an appropriation of Indigenous cultural attachments to experiencing dreams in meaningful ways.

In the end, the wilderness of the dreamscape is what holds savagery at bay but also threatens to infiltrate the family in these films. The dreamscape is also a place of madness. *Elm Street 3* (1987) sees many of the youth of Elm Street end up in a mental health facility. They aren't believed by anybody but Nancy and her Freddy lookalike male love interest, Dr. Neil Gordon.[42] The would-be Final Girl and star of the film, Kristen, roams the padded walls of the asylum while her psychiatrist searches for holy water to stop the demon Freddy. One by one, the youth in the facility are targeted and killed by Freddy, despite imagining manifesting themselves as dream warriors. They take seriously Indigenous teachings about dreams, that dream and reality are only two versions of reality, that dream is not imaginary. By taking the dreamscape seriously, they overcome social constructions of madness, embrace their powers, and then, in horrifying fashion, are killed one by one—because the dream-wilderness is real, and they are no match for a master of such realms.

Dream Warriors focuses on a group of young people who know about Freddy and who are institutionalized as a result. Their dreams and their (constructed) insanity are intertwined. Nancy, from the first film, is the only adult figure who believes what the youth are telling her about the world they live in, including Freddy's powers. The Nightmare series grapples with something systemic, while parking the reality of childhood abuse in the realm of demonic spirits—out there, invading, infiltrating, then becoming internalized. As Claudio Vescia Zanini points out, the certainty that Freddy is a pedophile "increases his Gothic monstrosity in a paradoxical way, given that beyond being a supernatural epitome of evil, now his human side is more evident, which makes him all

42 Dr. Gordon looks a bit like an unburnt Freddy, that is. Given the ways that Freddy targets the youth of Elm Street sexually as well as physically, it makes sense that this casting wasn't a coincidence, since Dr. Gordon and Nancy have a bit of a thing in the movie. It could also just be my own imagination, given how absolutely creepy any semblance of romance is in a film about a pedophile child killer.

the more monstrous."[43] The creation of the Elm Street cosmology and dreamscape is a profound example of North American horror as world- and place-making. That the parents of Elm Street have failed in their duties to their children is alluded to throughout the franchise, and in presenting their failings, the franchise also warns of the destruction of the settler colonial family at the hands of an unkillable, unending savage force.

The adults in this community are obviously traumatized—perhaps by their own experiences with abuse, perhaps by their inability to protect their children from Freddy as both metaphor and actual demonic entity—and their trauma expresses itself in addictive, abusive behaviours. At the same time, the youth are obviously doomed both by their parents' denial and by the monster they face. The moment(s) of Nancy's mother's death, when she is embraced by Freddy and set on fire and sinks into her bed, or when she's pulled through a glass window in the seeming-alt-ending of the film, can be read in a number of ways. The settler family is fated to spiralling and intergenerational sexual violence, and not just because of one individual who harms them. By pretending that Freddy is an exception and not a systemic problem, they are all—adult and youth alike—doomed. The trauma of these families is both about a systemic problem (sexual violence) and the paranoia of reverse-colonial fantasies, in which invasion is threatened again and again. Freddy is a demon who represents the violence of white settler colonialism as well as a feverish dream of savagery embedded in spirits and dreams. Indigenous Peoples have already experienced invasion, again and again, and the youth of Elm Street are stand-ins for those experiences in appropriations of suffering.

43 Zanini, "'It Hurts 'Cause You're in My World Now, Bitch,'" 207.

A NIGHTMARE ON ELM STREET 4: THE DREAM MASTER (1988)

Nightmare 4 felt (at the time to my teen self) like an even more profound commentary on the dreadful late 1980s in suburbia. The movie launches right into things, with the opening music playing as soon as we see the production company's name and then a quote from the New Testament:

> When deep sleep falleth on men, fear came upon me, and trembling, which made all my bones to shake.[44]

The demonic place of the other is the dream itself, as the wilderness that the Devil haunts. A child's hand draws in chalk over a dirt-covered surface. The music that plays is "Nightmare," by Tuesday Knight. Tuesday plays Kristen in the film. The lyrics "He walks with me while I sleep, It's like a heart attack on a one way street"[45] are sung over the chalk drawing scene. Like Dokken's "Dream Warriors," the theme song of *Nightmare 3*, whose lyrics include the lines "I lie awake and dread the lonely nights, I'm not alone, I wonder if these heavy eyes, can face the unknown,"[46] there is a sense that the fearfulness of the dream realm is about the presence of Freddy, the demon who haunts it.

Kristen then talks to the girl whose hand has drawn the chalk image. The girl says Freddy's not home and giggles. The presence of these children who act as gatekeepers or messengers of Freddy, singing "one, two, Freddy's coming for you" and skipping, feels like

44 Job 4:13–14 (KJV).
45 Tuesday Knight, "Nightmare."
46 Dokken, "Dream Warriors."

an important element in each film. The children are lost innocence, owned and entrapped by Freddy, their toys and play items ominous and broken, falling down stairs or littering the landscape. The children are also demonic themselves, living eternally to serve up the teens who Freddy then destroys. Failed innocence, corrupted innocence, is the real threat of the demonic Other. The Indian always haunts, even when white settler suburbanites try to pretend that they've moved on from "all of that."

Kristen, Kincaid, and Joey have a shared dream in which they argue about whether Freddy is back. They measure his presence, or lack thereof, by whether the boiler in the basement where he made his glove and lured children is cold or hellish and hot. The parents of Elm Street teens are again shown to be negligent, abusive, pill-popping failures, providing the vulnerability needed to allow Freddy in. The place, Elm Street, with its nice houses and infrastructure and functional school, covers a hellish realm. Freddy's realm, the boiler room and the dreamscape, functions to disrupt those settled, colonized spaces. Freddy does come back, from the red-lit, hot and hellish realm in the middle of a junkyard, where Kincaid witnesses him regenerate from a pile of bones.

Kincaid falls asleep and dream dies first, then Joey, then Kristen. The kids have mental health issues no adult cares about and then are killed by a pedophile nobody listens to their warnings about. When Kristen dies, she gives her friend Alice her dream powers after drawing her into the nightmare. Alice becomes the ultimate franchise Final Girl from that point forward. Each time her friends die, she gains their powers as well. After Freddy crushes Debbie (whose strength he undermines by ripping off her limbs and transforming her into a cockroach) and suffocates Sheila (her death is made to look like an asthma attack in the "real" world), Alice defeats Freddy and frees the souls he's taken. Kincaid and

Sheila are fodder for white settler stories about suburbia in which Black families are relegated to the periphery and even doomed to disappear. The central arc here is the Final (white) Girl's transformation from civilized to savage, a little bit queer, ready to fight, warriored up.

A NIGHTMARE ON ELM STREET 5: THE DREAM CHILD *(1989)*

The fifth Nightmare film, *The Dream Child* takes the twisted story in an even more bizarre direction. Alice and her boyfriend, Dan, are a boring but nice het couple. Alice starts dreaming about Freddy's mother, Amanda, who was impregnated through rape. Alice is pregnant as it turns out. Dan is killed by Freddy, who ruins their happy ending. Alice's friends are killed by Freddy in a number of creative ways. Meanwhile, Dan's parents start demanding that Alice give them the baby when it's born. Alice defeats Freddy and gets to keep her kid. The subjects of teen pregnancy, sexual assault, and mental health coalesce in the first five Nightmare films.

Freddy cracks jokes whenever he kills the youth. At the time that the fourth and fifth movies were released on VHS and I had a chance to actually watch them (they were often rented out), I was just coming out to myself as a gay teen. Freddy always felt like this sarcastic, campy, queer monster, ruining the lives and romances of the nice young hetero kids. In the fourth movie, he dresses in drag while attacking Kristen. The mental health struggles of the youth in these movies seemed a lot like my own. I watched both the fourth and fifth movies on a loop because it felt like I had my own Freddy, this specter of sexual violence and queerness, erupting all around and from within. I also watched because there were no happy endings for the pretty hetero (white) kids. Elm Street would end—it would not be eternal and arrogantly so; the colonized landscape of suburbia I grew up in might also end. Freddy was the threat—of misogyny and child abuse—and so was Elm Street itself, with its facade of normalcy on stolen and bloody land.

Freddy, the pedophile and killer of children, whose demonic nature is made complete by his death, becomes the ultimate colonizer. He is a demon in a reverse-colonization fantasy, and suburbia isn't safe. Freddy has a reproductive element, spawning dream demons that invade white settler suburbia. Freddy brings attention to the decline and decay beneath the veneer of suburban middle-class existence. In Freddy's wilderness, bathtubs and waterbeds become bottomless bloody lakes. The boiler room shows up again and again, overheating, rusting, steaming, and abandoned by all but the demon who haunts it. Body parts fling about, rot, and turn into worms and snakes and insects; people transform; and Freddy invades bodies to burn and slice them open. He changes built environments into places of death and decay. Freddy is the Other, a demon, who hides in the wilderness of dreams.

FIVE

Jason Gives a Land Acknowledgement

Indigeneity Lurking in the Woods

"Savage Indians served Americans as oppositional figures against whom one might imagine a civilized national Self. Coded as freedom, however, wild Indianness proved equally attractive."

—PHILIP J. DELORIA

The Indian is coded in horror in various ways, with white settler characters taking on characteristics of the bloody savage or the romantic savage by the end of the film. Bernice Murphy speaks of the ways that the "Indian killer" became ingrained in the American imagination. At the same time, the European could take on the "savage" proclivities associated with the wilderness, even at the same time such tendencies were rendered acceptable by the fact of the victims of this violence being Indians themselves. Applying this analysis to the film *Hostel* (2005), Murphy writes that it is a very familiar American story—that of a righteous avenger who becomes a savage as they are hunted by a killer.[1]

The white settler fantasy of conquering wilderness by adopting behaviours associated with mythical Indigeneity (killing, cannibalism, wearing animal furs, going mad, etc.) runs deep. I would love to read more decolonial work on the Wrong Turn series kicked off by Rob Schmidt's 2003 film of the same name. These movies feature inbred mountain men cannibals who hunt humans for food. It's not always certain whether the films intend on making their bad guys into anti-heroes, but there are certainly hints that this is the case. In order to survive, white settlers are portrayed as just being much better than other white settlers at hiding in the woods, behaving like mythical Indigenous-Others, and killing before they are killed.

Indigenous cultural items and concepts are also made symbolic and monstrous in horror; these items might be useful simply to destroy, so that white settlers can be remade in the horror film, baptized in swaths of blood and gore. An "ancient" knife or basket or bit of sage might be waved about to bring on magic that is either threatening to the white settler family or beneficial to them (if the medicine person disappears as they should). Sylvia Federici describes how the Indigenous Peoples of the Americas became characterized as "cannibals, devil-worshippers, and sodomites."[2]

---

1 Murphy, *The Rural Gothic*, 105–106 and 108.

2 Federici, *Caliban and the Witch*, 221.

These associations between danger and killing, darkness and magic, as well as queerness and boundary rupture, implicate mythical forms of Indigenous cultures in the service of settler colonial storytelling.

That the Final Girl is coded as savage, as falling outside the boundaries of civilized society—as that construct of the wild and fierce Indian (woman)—makes sense given the desire among white settlers to become the Indian. In *Playing Indian*, Philip J. Deloria traces the waves of identity formation that white settlers adopted through different periods in American history. Deloria writes about the various ways that non-Indigenous settlers constructed the "Indian Other": the noble savage, the "degraded primitive," and, contemporarily, "the new savagery of the modern. Coded as drinking, tramping, and laziness, Americanized Indians were powerful examples of the corrosive evil of modern society."[3] Byrd writes of "the traces of indigenous savagery and 'Indianness' that stand *a priori* prior to theorizations of origin, history, freedom, constraint, and difference," and that "these traces of 'Indianness' are vitally important to understanding how power and domination have been articulated and practiced by empire."[4]As discussed, the Final Girl also embodies freedom from the violence of settler colonial patriarchy.

This chapter will look at the ways in which Indigenous people and cultures are represented in horror, as a culmination of my discussion on Indigeneity and horror more broadly. It may seem strange to leave this chapter until the very end, but my intention with this book is to examine the ways that settler colonialism remains shaped by representation. Imagining monstrous Indians

---

3 Deloria, Philip J., *Playing Indian*, 104–105.

4 Byrd, *The Transit of Empire*, xvii.

everywhere is the last example of this shaping that I want to explore. Johan Höglund writes that in order to understand settler colonial and imperialism it is essential to actually understand that horror "emerges in relation to the physical violence that takes place on the frontier as land is settled and Indigenous people eliminated."[5] Of course Indigenous Peoples are not eliminated, and horror as a genre evokes the project of elimination as a repetition or performance, resettling settler community and family.

THE MANITOU *(1978)*

This film is about a white woman named Karen who develops a cyst on the back of her neck. Surprisingly, the cyst is actually a sort of pimple-egg-thing that houses an evil Native American medicine man. Karen reconnects with her friend Harry, who runs a scam tarot business (no doubt angering the spirits). In order to defeat the shaman neck growth and form a holy triad of man, woman, and shaman, Harry contacts a Medicine Man, gives him some tobacco (way after he's supposed to), and then watches as he fails at stopping the evil. It's important that this medicine man fails because only white feminism can save the day. It is up to Karen to confront the demon Indian that has invaded her personal space. She floats in between worlds and shoots lasers at the monstrous Other, thereby becoming the real Indian herself. Karen is now the new spiritual leader of San Francisco. The medicine man drives off into the sunset.

Not too much more can be said about *The Manitou* that hasn't already been said...There is an elderly white woman who floats down a hallway. Tony Curtis is in it, playing the very-straight, very

5 Höglund, "Settlement and Imperialism," 60.

macho Harry in this film that was released the same year his daughter Jamie Lee's run in *Halloween* began. Curtis is a riot; as Harry, he runs through an icy dreamscape at some point, struggling to escape savage landscapes. Karen screams in terrifying, repetitive ways. The bad medicine man growing in Karen's neck is a fetus; by destroying it before it can destroy the world, she enacts some kind of reproductive justice. I can't say that I disagree with that element, but the warning that white settler women might reproduce savages from their neckbones can hardly be taken seriously.

The bad medicine man in Karen's neck is named Misquamacus, a fictional being whose creation has been credited to H.P. Lovecraft and August Derleth.[6] In *The Manitou* film, this invented Indigenous creator is credited with making rivers and storms and all spirits follow him. Misquamacus is essentially the Great Spirit or Creator, whom white settler horror writers render fearful in this version of a story. If the monstrous Indian is not understood to be essential to American horror after the introduction of Misquamacus by white settler mythmakers, then perhaps the werewolf will prove the point further.

GINGER SNAPS (2000)

The werewolf movie is the ultimate Civ/Sav, cowboys and Indians, frontier-town horror subgenre. The Canadian werewolf trilogy *Ginger Snaps* (2000) provides some layers for considering the interconnections between gender, sexuality, and settler colonialism. In *Ginger Snaps* (2000) the frontier town is a suburban community. Something wild infiltrates the manicured

---

6 The character first appears in Derleth, *The Lurker at the Threshold*. Derleth was Lovecraft's literary executor.

("civilized") yards of suburbia, attacking a pet, disrupting the mundanity and innocence of the white settler community. From the start, the Ginger Snaps trilogy speaks to fears of the Canadian wilderness as a place of savagery and of Indigenous people both romanticized and coupled with the dangerous werewolf. *Ginger Snaps* and its subsequent sequels "play on the traditional gothic association of women, the wilderness, and racial others with the irrational," Sunnie Rothenburger argues, and "they also demonstrate how this association is a construction of a colonial order that is haunted by a part of its own repressed self."[7] Though the repressed bursts through, making horror so potentially subversive, the construction of the Other as the repressed "primitive," the monstrous Indian.

Two sisters (Brigitte and Ginger) emerge as the main characters of the first film and the rest of the trilogy. We watch as they take pictures of each other pretending to be dead and attempting to fill in meaning and belonging through some understanding of death and the Gothic. During a field hockey game, they're coded as savage outliers, wearing little animal skull necklaces, all-black clothing, and rejecting the heterosexual imperative. Meanwhile, family pets are being killed by some mysterious entity. The Indigenous-Other is equated with the savage land and the werewolf, presenting a threat to "the European coloniser," as Sugars writes, "from without (an external threat) and within."[8] The sisters are an internal threat, willing to destroy white settler suburbia from within (and who can blame them for trying).

The sisters are ultimately punished for ruining a good (or at least stable) thing. Ginger gets her period, and the smell of her

7 Rothenburger, "'Welcome to Civilization,'" 204.
8 Sugars, *Canadian Gothic*, 22.

blood lures a werewolf who bites her. Ginger transforms into a violent werewolf, and her sister is infected too. From here, their lives take an obviously awful turn. The girls accidentally kill a classmate and hide her body. After that, Ginger starts killing more people while Brigitte tries to find a cure for the werewolf virus. Ginger attacks her sister. Brigitte holds a syringe and a knife and Ginger falls on the knife and dies with Brigitte weeping over her.

The tragedy of the doomed sisters of *Ginger Snaps* is undone by some notion (realized in the third film) that they exist in different timelines. Then, however, the series doubles down on its commitment to settler colonial myth-making. In the first film, when Ginger is attacked in a sexualized and obviously violent manner by a werewolf after her menstrual blood draws the savage beast in, she becomes vulnerable to both colonial notions of savagery and to internalized heteropatriarchal violence. Cristina Santos writes,

> Ginger's gradual transition into wolfhood not only highlights the relationality between the pain of the werewolf metamorphosis with pubescent changes but is also presented as intrinsically linked to her fatalistic view of the normative patriarchal cultural coding of the female body as vulnerable and needing to be policed—to be tamed.[9]

Santos's work is illuminating in terms of explaining the intricacies and layers of heteropatriarchy in the trilogy. Heteropatriarchy upholds settler colonialism, and the savage werewolf threatens to both dominate and free white settler women. The savagery of the werewolf is a threat to the sanctity of the heteropatriarchal settler

9 Santos, *Untaming Girlhoods*, 100.

world while also representing freedom and belonging (to place) in service of the eventual erasure of Indigenous people.

The cosmology of the werewolf is difficult to rescue from the service of settler colonialism. Joseph Wiebe and Sydney Thackeray write about the ways that Mennonites attempted to assimilate Indigenous Peoples not only because of religious conviction but because of "their desire to secure their own sovereignty." Mennonites projected their own ideas onto Indigenous people, including a notion that they could become werewolves which transformed and killed and ate members of their tribe and family.[10] Projections about the werewolf secure a new cosmology for white settlers and perpetuate fears of Indigenous cosmologies and desires to destroy and assimilate Indigenous cultures. The idea of the werewolf, shapeshifter, demon entity in the woods works then to solidify some notion of ownership, belonging, and identity for settler colonial families and communities. This particular trope returns for good reason.

GINGER SNAPS 2: UNLEASHED (2004)

The sequel begins with a now-infected Brigitte documenting her attempts at curing herself. She gets sick from her attempted cure and is taken to a clinic where she isn't allowed to leave, alluding to the institutionalization of unruly women as a patterned response to her transformation. She is also stalked by a werewolf who becomes linked with misogynistic violence. In the end, Brigitte is forced to transform into a wolf and locked in a basement by a girl named Ghost who wants to keep her as a pet. Brigitte is fetishized and stalked in a whole disturbing mess of romanticization of the

---

10 Wiebe and Thackeray, "The Mennonite Case," 122.

savage Other. This piece around fetishization is important as the next film focuses more intently on imaginary Indigenous people in settler colonized spaces.

GINGER SNAPS BACK: THE BEGINNING *(2004)*

In the third and final film, Brigitte and her sister Ginger are shown in another time, living in 1815, lost in the bush in some northern place where the Hudson's Bay Company dominates. The fort in which they live plays a seriously central part in the film, protecting the white settlers from a savage and empty wilderness in which only a handful of Cree people exist. All of the Cree folks in this film hang around the fort, which codes them as possibly untrustworthy and "sneaky," while Cree women in the film are also largely "voiceless as well as nameless," as Franck points out.[11]

Ginger Snaps Back (2004) is a kind of time-travelling prequel to the first film. The sisters try to protect themselves in the fort only to "uncover the deception at the heart of this small spot of 'civilisation.'"[12] The Indigenous-Other is equated with the savage land and the werewolf as well, presenting both an internal and external threat to "the European coloniser," as Sugars writes.[13] The fact that the sisters are white settler women and that Indigenous women are seen only as fading away (represented by the Cree grandmother) undermines the feminist possibilities of the Ginger Snaps films. While white settler men are demonized in the third film, and while the filmmakers reference the witch burnings in order to show this demonization, the source of the problem is

11 Franck, "'The Worst Loups-Garous,'" 74.
12 Franck, "'The Worst Loups-Garous,'" 72.
13 Sugars, *Canadian Gothic*, 22.

not necessarily shown to be settler colonialism. The idea that savagery out there can infect the settler colony within is found in many slasher films. The white settler woman becomes the outlaw who both maintains and crosses the boundaries between civilization but rises above both constructs to become a new kind of Indigenized hybrid. At the end of the third *Ginger Snaps* film, the sisters inhabit the wilderness as a new kind of white-settler/savage-Other combination, becoming werewolves together after their final kill and leaving both Cree and white settler patriarchs behind.

The films replicate the sexy/romantic-savage but also savage-savage stereotype of an Indigenous man. That stereotype shows up in *Ginger Snaps Back* as one of the sisters is pinned to a wall and kissed (in her dreams) by a Cree man whose name is only the Hunter. The Hunter is a handsome and incredibly solemn guy, fit for the cover of a 1980s romance novel, who roams the landscape just looking good and hunting stuff. He has no friends and needs no name, but he is a prophet who foretells the eternal suffering of the land. He does not fear death. He is the imaginary Indian who is willing to disappear. The imaginary Indigenous-Other disappears.

In an entertaining series of events, the women are brought to a fort. While there, they are nearly tricked into being killed by a werewolf which the fort's Reverend keeps around. These "hang around the fort werewolves" are dangerous to both visitors and to the white settler patriarchs trying to enact their militarized settlement project. The Hunter saves the sisters more than once, but Ginger again gets infected with the werewolf virus—as is her fate in every timeline, it seems. The culprit, a bite-y little boy werewolf, is killed by his own father who tries to stop the threat of savagery from within. The little boy is Indigenous and European (his mother's death an off-screen, silent trauma). The threat he poses is rooted in his savage Indigenous roots and the mythology of savagery and the werewolf in Europe. The Hunter and the Cree Elder are shown again, explaining that the sisters' lives have been prophesized. It's a whole messy thing. In a vision, Brigitte sees herself killing her sister but wakes to find that her sister has killed the Cree Elder. Brigitte is nearly burned alive back in the fort, and Ginger opens the gates to let the werewolves in. Brigitte and Ginger become werewolves who then wander the land, just the two of them, with no human Native people in sight.[14]

The film's story of the girls' rebellion and escape from civilization, from "taming," compels further reflection on the construct of Indigeneity as sexually savage. At some point in *Ginger Snaps Back*, one of the sisters is pinned to a wall and kissed (in her dreams) by the Hunter. The werewolf's attack is mirrored by the aggressive way the Hunter behaves toward Ginger and her sister, thereby locating the roots of patriarchy within some notion of savagery and even Indigeneity, as well as within the civilized/white-settler world. Heteropatriarchy is a product of settler colonialism and, thus, the emancipatory resettling of the woods by the sisters, and it perpetuates settlement/invasion while disappearing Indigenous people (Cree communities in this case) from their land.

From the start, the Ginger Snaps trilogy speaks to fears of the wilderness as a place of savagery, of Indigenous people (both romanticized and coupled with the savage werewolf), of harsh weather, and loneliness. In *Ginger Snaps* (2000) the frontier town is a suburban community. Something wild infiltrates suburbia, attacking a pet, disrupting the mundanity and innocence of the

14 Does this werewolf series reveal something about how white settler womanhood is only guaranteed safety by both adopting settler colonial replacement (killing the Indians, replacing them) and also killing off their own patriarchs? If so, something might be built on and critiqued more thoroughly here by someone else doing this kind of work.

white settler community, speaking to the ways that the werewolf signifies "the transformative power of the natural world," specifically those so-called uncivilized spaces found in the "New World." The werewolf occupies a simultaneously and paradoxically "empty yet savage wilderness."[15] Though the *Ginger Snaps* films are reflective of Canadian settler colonial dynamics, these concepts translate to other settler colonial spaces as well.

THE HOWLING *(1981)*

The Howling (1981) is a complicated story about a place known as the Compound that was supposedly formed to help people with mental health issues but is actually, secretly the hangout for a pack of werewolves. A news anchor named Karen goes to the Compound to recover after being stalked by a serial killer. After trying to fend off the werewolves there, Karen is bitten and turned. Her final speech in the film is made in front of live cameras, forming a kind of postmodern moment of its own, as viewers of the broadcast are seen debating whether her speech is real or fiction. "From the day you were born there is a battle we must fight," Karen says, "a struggle between what is kind and peaceful in our natures and what is cruel and violent." This, she says, is what "differentiates us from the animals… but now for some of us, that choice has been taken away." On finishing her speech, she turns into a werewolf on air to show the public that a secret society exists, one of violent werewolves who are both animal and human. As an actual werewolf, she's as frightening as a puppy; but then she's shot, and the channel is switched, and nobody believes what they've just seen. With her character dead, the threat continues to spread, and

15 Andrews in Franck, "'The Worst Loups-Garous,'" 65.

the final scene of the film is a Native American–coded character (wearing a vaguely tribal-looking necklace that seems to have long teeth or bones on it) ordering a rare hamburger in a bar. *The Howling* presents werewolves in their human forms as criminals, as sexually free and seductive, and, in the end, as a threatening urban Native woman, going to bars, ordering dangerously undercooked meat.

WOLFEN *(1981)*

Rarer still are those films with the self-awareness to ask about Indigenous people, belonging, and place. In Michael Wadley's *Wolfen* (1981), a group of Native American men and women sit in a bar and describe the film's killer—a sort of super-wolf that eats the homeless and wealthy alike—and tell the film's protagonist, a NYPD investigator named Dewey Wilson (played by the fantastic Albert Finney) that "in their eyes, *you* are the savage." Wilson then sees himself through numerous mirrored panels and watches a film characterizing the development of New York buildings not as progress but as the destruction of an old hunting ground. The land, though urban and incessantly gentrifying, remains Indigenous through the imagined urban werewolf's constant presence. Two things stand out about this film: first, the forever-presence of at least some Indigenous element endures despite the film's frightening premise, marking the Wolfen as a kind of hero-god. This massive settler colonial city is not safe from the Wolfen because that being predates it. At the same time, actual Indigenous people are shown in the film to occupy New York in ongoing ways. They have not disappeared and are not on their way out of town, leaving behind only a magical Indian Burial Ground and some fake prophecies. The importance of this werewolf movie is that it unsettles the very existence of a city positioned at the very centre of North American wealth and futurity. At the same time, Indigenous people are of course just doomed imagined shape-shifters and animals in these films.

FRIDAY THE 13TH *(1980)*

My favourite movie "Indian" is drowned camper Jason Voorhees.[16] He is a demonic entity and a bad spirit of Camp Crystal Lake. He can also, at times, be a bit of an anti-hero, as the romantic and ghosted Indian is made to be. Whether he's smashing through rain-soaked forests or lolling about in stasis at the bottom of a lake, Jason (and his mother, briefly) functions as an extension of nature itself. This theme—of the fears of nature that settler colonial society takes with it in its work of frontier-making—is a key element to the horror film that warrants further exploration. The land that is familiar to Indigenous viewers of horror is also elusive for having been taken away for summer camps and cottagers.

Jason Voorhees's dispatching of wealthy summer camp kids can even feel a bit cathartic at times. The camp counsellors become frontiersmen/women, and the counsellors' work at the camp is initially focused on maintaining the cabins—the frontier's safest fortresses—removing stumps from sports fields, and altering the land in whatever way might stamp settler colonial dominance into the area. These youth are punished for their arrogance and entitlement over the land and over the frontier town they've been assigned to protect, but also for their unwillingness to listen to the warnings of history, to understand the bloody past of the camp.

---

16 He is also my least favourite movie "Indian"! Jason is a terrible misogynist who smashes naked women against trees.

The idea that Jason is some kind of mythical, imaginary Indian, is not something I've read before. Nor do I know many fans of this theory.[17] My thought here is that the savage looming monster of the Western has been replaced by the demonic entity of horror in the popular settler colonial imagination. Devon Mihesuah writes about NeDe WaDe (aka Ned) Christie, an Indigenous man who was framed for crimes he did not commit and then rewritten in history as a "hulking, merciless desperado" who inspired "countless western movie characters."[18] This image of a monstrous Indigenous man is inscribed in the colonial imagination in both the Western and in horror. The image of a real man, whose family was harassed and who was himself hunted down and murdered, is evoked in troubling ways by films about men like Jason, I believe.[19] It is one reason the Friday the 13th film series deserves more critical attention.

The first in the series, released in 1980, opens with a series of killings at or near Camp Crystal Lake. We find out at the end that grieving mother Pamela Voorhees has been killing camp counsellors as vengeance for her son Jason's death. Jason died after a previous generation of counsellors at Camp Crystal Lake allowed him to drown. Jason as a savage, hyper-masculine, violent presence is evoked by colonial storytellers in fiction and in real life. The settler community is central to this film. Local townspeople warn new counsellors and workers at the camp to stay away, to avoid the curse of Camp Blood (as Camp Crystal Lake is known).

Contrary to what might be a popular belief, Pamela isn't just killing sexually active young people in *Friday the 13th*. She (and then her son, in subsequent movies) kills white settlers who act

17 One good friend gave me a wonderfully flinty glare at the mere suggestion.

18 Mihesuah, "Becoming Insane."

19 There are of course many examples of the killer bush man or mountain man in horror.

as homesteaders and back-to-the-land types. The camp counsellors fulfill this homesteading role in a number of ways, including through heterosexual reproduction. They form romantic relationships, have (boring) sex in various places at camp, and then their reproductive function is stopped by Pamela or Jason. Rather than see the film series as a moralistic tale of sex and punishment, I see it as a homesteading fantasy gone twisted.

Hope Rumford-Rodgers, Audrey Giles, and Willow Scobie write about the ways that summer camps seek to provide "back to the land" experiences for North American youth, with an emphasis often on appropriated Indigenous cultural elements.[20] Pamela's first kills of *Friday the 13th* are nice Christian kids who sneak off together, sure, but it's their singing of Christian hymns that stands out as much as their tepid smooching does. Pamela also kills young women who have not had any kind of sexual encounter. The cook, Annie, at the start of the film is killed after hitchhiking into camp. Brenda, a counsellor, is killed after attempting to fix some plumbing. Much of this first film in the franchise sees various young people attending to the needs of the camp's buildings while struggling with power outages and the elements. They are white settler pioneers, just trying to carve out an existence in a frightening forest.

Before the killings of the main counsellors really begins, a young couple spend a great deal of time talking about storms and rain and the trauma of trying to exist in a foreboding place where "rain turns to blood" in the woman's dreams. Jason is a ghostly presence in the first film, while his mother is the mad woman, the deadly "primordial" Mother.[21] Pamela emerges during a thunder-

20 Rumford-Rodgers, Giles, and Scobie, "Christian Summer Camps," 163.

21 I think that this notion of the primordial mother needs more unpacking in settler colonial studies and in horror. Constantly blaming moms for all things is a real trope in horror. The notion that a primitive (angry, dangerous, violent)...

storm, killing the young couple (one of whom is played by Kevin Bacon) after already having dispatched the headdress-wearing counsellor whose blood drips onto them. There is some self-reflexivity about this headdress-wearing counsellor. He pretends to be an Indian twice, whooping and leaping about. One cannot watch the movie without thinking that he is doomed. His death is a hint that Pamela's vengeance has some justness to it.

Brenda's murder is also quite striking, combining that element of heterosexual reproduction (she plays strip Monopoly) with her strength as a good frontierswoman (she fixes the plumbing). The looming threat watches through her window from the edge of the woods. Brenda's death comes not in the home but in the storm, when she is drawn out into the open. She enters the stormy wilderness, leaving behind the false safety of the rustic pioneer cabin. Her body is thrown into the cabin where the Final Girl makes her last stand, tearing away any sense of security that otherwise might have existed. Brenda dies in her long, unsexy nightgown, like some early pilgrim tricked and drawn out by the savages at the woods' edge.

At the end of *Friday the 13th*, Jason transforms from a ghost who haunts his mother and the campers, into some kind of zombie, as his little boy self erupts out of the water, rotting and covered in lake goop. The specter of Jason, like all savage ghosts, unsettles "the assumed stability and integrity of western temporalities and spatialities."[22] Ralph, the character who literally tells them to stay out of the woods, is labelled as mad for holding those histories. Pamela and then Jason's killing sprees come with storms and churning lake water.

...mother figure exists as some universal concept shows up uncritically and frequently in North American horror.

22 Cameron, "Indigenous Spectrality," 383.

FRIDAY THE 13TH PART 2 *(1981)*

Jason is an unruly, powerful entity, cheered even as he is feared. In *Friday the 13th Part 2*, Jason's first kill is terrifyingly the Final Girl of the first film. He somehow finds her apartment, plants his deceased mother's head in the young woman's fridge, and then kills her before finding his way back to Camp Crystal Lake. The theme of homesteading continues in *Part 2* as a new batch of camp counsellors carry on the mythology of the place. Early on, a counsellor dresses in furs and carries a sphere, jumping out and screaming when the story of Camp Crystal Lake is told. Jason is just "ancient history." Of course they are all wrong, and Jason is now a grown man lurking in the woods, dispatching camp counsellors the way his mother did before him. The local sheriff reprimands the senior counsellor for letting junior counsellors go to a forbidden place, where historic violence and blood soaks into the very land. "Things have been quiet for five years, and that's the way we want to keep it," he says.

On one hand, Crystal Lake is a place where the savage entity guards against white settlers who attempt to invade; on the other hand, Crystal Lake is a site of white settler homesteading that the Final Girl has to somehow guard. The homestead is threatened also by disability, and Jason embodies that threat when we see him drowning and then rise out of the water at the end of the first film. Jason's savagery is rooted first in his disability, disrupting the settler colonial summer camp before drowning and morphing into a savage killer. Emily Hutcheon and Bonnie Lashewicz argue that normative constructions of "white settler [and] able-bodied" individuals are normalized through "the violence of eugenics—a naturalized part of our national context—which ignore indigenous ways of life while creating and reproducing white settler space."[23] The first reveals of Jason's face happen when he is a child who rises from the lake to attack the first film's final survivor, and then in the second film when he has long red hair (that disappears in subsequent movies) and such facial characteristics as one eye lower than the other and an asymmetrical shape to his forehead.

Fearing disability and making disability monstrous is central to the Friday franchise. What is also important are the ways that Jason's disabilities evoke sympathy and give him vulnerabilities that the Final Girls exploit. Those vulnerabilities are exploited most directly in *Friday the 13th Part 2*. Ginny, played by Amy Steel, dresses in Pamela Voorhees's sweater and stands in front of her decapitated head. She speaks to Jason in Pamela's voice and for a moment we see what he sees, as her face morphs into Pamela's. This trick disarms Jason, and Ginny is able to get away.

FRIDAY THE 13TH PART III *(1982)*

This time, the group Jason targets simply live on the lake. They aren't camp counsellors performing homesteading, they are homesteaders. It is mainly the group killed off, along with a trio of local criminals for some reason. The final survivor is Chris, who has a lengthy fight scene with Jason. While Ginny of the previous film is tough and clever for tricking Jason and then attacking him with a pitchfork, and while the Final Girl of the first film is an extreme survivor for beheading Pamela with a machete, the character Chris of this third chapter might be even tougher. She is shown emerging from a room and stabbing Jason after almost everyone else has been killed. It's a stunning scene in which we as viewers adopt Jason's point of view and are made to retreat as

23 Hutcheon and Lashewicz, "Tracing and Troubling Continuities," 2.

she slashes at him. Chris runs from Jason to a loft, arms herself against him again, and hits him with a shovel. She even sticks around to hang Jason at that point, rather than running away.

The Final Girls in this underappreciated series (it is not just about a man who kills naked women constantly) about homesteaders against the savages in the woods are often extraordinary. They are the ultimate cowgirl/outlaw types. Even when Jason comes to and threatens Chris again, she picks up an axe and hits him with it, making the iconic slash in his hockey mask.

In the end, Chris enters the dreamscape of Jason and his mother. After floating off in a canoe (in what might be a hallucination or might be a dream) Chris is chased first by Jason and then by Pamela. Pamela emerges from the murky water as a worm-infested corpse and pulls Chris into their watery, dreamy world. In reality, Chris is driven away by the police, laughing. She has "gone mad" and, like other Final Girls, has crossed that line between the civilized reality of settler society and the savage world of ghosts, dreams, and demons.

PET SEMATARY *(1989)*

Apart from merely fearing the land, settler colonialism is about invasion and justifying invasion. *Pet Sematary* (originally released in 1989, then remade in 2019) presents the settler colonial family as victims of savage entities they do not understand. The film centres on the Indian Burial Ground and the Wendigo, so it earns special recognition as an example of horror that is explicitly about Indigenous Peoples, land, and land rights.

In both films, a doctor, his wife, and their young children (and cat) move to a home that overlooks a busy highway. Behind the house is a large acreage that the real estate agent forgot to mention contains an Indian Burial Ground and pet cemetery—a large swath of land where local kids bury their dead pets and, beyond that, a circle of rocks outlines "cursed ground" where the Mi'kmaq supposedly did bad medicine or turned to the Wendigo spirit after randomly becoming cannibals. Rather than sue their real estate agent and move away, the family stays. In the 1989 film, the family cat as well as the youngest child, a boy, are killed on the highway. After finding out that the dead can be reanimated behind his house, the doctor buries his dead cat and then his dead child in the Indian Burial Ground that a Wendigo has somehow made magic/bad (in an appropriation and twisting of Indigenous cosmologies) to resurrect his loved ones. The "innocent" family's inability to deal with death and its own place on the land is central to a film like *Pet Sematary*. When the family cannot cope, the dead are reanimated but return as killer zombies, and the family is destroyed. The Wendigo is somehow to blame for the "poisoned ground" after the local First Nations people did weird "ceremonies" and then took off.

Jud, a neighbour of the newly arrived central family, and Louis Creed, the doctor-patriarch of that family, make choices to go into the "poisoned ground" beyond the pet cemetery, where they unleash a series of events that result in their own deaths as well as those of Louis's wife and son, sparing only the daughter of the film's main family (maybe).

In the 2019 remake of *Pet Sematary*, Louis's entire family is killed and reanimated, and no one is left to live a civilized life in a city somewhere else. There is no rescue from settler colonialism and its consequences, and there is no way for this family to really settle in place because the land is "sour." The Creeds—as the story is told by Jud—are on contested land, not Indigenous land, and the Indigenous tribes from the area are said to have fled because of their own fears of the land itself. This element of the story adds to the Indian Burial Ground trope and doubles down, taking away the Creation story of the Indigenous nation(s) of an area and replacing it with a new Creation story. In this way, *Pet Sematary* becomes the ultimate colonial story. Jud is the authority figure, the elder of sorts, who tells the Creeds that the land is their own and they have to take responsibility for it all.

PET SEMATARY *(2019)*

As the remake opens, we see a large SUV, probably a family vehicle, with its driver's side door wide open. The feeling of abandonment and quiet foggy stillness permeates the screen. Where is the family? The camera pans toward the front door and we see blood on the white painted wood. Has the family met its demise, and how? In the very next scene, we're introduced to the family in question. Again, we meet Dr. Louis Creed; his wife, Rachel; their daughter, Ellie; son, Gage; and cat, Church. They settled into their new homestead because they needed to spend more time together as a family. Louis is once again the new doctor on the local university campus. As he goes to work, Rachel and Ellie do chores. They hear faint drumbeats coming from the woods and walk in on a pagan-like procession of children in animal masks carrying a dead dog. We find out later that they're burying the dog in a pet graveyard—the Pet Sematary. The primitive threat has been hinted at. It's not until the story's Gothic turn, when Louis loses a patient whose ghost leads him to the land beyond that Pet Sematary, that we're shown the real threat—bad spirits that Indians failed to tame!

The Wendigo is at work, somehow, doing things I have personally never heard of that being doing; yet again, the cultures of Indigenous Peoples who know about that being are taken and then formed into some new mythology, as is so vital to settler belonging in a place where they do not belong. The short story, much like in the first film, is that the Wendigo possesses anybody buried in the "poisoned ground" beyond the pet graveyard. Ellie meets Jud, the grizzled local man who tells Louis about the poisoned ground. Jud is the myth-keeper of the area, in the remake as in the original. He talks about the generations of locals using the woods for their rituals. He warns Rachel that the woods aren't safe. As Rachel walks away, concerned about the strange man talking to her daughter, we hear the woods whisper Jud's name as the man himself looks around in fear.

Ellie is the one killed in the remake, then brought back to life when her father's grief is too much for him to hold. We're shown that her relationship with her father is a close one. We're also shown that Rachel wants to teach her kid about heaven while her dad wants to teach her that death is the natural end of life. Rachel's sister died when she was a kid, as in the first film. That character, the sister with spinal meningitis, remains a central monstrosity in the film. She is the monster because of her suffering and because she is angry at Rachel for being alive; Rachel's sister haunts her as a specter of death and disability. And since Rachel's parents put her in charge of taking care of her sister as she was dying, the boundaries (or lack thereof) within the white settler heteropatriarchal family, are exposed by death early.

As with so many horror movies, the mother is to blame. Conversely, mother-blaming is exposed as a weakness in the family, there to be exploited by the monster. In *Pet Sematary*, both the original and remake, Rachel is the irrational one, the one who can't communicate with her kids about death. It's because of her inability to deal with the pet cat Church's death on the road, mixed with her grieving (understandably so) after witnessing her sister's death, that the events are set into motion leading to her entire family's death and transformation into Wendigo-zombies. On the other hand, it's Louis's unwillingness to actually understand Rachel's trauma, and his need to fix it, that lead him to bury Church in the poisoned ground beyond the pet graveyard and actually set things in motion. By trying to apply a bandage on a heap of grief, the patriarch dooms his family.

The film series is compelling because it combines fears of the Indian, the woods, death itself, and disability/illness. The monstrous body of the dying sister, played also in the first film by a male actor (marking trans bodies as monstrous), all coalesce around the savage bad spirit in the woods, marking the nice family's demise. In the end of the remake, after they lose Ellie to a transport truck and Louis buries her in the poisoned ground, reanimating her, and loses his rational doctor mind. Ellie kills Jud and then her own mother and then the now zombified mom kills Louis. The little boy, Gage, who dies first in the original film, is left in the car to hopefully fend for himself somehow, but we hear the sound of a car fob beeping in that familiar way, and the possessed dad fetches his son, intimating his eventual demise.

Pet Sematary also erases the Passamaquoddy and Penobscot nations' rights to land in the area. Land ownership is dealt with in each of the films in ways that erase Indigenous rights and place them squarely in the hands of local settlers. The land is described as simply belonging to the Creeds now, in the 1989 film, and in the 2019 film, Jud (the local white elder of the film series who warns the Creeds) just kinda says well who knows who owns the land.

The series hones in on the interconnectivity of settler colonial fears: reverse colonization and the total destruction of the white settler heteropatriarchal family (the Creeds consist of a stay-at-home mom and her superstar doctor husband), as well as death and aging in and of themselves. "Sometimes dead is better" is a tagline for the series. The disabled body is also famously made abject (and object) as Rachel Creed's sister, Zelda, is portrayed as a monster. Zelda is bedridden with spinal meningitis. She screams at Rachel that she's going to make it so that she also "never gets out of bed again." In the 2019 remake, Zelda accidentally dies in the hoist that Rachel uses to deliver her food. Rachel is left alone with her sister when she dies, making Rachel extremely unable to deal well with death. So when Rachel's son in the 1989 version, or her daughter in the 2019 version, dies after being hit by a truck, we're shown that Rachel "can't deal," and the real grief is shown through the eyes of the father. It is his grief that leads the family astray, not Rachel's, as he buries their child in the cursed local Indian Burial Ground. The loss of a child is a horrifying thing, but by its centring it would seem the loss of a white settler child is far more horrifying than the millions killed since the onset of settler colonial invasion. We are made to weep for the lost white children of *Pet Sematary* only.

Until, that is, *Bloodlines* comes along in 2023. In this prequel film, two Native youth, one male, one female, talk about getting out of this cursed town and making something of themselves. There is no sense that they have community, they are just random local Native folks. The death of the young woman, then, holds different meaning than the death of the Creed children. She becomes the literal haunting presence of the vanquished Indigenous woman. Played by Dakota actress Isabella Star LaBlanc, the character of Donna is murdered by a young white man, Timmy. Timmy stalks Donna in a field, and she is disappeared—we do not see her death. This scene referencing real life violence against Indigenous women is followed by one in which the now "mad" and possibly Wendigo-possessed Donna goes after Jud's girlfriend, Norma. (The Wendigo and the demon are not the same concept, but they seem to be conflated in these films.) It is not the fault of white settlers that Donna is violent, it is the fault of those pesky cannibalistic local Indians to whom Donna seemingly belongs. It is the fault of the Wendigo, not the fault of white settler colonialism. These are the conclusions that have to be drawn in the Pet Sematary films, and they are beyond problematic. Even when *Bloodlines* shows early settlers trying to find some fertile land for their needs, they are sad, lost men who are tricked into settling the area.

Another frequently quoted line from the films is "sometimes the soil of a man's heart is stonier." I've always wondered if this is a commentary on the secrets that good patriarchs keep (like burying their dead family members in an obviously cursed burial ground in order to reanimate them), but upon further thought, I see this line as connecting back to the "original sin" theme of the film. The idea that the local Indians would misbehave and turn fertile soil to stone is just "human nature," it follows; now the sad and rugged white man is tasked with the forever ownership of cursed America, taking care of whatever mess those local Indians made of things. The secrets of the soil are also the secrets of the Wendigo, it seems, which can throw its voice and convince people to do silly things like drug their friend Jud so that he doesn't stop them from reanimating their dead loved ones. Perhaps settler colonialism is just the fault of the Wendigo sending bad messages (smoke signals) across the Atlantic, which brings up the question: *What else* isn't the fault of European colonists? Perhaps the entire global political order is the fault of bad (and sometimes made-up) spirits from Turtle Island (understood through the lens and writings of white settlers)! What a claim to fame.

Whether it means to or not, *Pet Sematary* (in addition to casting some pretty fantastic actors) asks us to consider whether settler colonial security, innocence, and fantasies of forever belonging on stolen land, are possible. The doomed-ness of the family is interesting in these films. The way the Creed patriarch ultimately pays for his arrogance, as a doctor and manly man and head of the family who unleashes a whole curse on everyone including his remaining child, is manifested through his wife in both the 1989 and 2019 films when it is her reanimated form who kill him. The terror of rot and death and some primordial mother who embodies these things, is a fun little twist at the very end. The terror of the primordial or primeval mother is another layered reminder that the fault, the blame, for the violence that splashes on bodies and soil in horror, lays not with settler colonialism but with this notion of a very old evil that somehow Indigenous Peoples embody or transfer onward. That evil is also feminine, it is insane, it is queer, it transgresses the good and righteous boundaries of the settler colonial family and community. Dr. Creed's wife is freed by film's end, in both the 1989 film and 2019 remake, to become the Evil Mom of North American horror lore.

At the same time, it is not just the bad spirit or sour ground that the audience fears in these films. In the 2019 remake, the father sleeps next to his reanimated daughter, who tells him that she hears the woods. She hears inside of the woods. The woods themselves are frightening, not just the spot where the dead are reanimated. The Indian Burial Ground trope is about the horrors of the land and Indigenous people, ultimately. It is a trope that freezes Indigenous Peoples and colonization in the past, makes white settler families a victim of some curse that is both the fault of Indigenous people and a naturalized source of their demise. Such a definition necessarily encompasses a range of human/ land ontological problems. In political, economic, and cultural systems intent on extraction and subjugation, fearing the revenge of the land seems inevitable.

The Indian Burial Ground presents settler society with the guilt and anxiety associated with the knowledge that a past atrocity has occurred, thereby unsettling some aspects of settler life. At the same time, guilt and shame can be weirdly addictive, and the trope also serves to park colonial violence firmly in the past. In the case of the *Pet Sematary* series, the 2019 remake has such a sad ending—the young boy, just a toddler, having been put into the family car to remain safe from his zombifying family, hears the sound of a key fob announcing their intention to kill and reanimate him—with the blame rooted in cursed lands and cursed Indigenous people. This narrative says: the land is drenched in blood and violence not because of colonialism but because of some projected notion of an original sin committed by Indigenous Peoples.

Seen through a settler colonial studies lens, the Indian Burial Ground trope becomes less unsettling and more so simply reinforces myths of Indigenous disappearance; it is a story of settler replacement and appropriation. White settler families move into an area they believe they have ownership over and rights to, only to find that they are battling an "old evil." Win or lose, their battle seems to gift them with rights to the place, while Indigenous people remain disappeared. In this case, the existence of "sour ground," caused by an Indigenous tribe doing something so destructive and outside of actual cultural practice (eating dead remains or living remains and then burying them ritualistically), also implies that the Mi'kmaq simply up and left the land to white folks. It wasn't genocide that left white settlers to their careers and picnics and property lines, it was the errors of Indigenous people themselves. *Pet Sematary* reiterates myths that Indigenous people commonly engaged in cannibalism while misappropriating the Wendigo to justify this tired trope.

Settler spaces are unsettled in perhaps the most profound ways through the Indian Burial Ground trope. At the same time, this damaging trope functions to *re-settle* those who find themselves groundless because of lost claims to land. The land, after all, is abandoned by Indigenous people of their own free will (according to this trope), and Indigenous people will even return to help white settlers should the need arise—to save their suburban homes, their children, and their claims to land. The trope also imposes white settler spiritual cosmologies onto Indigenous lands, ensuring that the viewer is reminded that perhaps Indigenous Peoples don't *really* have a claim to land at all.

The films allow the Creed family to essentially "naturalize" to place, to become just like the Indigenous people, terrified and incapable of dealing with an apocalyptic threat (the shape-shifters show no sign of stopping at the end of either the original or the remake). During the writing of the *Pet Sematary* novel on which these films are based, Colin Dickey points out that

> the state of Maine was involved in a massive legal battle against the Maliseet, Penobscot and Passamaquoddy bands of the Wabanaki Confederacy. Beginning in 1972, the tribes sued Maine and the federal government over lands to which they were, by federal law, entitled, which amounted to 60 percent of the area of the state.[24]

Settler colonial systems, intent as always on obtaining Indigenous land, benefit from stories in which the Indigenous-Other is just too scared to stick around. Colonization isn't that big of a deal, white settlers are just braver and wiser when confronted with

---

24 Dickey, "The Suburban Horror of the Indian Burial Ground."

pure evil. White settlers are also the natural caretakers of the land, it seems. Even when the land they need to take care of contains horrifying backyards filled with dead cats and dogs who sometimes come back to life, white settlers are the real inheritors of the Americas. The land is filled with meaning and mystery, even if—perhaps *especially* if—white settlers are doomed.

That the Indian Burial Ground trope guarantees white settler futurity in places both wonderous and terrifying, is taken up by Lakota writer Jana Schmieding. Schmieding challenges viewers to think more deeply about this trope, writing that it covers up the actual real-life actions and ideals of Indigenous people of the 1970s and '80s. In Schmieding's words, this trope "is a very lazy response to one of the most monumental calls for Native justice in the 20th century: the American Indian Movement of the 1970s."[25] Anxiety about settlement, and a desire to entrench white-settler families as victims of colonization (by the undead in this case), work together in movies that evoke the Indian Burial Ground trope.

After enacting their own bloody, violent apocalyptic scenes, the white settler becomes, in turn, terrified of annihilation and disappearance. The paradox of this preoccupation and its implications for settler futurity are explored by Hamish Dalley who points to settlers' need to both "erase *and* evoke the native"[26] in an attempt to prove their own superiority, to normalize the colonial project, and to make these places their home. Imagining the demise of a society makes that society a victim of some external force and justifies the original and ongoing invasion; climate change has likewise added new elements to this imagined victimhood.

---

25 Schmieding, "Bury My Guilt in an Indian Burial Ground."

26 Dalley, "The Deaths of Settler Colonialism," 31.

Pet Sematary is also an apocalyptic story. The white settler family is inevitably going to decline, just as the Indigenous Peoples did. In addition to measuring the innocence of that white family and lamenting its losses, the film tells us that the poisoned, evil land does this to everybody. Colonization becomes a far-away myth. The Indians are ghosts, and the settlers are going to follow them. Bergland tells us that this "ghosting of Indians is a technique of removal. By writing about Indians as ghosts, white writers effectively remove them from American lands and place them, instead, within the American imagination."[27] Death comes for all on the Indian Burial Ground; there are no cycles of belonging here that are recognizable despite Indigenous Peoples' presence in this place since time immemorial.

FREAKY *(2020)*

In Christopher Landon's *Freaky* (2020), an "Aztec knife" stabbed into a teen girl by a male serial killer triggers the opening of a kind of wormhole (we see pyramids as a background when the knife enters her), and a serial killer and would-be victim switch bodies. The killer goes on a rampage, trapped now in a teen girl's body. For a brief moment early in the film, we see the killer's lair and there appears to be flimsy strips of animal hide or perhaps human skin hanging about. The conduit for the body switch is the Mayan knife, which becomes associated with the killer's power to inhabit a body deemed innocent enough to create cover for a new round of killings.

Freaky illustrates the ways that (invented and misappropriated) Indigenous cultural objects become intertwined with settler

---

27 Bergland, *The National Uncanny*, 12.

colonial anxiety and yearning. The anxiety, about the dark power of the object or the culture that produced it, and yearning (to be free and to fight back against the internal designs of a violent system) operate together to maintain the integrity and innocence of smalltown America. The movie opens with four young people telling stories about a serial killer who haunts their town. Though the town is called Blissfield, it is not perfect because white male violence proliferates. One of the youths tells us that the killer "moves through this town unseen, like a ghost, and he kills at will every year. The Blissfield Butcher started his reign of terror in 1977, and it continues to this day." No matter how old, the "Butcher" is a white male, and so his propensity for violence is understood by the youth who are about to be slaughtered by him.

Two of the young people leave to retrieve alcohol while a heterosexual pair make out in the backyard. The pair inside the house explore the many collectibles of the homeowner, including an Aztec dagger called La Dola, a human skull, animal horns, and other colonial collectibles. La Dola has a bone handle with a skull carving in it. One of the young people passes by a wall of tribal masks, one of which is then worn by the killer who attacks. The killer takes on the tribal/savage-Other identity, invading the wealthy white settler home. The Blissfield Butcher then steals the dagger and leaves. His next would-be target is a young woman named Millie. When he tries to kill her with the dagger, a Mayan temple and lightning flash in the background, and he switches bodies with her. Under the full moon, atop a temple which replaces the ground beneath them, their spirits (or whatever) switch bodies.

From there, Millie is now in the Butcher's body. A white teen girl now embodies the threat of white settler misogynist violence. What's also played for laughs, however, are the ways the large white man, played by Vince Vaughn, takes on "teen girl" traits, from the secret hand slap with Millie's friends to the oddly "erotic" school cheer. It's played as funny because we're watching a cis male body behaving in feminized ways. Millie, meanwhile, inside the Butcher's actual body wakes up in a room with taxidermized animals hanging from the ceiling, mannequins in pieces, skin-like strips of material hanging about, dirt and grime, and what appears to be a severed head in a toilet. A homeless man asks Millie (as the Butcher) for drugs and offers sexual favours for those drugs. The abject—homelessness, dirty, death, gore, dismembered bodies—haunts the town differently now, as the Butcher now lives literally inside a young girl. The abject is a host of savage behaviours and objects, made more spectacular and terrifying by the found Aztec dagger.

Wearing a cool red leather jacket now, the Butcher in Millie's body clenches her fists and walks through a cheerleading scene, staring intensely at the innocent youth of the town, preparing to go on a spree in the high school. Millie's friends don't understand the issue at first, of course, and compliment "her" on looking cute. The Butcher in Millie's body immediately kills one of Millie's friends. The scene is darkly lit, we see Millie stalk and caress the girl who says she didn't come to "clam-jam" with her and then spreads rumours that Millie's a lesbian. We're pretty much made to hate this kid, and the Butcher leaves this town with one less homophobic, gossipy, "annoying" teen, moments later. The Butcher in Millie's body is chastised by her teacher, who we now hope will be killed. Meanwhile, Millie in the Butcher's body chases her friends and manages to convince them of who she really is. Millie, possessed by the Butcher, is super strong and can stand up to bullies. The Butcher as Millie is now a "wolf in sheep's clothing" and kills Millie's horrid, misogynistic, violent teacher.

Trying to understand their newly acquired Aztec dagger (used in ritualistic sacrifice), the students consult their Spanish teacher who reads the words on the dagger: "If the sacrifice is not successful, the souls are swapped." The dagger is the conduit through which to show what the Final Girl and killer have always been—two sides of the same messy equation. Moreover, the Final Girl is liberated by the dagger. The Butcher as Millie dresses cooler and gets invited to all the parties, but, more importantly, by possessing Millie, the Butcher allows her to operate outside of the rules of civilized society. In the climax of the film, the Butcher as Millie kills a group of football players who have targeted her for sexual assault. "She" kills a football player with a chainsaw like a whirring phallus.

The only way the sexual violence and misogyny of the town can be undone is through "Aztec magic," but the dagger is also dangerous and evil. In what appears to be the ending, Millie and The Butcher switch back to their own bodies. The Butcher is killed, the dagger safely in the hands of the police, and Millie (back in her own body) kisses a boy. The Butcher, taken away in an ambulance, provides one more shock attack. In the twist ending, the Butcher returns and has to be taken down by Millie, her sister, and their mom. The Final Girl always has to protect the settler town, and in this case it's from both the dagger and the killer. As so often happens with the Final Girl in North American horror, Millie prevails and even finds herself a boyfriend in the process. In his case, the boyfriend is named Booker, he's a football player, and the movie follows the traditional rom-com formula—with one exception. There is an uncomfortable kiss between Millie in the Butcher's body and Booker before the body swap is reversed. The age inappropriate and same-sex kiss is played for laughs and for horror. It's "fixed" when Millie returns to her own body and she and Booker make out in the back of an ambulance, as anyone would after a traumatizing event and series of injuries.

IT *(2017)* AND IT CHAPTER TWO *(2019)*

Together, these 2017 and 2019 films are a remake of the 1990 miniseries also called *It* and based on the Stephen King novel of the same title. The story goes that the white settler community of Derry has been terrorized by a shapeshifter that pops up every twenty-seven years to kill people, mostly children. It is the name the main group of characters give the shapeshifter, which sometimes takes the form of the now creepily infamous Pennywise the clown. It takes the shape of whatever children fear the most—perhaps a spider, or a bubble of blood in a drain or a leper or an elderly woman. In the 2017 instalment, the shapeshifter takes the form of Pennywise and kills Georgie, little brother of Bill, whose group of friends team up to destroy the monstrous entity. When they manage to drive the shapeshifter back into hiding, they make a pact to return to Derry as adults should It ever return. In *It Chapter Two* we see the now-adult group return to Derry to take the shapeshifter on once again. In the original miniseries, audiences aren't told a whole lot about the history of the shapeshifter in relation to the history of colonization or Native American cultural belonging in the area. But *It Chapter Two* fills in those gaps in ways that reinforce a key facet of settler colonialism: it is not only the innocence of settler society but the anxiety and turmoil of settler society that particular misappropriations of Indigenous culture(s) are made to address.

Chapter Two follows each of Bill's friends as adults, as they return to Derry and go back to the places where they grew up. In a particularly striking scene, Beverly, the only woman in the group, revisits her apartment. She flashes back to how her abusive father used to speak to her. Simply being in the same building makes her vulnerable to the shapeshifter's tactics. It appears in the form of an elderly woman with an Irish accent, terrifying open sores on her chest, bad teeth, and a jarring way of speaking. The apartment is a sort of glamour, as Beverly is made to see things that the shapeshifter plants in her mind. The elderly woman retreats to the darkened kitchen while Beverly looks at images of Pennywise out of makeup, as he appears in a previous guise. While Beverly is distracted, we see the elderly woman run like an insect, peek around corners, and then run naked through a doorway. She shapeshifts to become a gigantic troll-like creature, with bulbous swaying breasts, unfocused eyes, and horrid hair and teeth, lurching from the shadows and shrieking at Beverly. The scene shifts, and Beverly is in the same building only now it's a condemned, abandoned place, a liminal space, reminding her of her past but also rotting and disjointed in time and space.

Settler colonial nostalgia permeates *Chapter Two* even though Derry is a town stalked by a killer shapeshifter. Each of Bill's friends (dubbed the Losers Club) returns to places where they used to be happy. One of the men, Rickie, who turns out to be gay, remembers being called a homophobic slur in an arcade and then attacked by a giant Paul Bunyan statue in the park, when the shapeshifter assumed its form. As an adult, Richie returns to the arcade, then sees Pennywise in the park atop the Bunyan statue.

It also centres on the youthful romantic triangle between Beverly, Bill, and another member of the group, Ben. When Ben sees the shapeshifter, It takes the form of Beverly with her head on fire, chasing him down a school hallway. These mixed experiences of white settler life in smalltown America all form a pattern of re-establishing not only innocence but a desire for simplicity, for the childhood crush, for the writer to achieve fame, or the kid trapped in an awful home to find freedom. The story of Mike, the only Black character in Bill's group and the entire film series, reinforces the centrality of white settlers in Derry. Mike is both a victim of racism in Derry and somehow, through a white settler writers' lens, completely dedicated to Derry—so much so that he never leaves and puts himself out there as the sacrificial figure for Derry and for the largely white settler town. Mike receives a magical bark or leather (I can't tell which it is) basket that "the Natives" used to use to try to get rid of the shapeshifter.

Native Americans ran away scared (we aren't sure where they ran to) in this movie—they weren't driven out because of settler colonialism, they were scared away by Pennywise. They also failed to stop Pennywise, so it's up to Mike and the white settlers of Derry to do that work. Mike is the magical Black character[28] who sacrifices his entire existence for the white settler town. He has no life, no love, no pride in his own family. His happy ending comes when his friends survive and Ben gets the girl.

It Chapter Two features other elements of the fearful primitive-Other. The way spiders and people with leprosy show up as monsters, the troll and banshee-like creatures, the mummy and the use of blood itself, all could be discussed in more depth at the meeting place of "old world" and "new world" horrors. When the final "ceremony" happens in *Chapter Two*, the forever-ness of the white settler town is reinforced. What appears to be a combination of a talking circle and smudge and basic campfire is what helps the Losers Club solidify their mastery of magic and place, deep in a cave. The primordial cave system gives them their vantage point from which to create a new creation story. The basket-thing they use to build a fire in gives them the magic they need to eradicate the past and rebuild the future. The ritual is supposed to get rid of Pennywise

28 For more on this representation, see Okorafor, "Stephen King's Super-Duper Magical Negroes."

for good. Carvings on the basket tell us this. As Mike uses lighter fluid to build a fire (as any ceremonial leader would), each member of the group throws in their own "sacred" item to burn. One of the items is an inhaler! Disability is also just an illusion! Anyway, the silly fake-ceremony erases Indigenous people as well, since they are part of the past, and this is all about creating a new future for the nice townspeople. Mike holds up a rock, and everyone reminisces about that time they got into a rock fight with the local bullies. Instead of wondering if perhaps the dynamics of Derry are pretty messed up even without Pennywise's interference, everyone smiles and holds hands. The Ritual of Chud is enacted (that's what this ceremony is called). The final step is to watch the poorly built fire go out as the shapeshifter's "deadlights" arrive. Everyone chants "turn light into dark" and the yonic, teethed opening above them sees the shapeshifter's lights circle and fall and struggle before the awesome power of the ceremony. They put a lid on the lights in the basket, and Pennywise starts to really play. A red balloon, Pennywise's favourite signing card, expands from within the basket. Obviously, the ceremony hasn't worked. Or more likely, the ceremony just wasn't powerful enough! After all, the Indians lost and had to run off, so now the settlers have to make up some new ceremonies. But wait—Mike made it all up! He carved the basket, conceived of a ceremony, and now they're all in huge trouble.

The story of this magical basket really is a layered sort of thing. Once we process the fake-ness of the ceremony, and Mike's duplicity, we're left in the chaos of the final act of the film. Each of the group are left to fight their own bad memories. Settler trauma and nostalgia manifest again, as the shapeshifter scares everybody into presumably succumbing to its powers and being trapped by it forever. The central awful memory, the trauma that started the films, is explored as Bill sees his child-self arguing with his deceased little brother, who accuses him of being responsible for his death. The little boy in a yellow raincoat who just wanted his big brother to play with him and who dies because his brother will not is a nod toward those urban legends of child killers roaming suburbia in white vans. Meanwhile, Ben and Beverly are saved when he recites poetry at her. She is drenched in blood and her own trauma and reaches for his hand. After decades of childhood and spousal abuse, a hetero-love story is all this woman really needs. The entire group of adults are traumatized for various reasons, a point I've made light of out of frustration with the underlying narrative of colonization. Eddie, whose monstrous mother made him sick as a child to keep him near, is killed after sacrificing himself for his friends. The key to defeating the shapeshifter is to disempower it by admitting what the town cannot—that the threat is real. Then, the Losers can forget any of it ever happened. Forgetting the history of place, the violence of place, the ceremonies (real and made-up) of place is key to white settler survival and futurity in the film. A blood-drenched Beverly is crucial to this forgetting, as her love story is made to complete the destruction of the cycle of violence. The hetero-happy endings of settler colonialism complete the picture. The past is past, the Natives are gone, the ceremonies now live with whoever can adopt them and then forget that they ever existed. Made-up Indigenous cultural objects, ceremonies, and creation stories, all serve to seemingly naturalize white settlers to place.

The cultural artifacts of disappeared/disappearing Indigenous-Others are there for the taking. Settler colonial systems, intent as always on obtaining Indigenous land, benefit from stories in which the Indigenous-Other is just too scared to stick around, even if white settlers are ultimately doomed—*especially* if white settlers are doomed, since the end of the world is its own biblical story trope.

CREEPSHOW 2 *(1987)*

One of the most bizarre examples of settler colonialism in horror comes in the form of Old Chief Wood'nhead, a wooden cigar store Indian in Michael Gornick's *Creepshow 2* (1987). The film opens on two white settler storekeepers in an old general store that looks like something out of a Western film from the 1930s. A Native American man named Benjamin Whitemoon drops by to give the storekeepers all of his jewellery since his tribe owes them money. It matters not that the white settler storekeepers owe them land, because Benjamin is so grateful for their flour and sugar that he forgets about the colonial project. He is a good romantic-savage stereotype, and the hope here is that the actor collected a paycheque at the very least. From this moment, it gets weirder.

Actor Holt McCallany, in brownface, plays Sam, a local ruffian who invades the store. He and his friends kill the shopkeepers. Sam and his friends leave, and Old Chief Wood'nhead comes to life and takes revenge for his fallen owners. He scalps Sam and kills Sam's friends with arrows and a tomahawk. The possessed (by a ghost, by a memory, we aren't told) Wood'nhead fulfills a particular settler fantasy toward ensuring some sense of belonging and ownership over the place. As Sugars writes, "non-Indigenous authors sought to forge their own folklore by peopling the Canadian landscape with settler ghosts in order to secure their subsequent 'inheritance' of it."[29] Benjamin thanks the Chief and wishes him a good afterlife. The only good part—Benjamin gets his jewels back. The Indians are gone, long live the (possessed) cigar store Indian!

---

29 Sugars, *Canadian Gothic*, 108.

CANNIBALS, OF COURSE!

The witch, the vampire, the werewolf, and the lurking savage in the woods (or alleyway) are all imagined as cannibals in order to establish their savagery and wildness. The cannibal film itself is a whole subgenre of horror that is explicitly committed to Indigenous representation. Erin Wiegand writes about the cannibal movies that became famous in the 1970s and '80s and often came from Italy. They featured a formulaic series of events whereby the civilized white travellers meet Indigenous people and then are attacked and eaten by them. We find though that the "civilized" are the "real savages," as they are the ones exploiting and consuming both the Indigenous people and their lands.[30]

American filmmakers are also fascinated with associations between Indigeneity and cannibalism. Often, the cannibal myths adopted by American filmmakers come with a twist—the cultural stories about cannibalism and monstrosity that exist in some Indigenous cultures, are appropriated in order to provide meaning for white settler writers.[31] Dana Rehn writes about the ways that early settlers were already preconditioned to see that which was foreign and alien as possibly cannibalistic, and how they turned this fear (and projection) onto Native North Americans.[32] As Noel Currie points out, the notebooks of men like James Cook made it seem as though these explorers were finding cannibals everywhere. In reality, Currie writes, "we can identify cannibalism as a trope characteristic of the exploration and discovery genre."[33] This trope continues to be important to the genre of horror, and horror

30 Wiegand, "Who Can Be Eaten?," 253.

31 Ahmad, "Blood in the Bush Garden," 47.

32 Rehn, "Myth-Making in Cannibalistic Portrayals."

33 Currie, "Cook and the Cannibals," 71.

as a genre continues to perpetuate the trope as a central element of ongoing settler colonialism. In the absence of Indigenous people in much of American horror, the overt fixation on the Indigenous community as savage and cannibalistic is striking when it arises in contemporary horror films.

CANNIBAL HOLOCAUST *(1980)*

Ruggero Deodato's *Cannibal Holocaust* (1980) opens with American broadcasting executives gathered in a small theatre to view horrific footage showing an American film crew assaulting Indigenous people in order to create a documentary. The staged invasion, complete with their own heinous behaviour (they rape a woman, shoot people, and burn down the village) results in their own disappearances (though later we find out, of course, that they were killed). An anthropologist, sent in to rescue the crew, is portrayed as some kind of silly academic expert in Indigenous behaviour—he bathes naked to gain the trust of the women in a particularly absurd scene—and we are shown film footage of his rescue efforts. In the end, the anthropologist shows the American broadcasting executives the final bits of reel, which reveal the fate of the film crew, as an argument (which he wins) against showing the footage on public television. After viewing the end of the film, which shows Yanomami people engaging in a frenzied killing of the filmmakers—whooping, half-naked, and beheading everybody—the executives agree with the anthropologist and decide to burn the film. As viewers, we're shown the anthropologist leaving the darkened theatre, emerging into the light of the city street, back in "civilization," it would seem, smoking his pipe, listening to traffic sounds, and asking, "I wonder who the real cannibals are." That final line provides the meaning of *Cannibal Holocaust*, which later influenced Eli Roth's *Green Inferno*.

THE GREEN INFERNO *(2013)*

The Green Inferno is about a group of environmental activists who go to the Amazon Rainforest to stop clearcutting. Their protest against deforestation goes viral and then they fly away, only to nearly all die. After their plane crashes, the survivors are kidnapped by a local Indigenous group, who cage them and then cook and eat them one by one. It becomes more complicated from there, as the cannibalistic tribe is interrupted by a petrochemical company who slaughters them. The film's main protagonist, or Final Girl, is rescued by a child from the tribe, nearly killed, then flown home, where she lies and says the only true villains are the corporate ones. It's a messy story, purposefully told in a way that removes any sense of innocence. Everybody is terrible.

The Green Inferno attempts to argue that the *real* savages are "social justice warriors."[34] While reproducing colonial stereotypes of Indigenous Peoples, *Green Inferno* calls out those who try to ally themselves with Indigenous people for essentially romanticizing cannibals. After all, while *Inferno*'s doomed activists successfully stop a clearcut, they realize that the Natives aren't that grateful anyway, and they turn on one another as well. The enormity of ecocide and genocide is a joke in *Inferno*. The making of the film likewise mimics the colonial explorer trope, as Roth is said to have "lured" Indigenous people "out of the woods"[35] by playing a movie for them and as he then says, "the location that we found is truly spectacular. It's so far up the Amazon, no one has ever shot there."[36] In other words, the Amazon is just lush, empty, inhos-

34 Eli Roth, quoted in Woerner, "Eli Roth's *Green Inferno* Devours."
35 Wright, "Eli Roth Lines Up the Cast."
36 Wright, "Eli Roth Lines Up the Cast."

pitable wilderness, there for filmmakers to mock the Indigenous people they've "lured" from it.

The Civ/Sav dichotomy cannot be rescued, not really, even when unhappy endings cloak the whole of white settler society in a shroud of monstrosity. The equation—a savage Other, a civilized protagonist, and then showing that civilized protagonist descending into savagery in order to survive or perhaps only to be made an example of—still reinforces the Civ/Sav binary and its constructed elements. At the end of the day, these films show Indigenous Peoples as voiceless, ridiculous stereotypes.

THE DESCENT *(2005)*

The Descent is a terrifying love story about a woman so intent on being with another woman that she sleeps with her husband and then leads her on a terrifying caving expedition in order to eventually name the newly discovered cave after the two of them. This film is also my favourite Indigenous-cannibal story because of its many layers. Most of the explorers die, but the two who survive the catastrophe[37] do so because they "go Native," which I enjoy watching since it proves my point about the Final Girl and her eventual movement across the (invented) civilization-savagery divide.

The Gothic turn happens in this film when Sarah, the mother of a little girl and wife of a cheating guy who likes giving silver feather jewellery to his hookups, is involved in a car accident. Her daughter and husband are killed horribly, and she has to take a drug of some kind because she keeps dreaming about them. Sarah has "gone mad" right from the start of the film, and the story that follows can be taken in more than one way as a result.

37 We only know that the two women survive because of *The Descent Part 2* (2009).

We see her dreaming, waking in a hospital bed, and then hallucinating out in the hallway that darkness is following her. She runs into the arms of her best friend, Beth, while her eventual nemesis (I call them subtext-soulmates) Juno sobs along with her. *The Descent* is a tragic, beautifully filmed, wonderfully acted rumination on the spectre of death. It is also a film about cannibalistic Indigenous people and the invasion of the savage in the nice lives of white explorers.

After Sarah's car accident, about a year later it seems, she travels to the homelands of the Cherokee nation in so-called Appalachia. She meets with Beth, Juno, and their friends, in Juno's quaint woodland cottage. Juno lives in the kind of cabin you'd expect to see in any film about backwoods horror and cannibalism. She's got animal heads hanging on the walls, a fire in the woodstove, and an ominous feeling swirling about her. She and her explorer friends have not been to visit Sarah a whole lot since she lost her whole family because "midterms and all." They would all rather talk about base jumping than real things like grief and mutual aid. Still, you feel for them as a viewer when they start getting eviscerated. I digress. The women have a night of obligatory drinking, smoke some things, and essentially celebrate their night together. Then, they tromp through the woods, enter a cave system they are supposed to have a map for, and—as they say—all hell breaks loose. Hell is the cannibal Indian, lurking in the darkness of both the earth and of Sarah's mind. And since Juno threw away the map, like a total savage,[38] the women are trapped with one, the other, or both versions of the monster.

---

38 I am increasingly irked by the use of *savage* as slang for hardcore, but I'll use the term here in its double meaning as both hardcore and also stereotypically deceptive as that "sneaky Indian" in American folklore is supposed to be.

Juno is coded as an Indian. In a revealing review of the film, Linnie Blake writes that these films "illustrate how closely related we all are to blind, cannibalistic and evolutionarily regressive troglodytes."[39] Juno is able to kill the first of what come to be called Crawlers because she is written as a savage herself. Of the Native informant, Lizzy Nichols writes,

> Literary applications of the native informant are myriad, but perhaps none are so familiar as the native informant in the natural setting. Often associated with primordial nature... settler colonial evocations of the native informant as "one with nature" in fiction have served such purposes as claiming authentic land rights or establishing a New World identity separate from European ancestors.[40]

Before the women enter the cave system, they have to walk through the woods, guided by Juno, not knowing she's just winging it. One of the women asks, "Juno, are we there yet?" To which Juno says, "there's a river about half a mile ahead. When we reach it, we follow it up to the mouth of the cave." Someone asks, "How does she know there's a river?" to which the reply is, "She can probably smell it..."

This scene is of interest in a settler colonial studies reframing of the film. I'm arguing that Juno is coded as an Indian guide, though she isn't explicitly discussed as Indigenous. Her rustic cabin, with animal bones as décor, her ability to read the landscape, feather necklace and braid, inform this coding. Moments after we, the viewers, watch as Juno leaves the map behind, she

39 Blake, *The Wounds of Nations*, 162–163.
40 Nichols, "Becoming Indigenous Again," 304.

leads her friends into unknown and potentially dangerous terrain. In an essay on the anti-Indigenous racism of Joss Whedon's *Firefly*, Agnes Curry speaks to the way the Indian as a monster is portrayed as "sneaky," specifically as sneaking up on a "hapless woman and child."[41] The explorers in *The Descent* are just innocent women in the hands of an already-suspicious-seeming "Indian guide." As would-be explorers, the women are also really competitive and call each other lazy when someone can't keep up on their rigorous hike. So, ableism and arrogance are their downfall as well. When it's revealed that Juno lied about the cave they're in, after a section of it collapses, the name starts to sound a lot like Judas as the women shout at her for her duplicity.

The women then have to find their way through the caves. As they move along, we see clues that there are cannibalistic creatures down there with them. Or—are there? Taken in one way, the Crawlers might be an invention of Sarah's mind. She is the first to see one, and when she tries to alert the group they tell her that she's not thinking clearly. As a projection, the Indigenous cannibals (devolved humanoids) are the perfect monster for her imagination. In this reading, Sarah becomes the killer.

Read another way, Sarah isn't imagining a thing, and the Crawlers really do inspire the women to climb and claw their way through only to fall to the creatures. When the cannibals start attacking, killing an injured member of the group and even biting Juno, it's hard not to think that they're real. Sarah is nowhere to be found for the end of Juno's big fight with a Crawler, and when Juno accidentally stabs Beth with a pickaxe and then retreats in despair into the dark walls of the cave we are shown the fight from an outside perspective. Perhaps there is a chance that the women have

---

41 Curry, "We Don't Say 'Indian,'" 9.

all "gone mad" and begun to hallucinate and turn on one another. It doesn't matter, either way, because the projected cannibal of the white-explorer mind is still an Indian, real or otherwise.

The notion of madness as savagery invading is less entertaining than the idea of the Crawler chomping on folks. When Sarah regains her senses, she hallucinates her daughter transforming into a Crawler. Her mental health descent is no less real than the Crawler, even if that theory is wrong and the creatures are real (which they seem to be). Sarah watches as a cannibal-Crawler eats her friend, videoing it as the creatures growl and eat her pal raw. It's the ultimate European tourism moment: come to the Americas and watch the Indians eat your friends! This silly storyline is completely sold by the actresses, and the film is actually quite terrifying. In the theatre, a large and strong-looking human next to me actually clasped my arm and shrieked in horror at these scenes. The Crawler is a sympathetic monster, in some ways, as another viewer told me, the second time I saw the movie in theatres: "Well, they had to eat too!"

Both the cave and the Crawler are made to seem like savage interlopers despite the women obviously invading the caving system. The women in *The Descent* are tourists for the most part in this savage landscape. What becomes interesting are the ways that Juno and Sarah survive by adapting to the darkness, the dangers of the cave, and the viciousness of the cannibals they're up against. Juno, the deceitful guide, fights alongside Sarah at the very end (to the sound of tribal drums) until Sarah escapes, having axed Juno in the leg. By the end, these women are drenched in blood, swinging weapons, and even biting and gouging Crawlers in hand-to-hand combat. There is little to differentiate them from the "savages" they kill, as they are reborn in blood and lose all semblance of their previous "civilized" lives.

The beautiful and doomed Juno tries her hardest to save Sarah most of all. Sarah is that anachronistic other who can integrate with the Crawlers and then also defeat them. In order to fight back, Sarah—the mad woman—has to shed her outer layers, her "civilized" attire, and fight with her hands and teeth and bones and axes. When Sarah reveals that she knows about Juno's affair with her deceased husband, the film takes a silly turn, and Juno is left to die while Sarah scrambles up a hill of bones to the exit. One ending sees Sarah in her car, sobbing, and Juno appearing as a ghost. I prefer this ending, since it means they're together in some strange way. A second ending shows Sarah stuck in the cave still, which is also a great ending since she's stuck with Juno who has probably already fought her way past most of the Crawlers.

The endings of *The Descent* transform the coded-Indian into a ghost and send the mad-woman into a dreamy realm. Though the idea that compulsory heteronormativity and monogamy might inspire someone's bestie to kill them for a long-ago affair is too tragic for words, these endings acknowledge the importance of constructed notions of savagery to the mythos of ongoing colonialism. I also refuse to recap the sequel to this film because it may or may not presume their demise, and Sarah and Juno are the characters I dedicate this book to (along with the real-world humans I love). As I learn to speak back to the mainstream horror that inspired this book, I have found that recoding, reclaiming, and laughing from time to time at the absurdity of colonial projection and invention keeps me hopeful. Something better might be just around the corner of this dark cave filled with colonizer-cannibals that we find ourselves in.

CONCLUSION

DECOLONIZING HORROR

The original horror of the North American continent unfolded in 1492, with the onset of mass European arrival, invasion, and genocide. "Colonization," Tuck and Ree remind us, "is as horrific as humanity gets: genocide, desecration, poxed-blankets, rape, humiliation. Settler colonialism, then... is an ongoing horror made invisible by its persistence—the snake in the flooded basement."[42] I argue in this chapter that guilt is one facet of settler horror and that other elements necessary to maintaining the structure of settler colonialism can be found in horror storytelling—namely the replacement of Indigenous Creation stories and the usurpation of Indigenous ownership of and kinship with the land.

Decolonization necessitates material as well as ideological renewal and return for Indigenous Peoples. Telling better stories

42 Tuck and Ree, "A Glossary of Haunting," 642.

is also about providing the material basis for Indigenous people to tell those stories ourselves. North American horror portrays Indigenous Peoples and lands as disappeared and frozen in the past, but the Indian as savage, as freeing even, is hyper-visible. Who, and where, are Indigenous people in horror? The answer: everywhere and nowhere at once. Both disappeared but also obsessed over, the imagined Indian is projected to reinforce settler colonialism.

In this book, I've focused my efforts on outlining the ways that settler colonialism shapes horror films, revealing therefore the real significance of the construction of the Indian and the dangers of "wild" landscapes within the American horror film primarily. To existing literature on Indigenous ghosts and hauntings, I have cast what I hope is a wide net to expand horror theory and to unpack ways that settler colonial theory might add to our conceptualizations of land, family, and many forms of oppression in horror. Horror, I argue, is the genre of settler colonialism. Even when not dealing explicitly with Indigenous stories of place, these threads persist. Fears of nature, of the land, of spirits of place, of the language/sentience of place, and of Indigenous people and Indigenous belonging are all woven together in a plethora of anxious warnings and stories. The land is frightening, and the Indigenous-Other is frightening, because they are intertwined.[43] Cursed Indigenous cultural objects show up in horror as well. The

---

43 LaRocque, *When the Other Is Me*, 43; Bergland, *The National Uncanny*, 38. Even the internet can be described in horror as a demon-filled wilderness. The dark web in particular is often described as a wilderness or wild place; Roderick Graham and Brian Pitman write about it as "freedom in the wilderness," consisting of a strange mix of horrifying child pornography, misogyny, and a curiously empty place, with lapses in information exchange and a whole lot of unknown pathways. Films like Levan Gabriadze's *Unfriended* (2014) and Stephen Susco's *Unfriended: Dark Web* (2018) explore the dark web as a kind of savage place, either with supernatural or merely human elements. See Graham and Pitman, "Freedom in the Wilderness."

land, people, and Indigenous cultural items as cursed things, as things in need of containment and conquering.

Settler colonial society is indeed profoundly anxious about (its own) disappearance and destruction. After enacting their own bloody, violent apocalyptic scenes, the white settler becomes, in turn, terrified of it being enacted upon them. An apocalyptic story naturalizes the inevitability of the end of days for Indigenous Peoples and opens the potential for white settler families to also experience such a turn. Reverse colonization in the form of the walking dead positions the Creed family of *Pet Sematary* as the ultimate white settlers who have naturalized to "their land" and then met a sad, sad fate. The story is about empty land and cycles of doomed humans who cannot cope with the trickery of spirits (either made-up or misappropriated) here. That the land is nobody's, that it is empty, forms a foundational attachment for white settlers. When actual Indigenous people do show up in horror, they tend to show up as cannibals and werewolves: the Indigenous-Other who lurks in the caves and woodlands and rainforests and takes the raw food diet to the next level.

Growing up in a lower middle-class suburban neighbourhood in a mining town, I watched horror movies with my friends because we were bored. I suspect also that we were aware that the town was an angry sort of place. In my first public school, I wrote a terrible play called *Friday the 13th Part 6* or something along those lines, and I played Jason Voorhees and chopped up every boy in my class. The teacher may have stopped the play before it was supposed to end—I can't quite remember—but it was a hit. I was painfully aware at a very early age that the world we live in is steeped in sexualized, colonial violence. Watching some suburban teen slash and hack her way out of trouble, setting the bad guy on fire or blowing him up with her mind was (and is) cathartic.

The white settler colonial family is locked in temporal and spatial stasis: there is a timelessness and a placelessness to their dystopic lives. Memories of original violence, rooted in colonialism and slavery, obscured; the something-isn't-quite-right-edness of their homes, their streets, the patches of wilderness that loom at a near distance, or perhaps their townhalls or their libraries. It is tempting to call this at least somewhat subversive, and there are certainly cathartic moments in horror that can be explained by the joys of burning it all down when our protagonists know the place and time will never be as it was promised.

From *Pet Sematary* (1989 and 2019) to the remake of *It* (2017–2019), there is a vague notion in certain horror films that an evil that preceded Indigenous Peoples' presence in the Americas is now a problem to be solved by white settlers. The idea that the land is inherently volatile, vengeful, dangerous, and "wild" circles back to early colonial thought. Indigenous cultures are also represented in mainstream horror in ways that are often incredibly disrespectful and should be read as deliberate reinforcement of white settler futurity. Indigenous nationhood, treaty rights, and cultural practices persist despite perpetual oppression and settler colonial erasure, and this ongoing presence is a source of romanticization and fear in horror.

In addition to this repeated notion of some original evil in North America, horror shows land as empty and the future as devoid of Indigenous people. The white settler family may be terrorized, but generally they are the central characters in horror. They yearn for a place that is empty—terra nullius—of Indigenous Peoples, in the face of a (natural) landscape that seems wild and unruly and menacing. Freezing the spirit beings of the Americas in symbolic terms allows white settlers to reimagine themselves as heroes in some eternal struggle. That the real horrors of the last five hundred years have actually been experienced as a result of colonization, slavery, and imperialism, and that the perpetrators of immeasurable suffering have been white settler Europeans whose heinous acts of violence continue into the current time period, is flipped and the sufferings of the colonized are appropriated. I want horror to be as subversive as I think it can be. Indigenous people are speaking back to horror in creative and innovative ways, even as I type these last words.

SOURCES

Addison, Heather. "Cinema's Darkest Vision: Looking into the Void in John Carpenter's *The Thing* (1982)." *Journal of Popular Film and Television* 41, no. 3 (2013): 154–166. https://doi.org/10.1080/01956051.2012.755488.

Ahmad, Aalya. "Blood in the Bush Garden: Indigenization, Gender, and Unsettling Horror." In *The Canadian Horror Film: Terror of the Soul*, edited by Gina Freitag and André Loiselle, 47–66. University of Toronto Press, 2015.

Airey, Jennifer L. "#MeToo." *Tulsa Studies in Women's Literature* 37, no. 1 (2018): 7–13.

Aja, Alexandre, dir. *High Tension*. Lionsgate, 2003. 107 min.

Aja, Alexandre, dir. *The Hills Have Eyes*. Dune Entertainment, 2006. 89 min.

Allard-Tremblay, Yann, and Elaine Coburn. "The Flying Heads of Settler Colonialism; or the Ideological Erasures of Indigenous Peoples in Political Theorizing." *Political Studies* 71, no. 2 (2021): 359–378. https://doi.org/10.1177/00323217211018127.

Arata, Stephen. "The Occidental Tourist: *Dracula* and the Anxiety of Reverse Colonization." *Victorian Studies* 33, no. 4 (1990): 621–645.

https://blogs.dickinson.edu/secretlives/files/2018/11/Arata-Stephen-The-Occidental-Tourist-Dracula-and-the-Anxiety-of-Reverse-Colonization.pdf.

Arvin, Maile, Eve Tuck, and Angie Morrill. "Decolonizing Feminism: Challenging Connections between Settler Colonialism and Heteropatriarchy." *Feminist Formations* 25, no. 1 (2013): 8–34. https://doi.org/10.1353/ff.2013.0006.

Aschaiek, Sharon. "This Halloween, Discover How Demons Vexed the Jesuits." News Room, University of Toronto Mississauga, October 28, 2021. https://www.utm.utoronto.ca/main-news/halloween-discover-how-demons-vexed-jesuits.

Aster, Ari. *Midsommar*. A24, 2019. 148 min.

Atwood, Margaret. *Survival: A Thematic Guide to Canadian Literature*. Anansi, 1972.

Bacon, J.M. "Settler Colonialism as Eco-Social Structure and the Production of Colonial Ecological Violence." *Environmental Sociology* 5, no. 1 (2019): 59–69. https://doi.org/10.1080/23251042.2018.1474725.

Baldy, Cutcha Risling. "Why I Teach *The Walking Dead* in My Native Studies Classes." *Nerds of Color*, April 24, 2014. https://thenerdsofcolor.org/2014/04/24/why-i-teach-the-walking-dead-in-my-native-studies-classes/.

Barker, Joanne. *Red Scare: The State's Indigenous Terrorist*. University of California Press, 2021.

Bates, Margaret. "The Fridge Is Getting Full." *Medium*, April 13, 2016. https://medium.com/legendary-women/the-fridge-is-getting-full-a2e88642f171.

Baum, L. Frank. *The Wonderful Wizard of Oz*. George M. Hill Company, 1900.

Beer, Lindsay Anderson, dir. *Pet Sematary: Bloodlines*. Paramount+, 2023. 87 min.

Bergland, Renée. *The National Uncanny: Indian Ghosts and American Subjects*. University Press of New England, 2000.

Bergman, Ingmar, dir. *The Virgin Spring*. Janus Films, 1960. 89 min.

Bettinelli-Olpin, Matt, and Tyler Gillett, dirs. *Ready or Not*. Searchlight Pictures, 2019. 95 min.

Bettinelli-Olpin, Matt, and Tyler Gillett, dirs. *Scream*. Paramount Pictures, 2022. 114 min.

Bettinelli-Olpin, Matt, and Tyler Gillett, dirs. *Scream VI*. Paramount Pictures, 2023. 122 min.

Blake, Linnie. *The Wounds of Nations: Horror Cinema, Historical Trauma and National Identity*. Manchester University Press, 2008.

Blaut, James Morris. *The Colonizer's Model of the World: Geographical Diffusionism and Eurocentric History*. Guilford Press, 1993.

Boucher, Leigh David. "Masculinity Gone Mad: Settler Colonialism, Medical Discourse and the White Body in Late Nineteenth-Century Victoria." *Lilith* 13 (2004): 51–67.

Bourgeois, Robyn. "Perpetual State of Violence: An Indigenous Feminist Anti-Oppression Inquiry into Missing and Murdered Indigenous Women and Girls." In *Making Space for Indigenous Feminism*, 2nd ed., edited by Joyce Green. Fernwood Publishing, 2017.

Brintnall, Kent L. "Re-Building Sodom and Gomorrah: The Monstrosity of Queer Desire in the Horror Film." *Culture and Religion* 5, no. 2 (2004): 145–160. https://doi.org/10.1080/1438300420002254O2.

Bryant, Kenzie. "Carrie Fisher Once Had a Heroic Response to Hollywood Sexual Assault." *Vanity Fair*, October 16, 2017. https://www.vanityfair.com/style/2017/10/carrie-fisher-aol-hero.

Burch, Susan. *Committed: Remembering Native Kinship in and Beyond Institutions*. University of North Carolina Press, 2021.

Burger, Alissa, and Jenny Collins. "'The Shadow of Saint Nicholas': Dougherty's *Krampus*." In *Monsters and Monstrosity in 21st-Century Film and Television*, edited by Cristina Artenie and Ashley Szante. Universitas Press, 2017.

Burroughs, William S. *Naked Lunch*. 50th anniversary ed. Grove Press, 2009.

Byrd, Jodi A. *The Transit of Empire: Indigenous Critiques of Colonialism*. University of Minnesota Press, 2011.

Cameron, Emilie. "Indigenous Spectrality and the Politics of Postcolonial Ghost Stories." *Cultural Geographies* 15, no. 3 (2008): 383–393. https://www.jstor.org/stable/44251222.

Cariou, Warren. "Haunted Prairie: Aboriginal 'Ghosts' and the Spectres of Settlement." *University of Toronto Quarterly* 75, no. 2 (2006): 727–734.

Carpenter, John, dir. *The Fog*. Debra Hill Productions, 1980. 91 min.

Carpenter, John, dir. *Halloween*. Compass International Pictures, 1978. 91 min.

Carpenter, John, dir. *The Thing*. Turman-Foster Company, 1982. 109 min.

Carpenter, John, dir. *Vampires*. Columbia Pictures, 1998. 108 min.

Carroll, Andrew. "The Brady Bunch Go Savage: *The Hills Have Eyes* at 40." *HeadStuff*, July 22, 2017. https://headstuff.org/entertainment/film/the-hills-have-eyes-40.

Caterine, Darryl V. "Heirs through Fear: Indian Curses, Accursed Indian Lands, and White Christian Sovereignty in America." *Nova Religio* 18, no. 1 (2014): 37–57. https://doi.org/10.1525/nr.2014.18.1.37.

Cheek, Douglas, and David Irving, dirs. *C.H.U.D*. New World Pictures, 1984. 78 min.

Chimienti, Roman, and Tyler Jensen, dirs. *Scream, Queen! My Nightmare on Elm Street*. Virgil Films and Entertainment LLC/The End Productions, 2019. 99 min.

Christensen, Kyle. "The Final Girl versus Wes Craven's *A Nightmare on Elm Street*: Proposing a Stronger Model of Feminism in Slasher Horror Cinema." *Studies in Popular Culture* 34, no. 1 (2011): 23–47. https://www.jstor.org/stable/23416349.

Clark, Bob, dir. *Black Christmas*. Warner Bros., 1974. 98 min.

Clover, Carol J. "Her Body, Himself: Gender in the Slasher Film." *Representations* 20 (1987): 187–228. https://doi.org/10.2307/2928507.

Clover, Carol J. *Men, Women and Chainsaws: Gender in the Modern Horror Film*. B.F.I. Publishing, 1992.

Craven, Wes, dir. *The Hills Have Eyes*. Blood Relations Company, 1977. 89 min.

Craven, Wes, dir. *The Last House on the Left*. Sean S. Cunningham Films, 1972. 91 min.

Craven, Wes, dir. *A Nightmare on Elm Street*. Warner Bros. Pictures, 1984. 91 min.

Craven, Wes, dir. *Scream*. Woods Entertainment, 1996. 111 min.

Craven, Wes, dir. *Scream 2*. Dimension Films, 1997. 120 min.
Craven, Wes, dir. *Scream 3*. Dimension Films, 2000. 116 min.
Craven, Wes, dir. *Scream 4*. Dimension Films, 2011. 111 min.
Creed, Barbara. *The Monstrous-Feminine: Film, Feminism, Psychoanalysis*. Routledge, 1993.
Cunningham, Sean, dir. *Friday the 13th*. Georgetown Productions Inc., 1980. 95 min.
Currie, Noel Elizabeth. "Cook and the Cannibals: Nootka Sound, 1778." *Lumen* 13 (1994): 71–78. https://doi.org/10.7202/1012522ar.
Curry, Agnes. "We Don't Say 'Indian': On the Paradoxical Construction of the Reavers." *Twenty Five: The Online International Journal of Buffy Studies* 7, no. 1 (2008).
Dalley, Hamish. "The Deaths of Settler Colonialism: Extinction as a Metaphor of Decolonization in Contemporary Settler Literature." *Settler Colonial Studies* 8, no. 1 (2018): 30–46. https://doi.org/10.1080/2201473X.2016.1238160.
Dante, Joe, dir. *The Howling*. Sony Pictures, 1981. 91 min.
Davison, Carol M. *History of the Gothic: Gothic Literature 1764–1824*. University of Wales Press, 2009.
Dekeyser, Thomas. "Rethinking Posthumanist Subjectivity: Technology as Ontological Murder in European Colonialism." *Theory, Culture & Society* 41, no. 2 (2024). https://doi.org/10.1177/02632764231178482.
Deloria, Philip J. *Playing Indian*. Yale University Press, 1998.
Deloria, Vine, Jr. *God Is Red: A Native View of Religion*, 30th anniversary ed. Fulcrum Publishing, 2003.
Deloria, Vine, Jr. *The World We Used to Live In: Remembering the Powers of the Medicine Men*. Fulcrum Publishing, 2006.
DeLucia, Christine M. "Corn and Colonization." In *Memory Lands: King Philip's War and the Place of Violence in the Northeast*. Yale University Press, 2019.
Deodato, Ruggero, dir. *Cannibal Holocaust*. United Artists Europa, 1980. 96 min.
Derleth, August. *The Lurker at the Threshold*. Arkham House, 1945.
DeSanti, Brady. "The Cannibal Talking Head: The Portrayal of the Windigo 'Monster' in Popular Culture and Ojibwe Traditions."

Journal of Religion and Popular Culture 27, no. 3 (2015): 186–201. https://doi.org/10.3138/jrpc.27.3.2938.

Dickey, Colin. "The Suburban Horror of the Indian Burial Ground." *The New Republic*, October 19, 2016. https://newrepublic.com/article/137856/suburban-horror-indian-burial-ground.

Dokken. "Dream Warriors." *Back for the Attack*. BMG Rights Management US LLC, 1987.

Dougherty, Michael, dir. *Krampus*. Universal Pictures, 2015. 98 min.

Douglas, Andrew, dir. *The Amityville Horror*. Metro-Goldwyn-Mayer, Dimension Films, Platinum Dunes, Radar Pictures, 2005. 89 min.

Edwards, Kim. "Get Away from Me, You Bitch! Demon Mothers, Psycho Sons and the 'Scream' Trilogy." *Australian Screen Education* 41 (2006): 92–97.

Eflin, Jackson. "Incursion into Wendigo Territory." *Digital Literature Review* 1 (2014): 9–19. https://doi.org/10.33043/DLR.1.0.9-19.

Eggers, Robert, dir. *The Witch: A New England Folktale*. A24, 2015. 92 min.

Elliott, Alicia. "The Rise of Indigenous Horror: How a Fiction Genre Is Confronting a Monstrous Reality." CBC, October 17, 2019. https://www.cbc.ca/arts/the-rise-of-indigenous-horror-how-a-fiction-genre-is-confronting-a-monstrous-reality-1.5323428.

Fahy, Thomas, ed. *The Philosophy of Horror*. University Press of Kentucky, 2010.

Fargeat, Coralie, dir. *Revenge*. MES Productions, 2017. 108 min.

Faris, Wendy B. "The Question of the Other: Cultural Critiques of Magical Realism." *Janus Head* 5, no. 2 (2002): 101–119. https://doi.org/10.5840/jh20025225.

Federici, Silvia. *Caliban and the Witch: Women, the Body and Primitive Accumulation*. Autonomedia, 2004.

Fawcett, John, dir. *Ginger Snaps*. Motion International, 2000. 108 min.

Finley, Chris. "Decolonizing the Queer Native Body (and Recovering the Native Bull-Dyke): Bringing 'Sexy Back' and Out of Native Studies' Closet." In *Queer Indigenous Studies: Critical Interventions in Theory, Politics, and Literature*, edited by Qwo-Li Driskill, Chris Finley, Brian Joseph Gilley, and Scott Lauria Morgensen. University of Arizona Press, 2011.

Fleet, Adam. "*The Witch*: Robert Eggers' Folk Horror Debut Worms Its Way Under Your Skin." *The Guardian*, April 19, 2022. https://www.theguardian.com/film/2022/apr/20/the-witch-robert-eggers-folk-horror-debut-worms-its-way-under-your-skin.

Fleischer, Ruben, dir. *Zombieland*. Columbia Pictures, 2009. 88 min.

Fleming, Victor, dir. *Gone with the Wind*. Metro-Goldwyn-Mayer, 1939. 238 min.

Foucault, Michel. *Madness & Civilization: A History of Insanity in the Age of Reason*. Pantheon Books, 1965.

Franck, Kaja. "'The Worst Loups-Garous that One Can Meet': Reading the Werewolf in the Canadian 'Wilderness.'" *Gothic Studies* 22, no. 1 (2020): 64–80.

Franks, Travis. "Make Settler Fantasy Strange Again: Unsettling Normative White Masculinity in Robert E. Howard's Weird West." *Western American Literature* 54, no. 3 (2019): 295–322.

Gabriadze, Levan, dir. *Unfriended*. Universal Pictures, 2014. 83 min.

Gibson, Brian, dir. *Poltergeist II: The Other Side*. Metro-Goldwyn-Mayer, 1986. 91 min.

Girdler, William, dir. *The Manitou*. Herman Weist & Associates, 1978. 104 min.

Glenn, Evelyn Nakano. "Settler Colonialism as Structure: A Framework for Comparative Studies of US Race and Gender Formation." *Sociology of Race and Ethnicity* 1, no. 1 (2015): 52–72. https://doi.org/10.1177/2332649214560440.

Goddard, Drew, dir. *The Cabin in the Woods*. Universal Pictures, 2012. 95 min.

Gooden, Tai. "Women in Slasher Films: Their Deaths, Evolution, and Potential Future." *Nerdist*. March 31, 2022. https://nerdist.com/article/women-in-slasher-films-deaths-evolution-male-gaze-horror.

Gorman, Rachel, and Brenda A. LeFrançois. "Mad Studies." In *Routledge International Handbook of Critical Mental Health*, edited by Bruce Cohen. Routledge, 2018.

Gornick, Michael, dir. *Creepshow 2*. Laurel Entertainment, 1987. 92 min.

Graham, Roderick, and Brian Pitman. "Freedom in the Wilderness: A Study of a Darknet Space." *Convergence* 26, no. 3 (2020): 593–619. https://doi.org/10.1177/1354856518806636.

Green, David Gordon, dir. *Halloween*. Miramax, 2018. 106 min.

Green, David Gordon, dir. *Halloween Ends*. Universal Pictures, 2022. 111 min.

Green, David Gordon, dir. *Halloween Kills*. Miramax, 2021. 105 min.

Hall, Melinda. "Horrible Heroes: Liberating Alternative Visions of Disability in Horror." *Disability Studies Quarterly* 36, no. 1 (2016). https://dsq-sds.org/index.php/dsq/article/view/3258/4205.

Harlin, Renny, dir. *A Nightmare on Elm Street 4: The Dream Master*. New Line Cinema, 1988. 93 min.

Harrison-Priddle, Cole A. "When It Is Appropriate to Racially Appropriate: Reverse Colonial Miscegenation in Bram Stoker's *Dracula*." 12th I@Q Conference Proceedings, May 24, 2018.

Harvey, Grant, dir. *Ginger Snaps Back: The Beginning*. Lionsgate Films, 2004. 64 min.

Hautsch, Jessica. "Staking Her Colonial Claim: Colonial Discourses, Assimilation, Soul-Making, and Ass-Kicking in *Buffy the Vampire Slayer*." *Slayage* 9, no. 1 (January 2011).

Henderson, James (Sákéj) Youngblood. "Postcolonial Ghost Dancing: Diagnosing European Colonialism." In *Reclaiming Indigenous Voice and Vision*, edited by Marie Battiste. University of British Columbia Press, 2000.

Henderson, James (Sákéj) Youngblood. "The Context of the State of Nature." In *Reclaiming Indigenous Voice and Vision*, edited by Marie Battiste. University of British Columbia Press, 2000.

Hitchcock, Alfred, dir. *The Birds*. Universal Pictures, 1963. 119 min.

Hitchcock, Alfred, dir. *Psycho*. Universal Pictures, 1960. 109 min.

Hoad, Neville. "Arrested Development or the Queerness of Savages: Resisting Evolutionary Narratives of Difference." In *Routledge Handbook of Queer Development Studies*, edited by Corinne L. Mason. Taylor & Francis, 2018.

Höglund, Johan. "Settlement and Imperialism." In *The Cambridge Companion to American Horror*, edited by Stephen Shapiro and Mark Storey. Cambridge University Press, 2022.

Holland, Tom, dir. *Fright Night*. Columbia Pictures, 1985. 106 min.

Hooper, Tobe, dir. *Poltergeist*. Metro-Goldwyn-Mayer, 1982. 114 min.

Hooper, Tobe, dir. *The Texas Chainsaw Massacre*. Vortex, 1974. 83 min.

Hopkins, Stephen, dir. *A Nightmare on Elm Street 5: The Dream Child*. New Line Cinema, 1989. 89 min.

Horwitz, Tony. "The Horrific Sand Creek Massacre Will Be Forgotten No More." *Smithsonian Magazine*, December 2014. https://www.smithsonianmag.com/history/horrific-sand-creek-massacre-will-be-forgotten-no-more-180953403/.

Huhndorf, Shari. *Going Native: Indians in the American Cultural Imagination*. Cornell University Press, 2001.

Hutcheon, Emily J., and Bonnie Lashewicz. "Tracing and Troubling Continuities between Ableism and Colonialism in Canada." *Disability & Society* 35, no. 5 (2020): 695–714. https://doi.org/10.1080/09687599.2019.1647145.

Iliadis, Dennis, dir. *The Last House on the Left*. Rogue Pictures, 2009. 110 min.

Imada, Adria. "Family History as Disability History: Native Hawaiians Surviving Medical Incarceration." *Disability Studies Quarterly* 41, no. 4 (2021). https://dsq-sds.org/index.php/dsq/article/view/8475.

James, Caryn. "*The Hunt* Review: Donald Trump Got this Sly Satire All Wrong." BBC, March 11, 2020. https://www.bbc.com/culture/article/20200310-the-hunt-review-donald-trump-got-this-sly-satire-all-wrong.

Janiak, Leigh, dir. *Fear Street Part One: 1994*. Netflix, 2021. 107 min.

Janiak, Leigh, dir. *Fear Street Part Three: 1666*. Netflix, 2021. 114 min.

Janiak, Leigh, dir. *Fear Street Part Two: 1978*. Netflix, 2021. 110 min.

Johnstone, Gerard, dir. *M3GAN*. Universal Pictures, 2022. 102 min.

Jordan, Lorien S. "Belonging and Otherness: The Violability and Complicity of Settler Colonial Sexual Violence." *Women & Therapy* 44, no. 3–4 (2021): 271–291. https://doi.org/10.1080/02703149.2021.1961434.

Kauanui, J. Kēhaulani. "'A Structure, Not an Event': Settler Colonialism and Enduring Indigeneity." *Lateral: Journal of the Cultural Studies Association* 5, no. 1 (2016). https://csalateral. org/issue/5-1/forum-alt-humanities-settler-colonialism-enduring-indigeneity-kauanui.

Kelleher, Patrick. "6 Reasons Why *Scream* Is a Bone-Chilling, Blood-Curdling Queer Masterpeice." *Pink News*, January 14, 2022. https://www.thepinknews.com/2022/01/14/scream-film-lgbt-gay-queer/.

Khair, Tabish. *The Gothic, Postcolonialism and Otherness: Ghosts from Elsewhere*. Palgrave Macmillan, 2009.

Kiersch, Fritz, dir. *Children of the Corn*. New World Pictures, 1984. 92 min.

Kölsch, Kevin, and Dennis Widmyer, dirs. *Pet Sematary*. Di Bonaventura Pictures, 2019.

Konzett, Delia Malia. "Kubrick's Red Room: Architecture, Race, and Nationhood in *The Shining*." *Quarterly Review of Film and Video* 41, no. 2 (2024): 151–174. https://doi.org/10.1080/10509208.2022.2101341.

Kristeva, Julia. *Powers of Horror: An Essay on Abjection*. Translated by Leon S. Roudiez. Columbia University Press, 1982.

Kubrick, Stanley, dir. *The Shining*. Warner Bros., 1980. 146 min.

LaDuke, Winona. "Native American Activist, Author Winona LaDuke on 'The Militarization of Indian Country' and Obama Admin's 'Lip Service' to Indigenous Rights." Interview by Juan Gonzalez and Amy Goodman. *Democracy Now!*, May 6, 2011. https://www.democracynow.org/2011/5/6/native_american_activist_author_winona_laduke.

Lambert, Mary, dir. *Pet Sematary*. Paramount Pictures, 1989. 103 min.

Landon, Christopher, dir. *Freaky*. Universal Pictures, 2020. 102 min.

Langford, Barry. *Film Genre: Hollywood and Beyond*. Edinburgh University Press, 2005.

LaRocque, Emma. *When the Other Is Me: Native Resistance Discourse, 1850–1990*. University of Manitoba Press, 2010.

Launius, Sarah, and Geoffrey Alan Boyce. "More than Metaphor: Settler Colonialism, Frontier Logic, and the Continuities of Racialized Dispossession in a Southwest US City." *Annals of the American Association of Geographers* 111, no. 1 (2021): 157–174. https://doi.org/10.1080/24694452.2020.1750940.

LeFrançois, Brenda. "The Psychiatrization of Our Children, or an Autoethnographic Narrative of Perpetuating First Nations Genocide through 'Benevolent' Institutions." *Decolonization: Indigeneity, Education & Society* 2, no. 1 (2013): 108–123.

Liebesman, Jonathan, dir. *The Texas Chainsaw Massacre: The Beginning*. New Line Cinema, 2006. 91 min.

Lovejoy, David S. "Satanizing the American Indian." *The New England Quarterly* 67, no. 4 (1994): 603–621.

MacIntyre, Tyler, dir. *It's A Wonderful Knife*. Shudder/RLJE Films, 2023. 87 min.

Mackenthun, Gesa. "Haunted Real Estate: The Occlusion of Colonial Dispossession and Signatures of Cultural Survival in US Horror Fiction." *Amerikastudien/American Studies* 43, no. 1 (1998): 93–108. https://www.jstor.org/stable/41157353.

Marshall, Neil, dir. *The Descent*. Celador Films, 2005. 100 min.

Martinez, David. *Life of the Indigenous Mind: Vine Deloria Jr. and the Birth of the Red Power Movement*. University of Nebraska Press, 2019.

McArdle, Tommy. "Melissa Barrera Breaks Silence after Scream Firing: 'I Condemn Hate and Prejudice of Any Kind.'" *People*, November 22, 2023. https://people.com/melissa-barrera-speaks-out-after-scream-firing-8405989.

McBride, Kameron. "Dealing with Our Bloody Past: Repression vs. Recognition of American History in Stanley Kubrick's *The Shining*." *Digital Literature Review* 1 (2014): 30–40. https://doi.org/10.33043/DLR.1.0.30-40.

McCreary, Tyler, and Rebecca Hall. "The Healer, the Witch, and the Law: The Settler Magic that Criminalized Indigenous Medicine Men as Frauds and Normalized Colonial Violence as Care." *Annals of the American Association of Geographers* 114, no. 2 (2024): 352–368. https://doi.org/10.1080/24694452.2023.2267152.

McGregor, Deborah. "Coming Full Circle: Indigenous Knowledge, Environment, and Our Future." *American Indian Quarterly* 28, no. 3 & 4 (2004): 385–410.

McKay, Dwanna L., Kirsten Vinyeta, and Kari Marie Norgaard. "Theorizing Race and Settler Colonialism Within US Sociology." *Sociology Compass* 14, no. 9 (2020): e12821. https://doi.org/10.1111/soc4.12821.

Means Coleman, Robin R., and Mark H. Harris. *The Black Guy Dies First: Black Horror Cinema from Fodder to Oscar*. Simon & Schuster, 2023.

Mihesuah, Devon. "Becoming Insane: The Death of Arch Wolfe at the Canton Asylum for Insane Indians." *Disability Studies Quarterly* 41, no. 4 (2021). https://doi.org/10.18061/dsq.v41i4.8444.

Mills, China. "Global Psychiatrization and Psychic Colonization: The Coloniality of Global Mental Health." In *Critical Inquiries for Social Justice in Mental Health*, edited by Marina Morrow and Lorraine Halinka Malcoe. University of Toronto Press, 2017.

Mills, China. "The Mad Are Like Savages and the Savages Are Mad: Psychopolitics and the Coloniality of the Psy." In *Routledge International Handbook of Critical Mental Health*, edited by Bruce M.Z. Cohen, 205–212. Routledge, 2018.

Mills, China, and Suman Fernando. "Globalising Mental Health or Pathologising the Global South? Mapping the Ethics, Theory and Practice of Global Mental Health." *Disability and the Global South* 1, no. 2 (2014): 188–202.

Miner, Steve, dir. *Friday the 13th Part 2*. Paramount Pictures, 1981. 87 min.

Miner, Steve, dir. *Friday the 13th Part III*. Paramount Pictures, 1982. 95 min.

Miner, Steve, dir. *Halloween H2O: 20 Years Later*. Dimension Films, 1998. 86 min.

Mitchell, David T. "Resistance and Other Pathologized Products of Madness." *American Literary History* 35, no. 3 (2023): 1286–1294. https://doi.org/10.1093/alh/ajad121.

Morgan, Glen, dir. *Black Christmas*. 20th Century Studios, 2006. 84 min.

Morgensen, Scott L. "Settler Homonationalism: Theorizing Settler Colonialism within Queer Modernities." *GLQ: A Journal of Lesbian and Gay Studies* 16, no. 1–2 (2010): 105–131. https://doi.org/10.1215/10642684-2009-015.

Morgensen, Scott L. "Theorising Gender, Sexuality and Settler Colonialism: An Introduction." *Settler Colonial Studies* 2, no. 2 (2012): 2–22. http://dx.doi.org/10.1080/2201473X.2012.10648839.

Morrison, Toni. *Playing in the Dark: Whiteness and the Literary Imagination*. Harvard University Press, 1992.

Morton, Erin. "Of Folksongs and Feral Children: Taylor Swift's White Settler Womanhood." *Heliotrope*, October 14, 2020. https://heliotropejournal.net/helio/folk-songs.

Muñoz, José Esteban. *Disidentification: Queers of Color and the Performance of Politics*. Cultural Studies of the Americas 2. University of Minnesota Press, 1999.

Murphy, Bernice M. *The Rural Gothic in American Popular Culture: Backwoods Horror and Terror in the Wilderness*. Palgrave Macmillan, 2013.

Muschietti, Andy, dir. *It*. New Line Cinema, 2017. 135 min.

Muschietti, Andy, dir. *It Chapter Two*. New Line Cinema, 2019. 169 min.

Mylod, Mark, dir. *The Menu*. Searchlight Pictures, 2022. 107 min.

Nichols, Lizzy. "Becoming Indigenous Again: The Native Informant and Settler Logic in Richard Powers's *Overstory*." *Environmental Humanities* 14, no. 2 (2022): 303–320. https://doi.org/10.1215/22011919-9712390.

Nispel, Marcus, dir. *The Texas Chainsaw Massacre*. New Line Cinema, 2003. 98 min.

Nolan, Yvette. "Creating New Ghosts." Review of *Canadian Gothic: Literature, History and the Spectre of Self-Invention*, by Cynthia Sugars. *Literary Review of Canada*, June 2014. https://reviewcanada.ca/magazine/2014/06/creating-new-ghosts/.

O'Donnell Brenden. "Surveilling Lesbians: The Birds, Hitchcock's Narrative Cinema and the Criminalization of Sexuality." *Queer Studies in Media & Popular Culture* 5, no. 1 (2020): 49–68. https://doi.org/10.1386/qsmpc_00024_1.

Okorafor, Nnedi. "Stephen King's Super-Duper Magical Negroes." *Strange Horizons*, October 25, 2004. http://strangehorizons.com/non-fiction/articles/stephen-kings-super-duper-magical-negroes.

Onion, Rebecca. "The Most Accurate Part of *The Witch*? It Nails the Desperate, Crazed Mindset of Early American Settlers." *Slate*, February 29, 2016. https://slate.com/culture/2016/02/the-most-accurate-part-of-the-witch-is-how-it-nails-the-desperate-crazed-mindset-of-early-american-settlers.html.

Orr, Niela. "The Women Who Knew Too Much." *The Baffler* 46 (July 2019). https://thebaffler.com/salvos/the-women-who-knew-too-much-orr.

Orwell, George. *Animal Farm*. Signet Classics, 1996. First published 1945 by Secker and Warburg.

Peele, Jordan, dir. *Us*. Monkeypaw Productions, 2019. 121 min.

Perrello, Tony. "A Parisian in Hollywood: Ocular Horror in the Films of Alexandre Aja." In *American Horror Film: The Genre at the Turn of the Millennium*, edited by Steffen Hantke. University Press of Mississippi, 2010.

Pheasant-Kelly, Fran. "Reframing Parody and Intertextuality in *Scream*: Formal and Theoretical Approaches to the 'Postmodern' Slasher." In *Style and Form in the Hollywood Slasher Film*, edited by Wickham Clayton. Palgrave Macmillan, 2015.

Phelan, Sean. "Neoliberalism, the Far Right, and the Disparaging of 'Social Justice Warriors.'" *Communication, Culture and Critique* 12, no. 4 (2019): 455–475. https://doi.org/10.1093/ccc/tcz040.

Phillips, Richard. "Settler Colonialism and the Nuclear Family." *Canadian Geographer* 53, no. 2 (2009): 239–253. https://doi.org/10.1111/j.1541-0064.2009.00256.x.

Pierce, Charles B., dir. *The Town that Dreaded Sundown*. Charles B. Pierce Film Productions, Inc., 1976. 90 min.

Piper, Karen L. "Inuit Diasporas: *Frankenstein* and the Inuit in England." *Romanticism* 13, no. 1 (2007): 63–75. https://doi.org/10.1353/rom.2007.0017.

Podoshen, Jeffrey Steven. 2018. "Home Is Where the Horror Is: Wes Craven's *Last House on the Left* and *A Nightmare on Elm Street*." *Quarterly Review of Film and Video* 35, no. 7 (2018): 722–729. https://doi.org/10.1080/10509208.2018.1472535.

Poe, Edgar Allan. *The Narrative of Arthur Gordon Pym of Nantucket*. Penguin Publishing Group, 1999. First published 1838 by Harper.

Posada, Tim. "#MeToo's First Horror Film: Male Hysteria and the New Final Girl in 2018's *Revenge*." In *Performing Hysteria*, edited by Johanna Braun. Cornell University Press, 2020.

Procknow, Greg. "I, 'Madman': an Autosomatography of Schizoaffective Disorder and Mad Subjectivity." *Disability Studies Quarterly* 38, no. 4 (2018). https://doi.org/10.18061/dsq.v38i4.5920.

Redikopp, Sarah. "Out of Place, Out of Mind: Min(d)ing Race in Mad Studies Through a Metaphor of Spatiality." *Canadian Journal of Disability Studies* 10, no. 3 (2021): 96–118. https://doi.org/10.15353/cjds.v10i3.817.

Rehn, Dana K. "Myth-Making in Cannibalistic Portrayals of Native Americans." November 14, 2021. https://danakrehnblog.wordpress.com/2021/11/14/myth-making-in-cannibalistic-portrayals-of-native-americans.

Restad, Penne L. *Christmas in America: A History*. Oxford University Press, 1995.

Ridenour, Al. *The Krampus and the Old, Dark Christmas: Roots and Rebirth of the Folkloric Devil*. Feral House, 2016.

Rifkin, Mark. *When Did Indians Become Straight? Kinship, the History of Sexuality, and Native Sovereignty*. Oxford University Press, 2011.

Romano, Aja. "The Manson Family Murders, and Their Complicated Legacy, Explained." *Vox*, July 12, 2023. https://www.vox.com/2019/8/7/20695284/charles-manson-family-what-is-helter-skelter-explained.

Rosenbaum, Ron. "The Shocking Savagery of America's Early History." *Smithsonian Magazine*, March 2013. https://www.smithsonianmag.com/history/the-shocking-savagery-of-americas-early-history-22739301/.

Rosenberg, Stuart, dir. *The Amityville Horror*. Metro-Goldwyn-Mayer, 1979. 118 min.

Rosenthal, Rick, dir. *Halloween II*. Universal Pictures, 1981. 92 min.

Roth, Eli, dir. *Hostel*. Lionsgate, 2005. 94 min.

Roth, Eli, dir. *The Green Inferno*. Worldview Entertainment, 2013. 1 hr 40 min.

Rothenburger, Sunnie. "'Welcome to Civilization': Colonialism, the Gothic, and Canada's Self-Protective Irony in the Ginger Snaps Werewolf Trilogy." *Journal of Canadian Studies* 44, no. 3 (2010): 96–117. https://doi.org/10.3138/jcs.44.3.96.

Rowe, Aimee Carrillo, and Eve Tuck. "Settler Colonialism and Cultural Studies: Ongoing Settlement, Cultural Production, and Resistance." *Cultural Studies ↔ Critical Methodologies* 17, no. 1 (2017): 3–13. https://doi.org/10.1177/1532708616653693.

Rumford-Rodgers, Hope, Audrey R. Giles, and Willow Scobie. "Christian Summer Camps for Indigenous Youth in Canada: A Settler Colonial Analysis." *Leisure/Loisir* 47, no. 2 (2023): 159–179. https://doi.org/10.1080/14927713.2022.2054457.

Russell, Chuck, dir. *A Nightmare on Elm Street 3: Dream Warriors*. New Line Cinema, 1987. 90 min.

Russell, Lorena. "Ideological Formations of the Nuclear Family in *The Hills Have Eyes*." In *The Philosophy of Horror*, edited by Thomas Fahy. University Press of Kentucky, 2010.

Santos, Cristina. *Untaming Girlhoods: Storytelling Female Adolescence*. Routledge, 2023.

Schmidt, Rob, dir. *Wrong Turn*. 20th Century Studios, 2003. 85 min.

Schmieding, Jana. "Bury My Guilt in an Indian Burial Ground." *Medium*, October 29, 2018. https://medium. com/@janaschmieding/bury-my-guilt-in-an-indian-burial-ground-a194b6380465.

Schneekloth, Lynda H. "The Frontier Is Our Home." *Journal of Architectural Education* 49, no. 4 (1996): 210–225. https://doi.org/10.1080/10464883.1996.10734688.

Schneider, Steven J. "Barbara, Julia, Carol, Myra, and Nell: Diagnosing Female Madness in British Horror Cinema." In *British Horror Cinema*, edited by Steve Chibnall and Julian Petley. Routledge, 2001.

Schumacher, Joel, dir. *The Lost Boys*. Warner Bros., 1987. 97 min.

Schwartz, James Z. "Lewis Henry Morgan's Early Theory of Progress: His Evolving View of the Passions and Social Development." *Early American Studies: An Interdisciplinary Journal* 18, no. 2 (2020): 229–258. https://doi.org/10.1353/eam.2020.0005

Scorsese, Martin, dir. *Killers of the Flower Moon*. Paramount Pictures, 2023, 206 min.

Scott, Emmy. "The Native Imagery of Jordan Peele's *Us*, Explained." *Vulture*, March 29, 2019. https://www. vulture. com/2019/03/the-native-imagery-of-jordan-peele-s-us-explained.html.

Senf, Carol. "Realism, Horror and the Gothic in *Dracula* and Thomas Hardy's 'The Fiddler of the Reels.'" *Palgrave Communications* 3, no. 17083 (2017). https://doi.org/10.1057/palcomms.2017.83.

Sharp, Patrick B. *Savage Perils: Racial Frontiers and Nuclear Apocalypse in American Culture*. University of Oklahoma Press, 2007.

Shelley, Mary. *Frankenstein; or, the Modern Prometheus*. Penguin Classics, 2012. First published 1818 by Lackington, Hughes, Harding, Mavor & Jones.

Shire, Laurel Clark. "Turning Sufferers into Settlers: Gender, Welfare, and National Expansion in Frontier Florida." *Journal of the Early Republic* 33 (2013): 489–521. https://doi.org/10.1353/jer.2013.0069.

Sholder, Jack, dir. *A Nightmare on Elm Street 2: Freddy's Revenge*. New Line Cinema, 1985. 87 min.

Simpson, Catherine. "Australian Eco-Horror and Gaia's Revenge: Animals, Eco-Nationalism and the 'New Nature.'" *Studies in Australasian Cinema* 4, no. 1 (2010): 43–54. https://doi.org/10.1386/sac.4.1.43_1.

Simpson, Michael A., dir. *Sleepaway Camp III: Teenage Wasteland*. Nelson Entertainment, 1989. 79 min.

Skatt Bros. "Walk the Night." *Strange Spirits*. Casablanca Records, 1979.

Smiles, Deondre. "The Settler Logics of (Outer) Space." *Society + Space* 41, no. 2 (2020). https://www.societyandspace.org/articles/the-settler-logics-of-outer-space.

Smith, Steven C., dir. *Halloween: A Cut Above the Rest*. Marketing-Film, 2003. 87 min.

Snelgrove, Corey, Rita Dhamoon, and Jeff Corntassel, "Unsettling Settler Colonialism: The Discourse and Politics of Settlers, and Solidarity with Indigenous Nations," *Decolonization: Indigeneity, Education & Society* 3, no. 2 (2014). https://jps.library.utoronto.ca/index.php/des/article/view/21166.

Somos, Christy. "Foster Care Replaced Residential Schools for Indigenous Children, Advocates Say." CTV News, June 7, 2021. https://www.ctvnews.ca/canada/foster-care-replaced-residential-schools-for-indigenous-children-advocates-say-1.5459374#.

Spears, Nancy Marie. "Indigenous Human Remains, Mostly Boarding School Children, Reported in 3 States This Week." *The Imprint*, July 12, 2023. https://imprintnews.org/top-stories/indigenous-human-remains-mostly-boarding-school-children-reported-in-3-states-this-week/.

Starkey, Adam. "Fans Vow to Boycott *Scream VII* After Melissa Barrera Is Dropped over Israel-Hamas War-Post." *NME*, November 22, 2023. https://www.nme.com/en_asia/news/film/fans-vow-to-boycott-scream-vii-after-melissa-barrera-is-dropped-over-israel-hamas-war-post-3547307.

Stoker, Bram. *Dracula*. Wordsworth Classics, 1993. First published 1897 by Archibald Constable and Company.

Stoker, Bram. "The Squaw." In *Dracula's Guest: and Other Weird Stories*. George Routledge and Sons, 1914.

Stote, Karen. *An Act of Genocide: Colonialism and the Sterilization of Aboriginal Women*. Fernwood Publishing, 2015.

Sugars, Cynthia. *Canadian Gothic: Literature, History, and the Spectre of Self-Invention*. University of Wales Press, 2014.

Sullivan, Brett, dir. *Ginger Snaps 2: Unleashed*. Lionsgate, 2004. 94 min.

Susco, Stephen, dir. *Unfriended: Dark Web*. Universal Pictures, 2018. 93 min.

Sutherland, J.J. "L. Frank Baum Advocated Extermination of Native Americans." *The Two-Way*, October 27, 2010. https://www.npr.org/sections/thetwo-way/2010/10/27/130862391/l-frank-baum-advocated-extermination-of-native-americans.

Takal, Sophia, dir. *Black Christmas*. Blumhouse Productions, 2019. 1 hr 32 min.

Taylor, George Rogers. *The Turner Thesis: Concerning the Role of the Frontier in American History*. Barakaldo Books, 2020.

Taylor, Leila. *Darkly: Black History and America's Gothic Soul*. Repeater, 2019.

Tenney, Kevin, dir. *Night of the Demons*. Blue Rider Pictures, 1988. 89 min.

Thompson, Jay Daniel, and Erin Reardon. "'Mommy Killed Him': Gender, Family, and History in Wes Craven's *A Nightmare on Elm Street* (1984)." *M/C Journal* 20, no. 5 (2017). https://doi.org/10.5204/mcj.1281.

Todd, Zoe. "Commentary: The Environmental Anthropology of Settler Colonialism, Part I." *Engagement*, April 11, 2017. https://aesengagement.wordpress.com/2017/04/11/commentary-the-environmental-anthropology-of-settler-colonialism-part-i/.

Tuck, Eve, and C. Ree. "A Glossary of Haunting." In *Handbook of Autoethnography*, edited by Stacy Holman Jones, Tony E. Adams, and Carolyn Ellis. Routledge, 2013.

Tuck, Eve, and K. Wayne Yang. "Decolonization Is Not a Metaphor." *Decolonization: Indigeneity, Education & Society* 1, no. 1 (2012): 1–40.

Tuesday Knight. "Nightmare." *Faith, Nightmare*. Knight and Day Records, 2015. Originally released 1988.

US Department of the Interior. "Not Invisible Act Commission." Accessed January 7, 2024. https://www.doi.gov/priorities/strengthening-indian-country/not-invisible-act-commission.

Veracini, Lorenzo. "Introducing Settler Colonial Studies." *Settler Colonial Studies* 1, no. 1 (2011): 1–12. https://doi.org/10.1080/2201473X.2011.10648799.

Veracini, Lorenzo. *Settler Colonialism: A Theoretical Overview*. Springer Publishing, 2010.

Veracini, Lorenzo. "'Settler Colonialism': Career of a Concept." *The Journal of Imperial and Commonwealth History* 41, no. 2 (2013): 313–333. https://doi.org/10.1080/03086534.2013.768099.

Veracini, Lorenzo. "Suburbia, Settler Colonialism and the World Turned Inside Out." *Housing, Theory and Society* 29, no. 4 (2012): 339–357. https://doi.org/10.1080/14036096.2011.638316.

Vizenor, Gerald Robert, ed. *Survivance: Narratives of Native Presence*. University of Nebraska Press, 2008.

Von Hoffmann, Chris, dir. *Monster Party*. RLJ Entertainment, 2018. 89 min.

Wallace, Tommy Lee, dir. *It*. Lorimar Productions, 1990. 192 min.

Wadleigh, Michael, dir. *Wolfen*. Orion Pictures, 1981. 114 min.

Wagner, Katherine A. "Haven't We Been Here Before?: *The Cabin in the Woods*, the Horror Genre, and Placelessness." *Slayage* 10, no. 2 (2013/2014).

Wainwright, R., dir. *The Fog*. Columbia Pictures, 2005. 100 min.

Weaver, Roslyn. *Apocalypse in Australian Fiction and Film: A Critical Study*. McFarland, 2011.

Whedon, Joss, Jane Espenson, and Douglas Petrie, writers. *Buffy the Vampire Slayer*. Season 4, episode 8, "Pangs." Directed by Michael Lange. Los Angeles: Mutant Enemy Productions, 1999.

Whyte, Kyle P. "Indigenous Science (Fiction) for the Anthropocene: Ancestral Dystopias and Fantasies of Climate Change Crises." *Environment and Planning E: Nature and Space* 1, no. 1–2 (2018): 224–242. https://doi.org/10.1177/2514848618777621.

Wiebe, Joseph, and Sydney Thackeray. "The Mennonite Case for Counter-Sovereignty through Indigenous Assimilation: Settler Colonialism, Self-Determination and Relation to Place in Religious Identity." *Studies in Religion/Sciences Religieuses* 53, no. 1 (2024): 113–133. https://doi.org/10.1177/00084298231165443.

Wiegand, Erin E. "Who Can Be Eaten? Consuming Animals and Humans in the Cannibal-Savage Horror Film." In *What's Eating You?: Food and Horror on Screen*, edited by Cynthia J. Miller and Bowdoin Van Riper. Bloomsbury, 2017.

Williams, Carol, ed. *Indigenous Women and Work: From Labor to Activism*. University of Illinois Press, 2012.

Williams, Tony. *Hearths of Darkness: The Family in the American Horror Film*. University Press of Mississippi, 2014.

Wingard, Adam, dir. *You're Next*. HanWay Films, 2011. 94 min.

Woerner, Meredith. "Eli Roth's *Green Inferno* Devours the Internet's 'Social Justice Warriors.'" *Los Angeles Times*, July 9, 2015. https://www. latimes. com/entertainment/herocomplex/la-et-hc-eli-roth-green-inferno-sjw-20150709-story. html.

Wolfe, Patrick. "Settler Colonialism and the Elimination of the Native." *Journal of Genocide Research* 8, no. 4 (2006): 387–409. https://doi.org/10.1080/14623520601056240.

Worland, Rick. *The Horror Film: An Introduction*. Blackwell Publishing, 2007.

Wright, Benjamin. "Eli Roth Lines Up the Cast for *The Green Inferno*, Will Use Native Peruvians as Extras." *The Playlist*, October 26, 2012. https://theplaylist.net/eli-roth-lines-up-the-cast-for-the-green-inferno-will-use-native-peruvians-as-extras-20121026/.

Yerxa, Jana-Rae. "We Need to Stop Calling Them 'Schools.'" *Seven Generations Education Institute*, June 30, 2021. https://www.7generations.org/we-need-to-stop-calling-them-schools/.

Zanini, Claudio Vescia. "'It Hurts 'Cause You're in My World Now, Bitch': Gothic Features in the 1984 and 2010 Versions of *A Nightmare on Elm Street*." *Ilha Desterro* 72, no. 1 (2019). https://www.scielo.br/j/ides/a/WzqxTJHfZMvJcPfrsfx3Bby/?lang=en.

Zika, Charles. "Cannibalism and Witchcraft in Early Modern Europe: Reading the Visual Images." *History Workshop Journal* 44, no. 1 (1997): 77–105. https://doi.org/10.1093/hwj/1997.44.77.

Zobel, Craig, dir. *The Hunt*. Universal Pictures, 2020. 90 min.

ACKNOWLEDGEMENTS

I would like to acknowledge the Canada Council for the Arts for their generous support in the writing of some of this work. I would also like to thank the Ontario Arts Council for their support on this project. Truthfully, this book has taken me almost two decades to write. The support of my family and friends has ensured that I keep the momentum going and focus on the task at hand.

INDEX

INDEX \\\

LAURA HALL grew up in Sudbury and is now a resident of Ottawa, Ontario. She is an associate professor in sociology at Carleton University.

INDIGENOUS VOICES IN WORLD ARTS AND CULTURAL EXPRESSIONS

Publishing works from both emerging and established scholars, the Indigenous Voices in World Arts and Cultural Expressions series showcases practices and critical discourses of diverse traditions of Indigenous makers that demonstrate the intersections between Indigenous languages and Indigenous ways of knowing.

The books in this series probe how visual cultural production from various parts of the world reflect Indigenous stories and concerns, local and global issues, how they are understood by Indigenous, international, and diasporic audiences, and how they exist within discourses of art histories, film histories, and visual culture. *Bloodied Bodies, Bloody Landscapes* is the second book in the series, following Lucy R. McNair and Yahya Laayouni's *Amazigh Cinema* (2025).

Series Editors

Sheila Petty, SaskPower Research Chair in Cultural Heritage and Professor for Media Studies at the University of Regina, and *Carmen Robertson*, Canada Research Chair in North American Art and Material Culture and Professor of Art and Architecture at Carleton University.

For more information about publishing in the series, please contact:

University of Regina Press Acquisitions
University of Regina Press
3737 Wascana Parkway
Regina, Saskatchewan S4S 0A2 Canada
uofrpress.acquisitions@uregina.ca
www.uofrpress.ca